Feb 8, 2005
HAPPY BIRTHDAY!
ALL MY LOVE,
C

D0831859

THE BOOK

AN ACTOR'S GUIDE TO CHICAGO

Edited by Mechelle Moe and Jen Ellison

Published by Performink Books, Ltd. ~ Sixth Edition

PerformInk Books, Ltd.
3223 N. Sheffield
Chicago, IL 60657

Copyright © 2003
PerformInk Books, Ltd.
All rights reserved.

ISBN: 1-892296-03-9

Carrie L. Kaufman, *Publisher*
Jen Ellison and Mechelle Moe, *Editors*

Cover and Chapter Design by Arlo Bryan Guthrie
Graphics and Layout by Marty McNulty

Successor to "Acting, Modeling and Dance," Founding Editors: Allyson Rice-Taylor, Emily Gerson-Saines

From the Editors' Desk—

Welcome to the 6th edition of "The Book: An Actor's Guide to Chicago," a comprehensive resource guide for the actor, designer, director, producer, arts administrator and educator.

So why should you buy this book? First, no one involved in Chicago theatre (or film) should be without a copy. Not that you couldn't survive, but we can certainly make life a little easier. How? Well aside from providing updated contact information and a directory of services for just about anyone you'd want to contact in the arts, each chapter tackles a different aspect of the industry. Do you have questions about your taxes? Greg Mermel goes over the basics for individuals (Chapter 8) and theatre companies (Chapter 7). You want to turn Equity but you don't quite understand the logistics, then check out Chapter 5. We also offer advice on audience development, how to get health insurance, how to write a press release and where to live. And that's just a hint of what's offered inside these pages.

We would like to extend our thanks to the staff of PerformInk and our many contributors for their creativity and expertise in helping us bring this book to fruition. We would also like to thank the entertainment community in Chicago for providing us with the information to make it complete.

Mechelle Moe & Jen Ellison

Photo: Suzanne Plunkett

CHAPTER 1
COMING TO CHICAGO

Around the World in 80 Days
Lifeline Theatre

Chicago—More Than a Stepping Stone for Professional Artists

By Jenn Goddu

In the mythology that surrounds "making it as an artist," the two poles are the bright lights of Broadway or the movie magic of Hollywood. Smack dab in the center of the country, Chicago is too rarely recognized as a place for aspiring talent to make their mark. And, yet, many professionals who have accomplished star status, fame or fortune started out here, and there are so many more who have stayed on to enjoy the vibrant theatre scene, the strong sense of community and a quality of life that is difficult to replicate on either coast.

Ask professionals who have elected to make art in Chicago to explain the appeal of this sprawling Midwestern city on Lake Michigan's western shore, and the list of reasons are extensive.

"There is more work available per actor here than there is in New York or LA, [although] a lot of it is non-paying or not paying well," says Sheldon Patinkin, chair of the Theatre Department of Columbia College Chicago. "To actually feel like you're an actor, designer or director—that is, a working actor, designer or director—Chicago is better than New York or LA."

Chicago "inspires a little more sanity than you'll find on either of the coasts," says actor Lance Baker. The opportunities are also bountiful, continues Baker— a self-described "born and bred Midwestern boy" who came to Chicago to attend DePaul University and found an acting job immediately upon graduation, albeit an unpaid one.

"If you're not working, you can constantly be auditioning at least," he says. "There's very little chance that you will feel there aren't ears willing to listen to your voice. It is more difficult to disappear into the morass in Chicago."

Baker, now an Equity actor who performs regularly around the city and has been seen at Court Theatre and Steppenwolf, says, "It's a place where the cream does rise to the top and, when you get up to the upper tiers, you do tend to meet people who are passionate about theatre and performance and take what they do seriously. These aren't people who are hopping aboard some gravy train because they have the best cheekbones."

Those hiring in the industry are willing to take a chance on new people in Chicago, says lighting designer Jaymi Lee Smith. "Unlike in a lot of theatre cities, you are given opportunities a lot sooner here...It's such a tight knit community that people are willing to leave a little bit of a legacy and, in some ways, mentor younger artists."

Smith, whose designs have been seen at Victory Gardens, Steppenwolf and Next Theatre, is also enthusiastic about the supportive culture in the production community here, adding that, "Everyone works so closely together to help each other with shows."

As Chuck Smith, a resident director at the Goodman Theatre, concurs, "No one out here is standing all alone unless they want to stand alone...It's amazing how much theatre companies are willing to help one another here."

Chicago has a well deserved reputation as being an "extremely open theatre community," says Marj Halperin, executive director of the League of Chicago Theatres. Here, any group of artists can get a lease on a storefront and launch a season of their own. But it goes even deeper than that, Halperin says, "It's about individuals who are free to call each other and ask for advice, whether they're calling the oldest or newest theatre in the city...Theatre companies freely exchange information here in a way that I don't think other cities do."

That support network makes Chicago a very comfortable place to make art, and that translates to the artists' ability to learn and grow, she said.

Chicago is also a good place to learn your trade. Aside from great opportunities for hands-on experience, there are many training centers and universities offering programs in film, television and theatre.

Getting your training in Chicago can help, says Patinkin. "While you're in school, you get to know a lot of people who could hire you when you get out of school." Also, "There's already an in-road, minor though it might be, if you go to school in Chicago."

The students and faculty make a contribution to Chicago's theatre, but they are only part of the mix. At all times, there is a great deal of talent at various levels of experience in the city, says Chuck Smith, also a League of Chicago Theatres board member. "You've got all these bases covered. You've got new talent coming in, you've got the transient talent coming in and sort of stabilizing the industry, and you've got all these old-timers who sort of guide the ship along."

Chicago has a huge amount of talent, which is often impressively shown on very tight budgets, and the community is bolstered by a certain amount of urban pride, Patinkin says. "Chicagoans, whether they actually go to the theatre or not, seem very aware that we are a national theatre town and they like that."

A supportive funding community and political environment also help make Chicago an important center for theatre in the nation.

The city government's "conscious choice" to support the arts and culture as an engine for economic and social development has been critical in the development of a vibrant theatre community, says Joan Channick, deputy director of Theatre Communications Group, the national organization for American theatre.

Chicago is now a "self-sufficient theatre city" in a way that isn't true of many cities in this country, she said. "It's become one of the places that we look to for the development of new and exciting work, and a high caliber of work."

There is a desire to create a body of work and a style of performance that differs from what has been present in American theatre. "The Chicago influence can be felt through the theatre today in a way that wasn't true 30 years ago," Channick says. "Other cities now aspire to be like Chicago."

And, finally, it is the life available to artists still struggling to "make it" in Chicago that clinches the deal, these industry representatives agreed.

"Most artists live a kind of itinerant life, and Chicago is now one of those places that people can say 'I am going to move to Chicago and have a life in Chicago,'" Channick says.

After four years as a designer in the city, Jaymi Lee Smith says she is just beginning to hit a glass ceiling here as far as opportunities go. Still, she's reluctant to move full-time to either coast. "I can do what I love here and have a good life here," she says. "I enjoy my quality of life without artistic compromises."

Coming to Chicago doesn't mean you have to ignore the call of New York or LA, but for someone just starting out in the industry, this city is well regarded as a starting-off point. "For those who can act, will act and must act, Chicago—of the three, for me at least—seems the best place to be," says Baker. "In Chicago, work begets work, and if you're committed to it and you're looking for work, you can find it."

Welcome to Your First Taste of Chicago— Without a Pickle on a Stick

By Chris Gatto, with additional reporting by Mechelle Moe

"It's 106 miles to Chicago. We've got a full tank of gas, half a pack of cigarettes, it's dark and we're wearing sun glasses. Hit it!"—Jake and Elwood Blues

So, you've decided to make the leap to Chicago. Just what is the allure of this town? Something has drawn millions of immigrants and visitors to Chicago, whose name was lovingly coined from an Algonquin Indian word meaning "place of the onion" or, more alluringly, "place of the bad smell." The history of Chicago is unwittingly and yet accurately told by Michael Palin's Father character in The Holy Grail: "All I had when I started was swamp...other kings said I was daft to build a castle on a swamp, but I built it all the same...just to show 'em. It sank into the swamp. So I built another one...that sank into the swamp. I built a third one...that burnt down, fell over, then sank into the swamp...but the fourth one stayed up." Chicago is exactly that: a city built on a smelly swamp that, throughout its history, has had to be pulled out of the muck and rebuilt several times over. It is an incredibly resilient, diverse, and ever-changing metropolis made up of three million residents populating well over 100 diverse neighborhoods. For you, the next question is: Where do I fit in?

"There was no need to inform us of the protocol involved. We were from Chicago and knew all about cement."—Groucho Marx

In order to find a place to live, you need to know how to move about the city easily and efficiently. The streets are set up on a grid system, running north/south and east/west with an occasional diagonal street thrown into the mix. State Street is 0 E/W, Madison Street is 0 N/S, and addresses are counted upward in number value from this point. Main thoroughfares can be found just about every four blocks running every direction, so you're never far from a bus or 'L' stop (above/below ground subway system).

Car owners should keep in mind that morning rush hour generally lasts from 6:30 a.m. to 10 a.m., while the afternoon congestion is usually from 2:30 p.m. to 7 p.m. Then, once you get to your location (if traveling within the city), you must allow time to park, especially in neighborhoods where most of the theatres are located (Lakeview, Lincoln Park, Rogers Park, Old Town, Downtown). Don't cheat with parking; if the sign says "No Parking," they mean it! They will ticket and/or tow your car (tickets average $50+ and tows are generally $150+) without a second thought. Lastly, add additional time to your commute if the weather rears its head. Chicagoans will often tell you that the city has two seasons: winter and construction.

"I miss everything about Chicago, except January and February."— Gary Cole

There is no surefire way to approach the housing quandary; however, a good method is to pick your neighborhood first. After you've put your bags down and caught your breath, you will be greeted by an amazing array of intricately interwoven and vibrant neighborhoods. Each neighborhood in Chicago has its own distinct personality. To aid you in your search, "The Book" has provided you with some neighborhood profiles for areas throughout the city that are popular with actors and artists. We are providing you with the most current 2003 information about rent rates, crime safety, and general neighborhood flavor. The rent information was collected from the CHICAGO READER (www.chicagoreader.com), and the crime statistics were taken from the Chicago Police Department Web site. Please note: Violent crime "grades" given to a neighborhood include person-on-person crimes like assault, sexual assault, murder, battery, and mugging, while total crime includes that number plus things like vandalism, theft, and arson. So, if you see a neighborhood with an "A" for violent crime and a "D-" for total crime, you might assume that your body will be safe, but your property may not.

"My first day in Chicago, September 4, 1983. I set foot in this city, and just walking down the street, it was like roots, like the motherland. I knew I belonged here."—Oprah Winfrey

Remember, the profiles are intended to be guidelines as neighborhoods are always changing. Most importantly, you need to go visit the neighborhoods that sound interesting to you. Make sure you feel safe, that the neighborhood meets your requirements for transportation and/or parking, and that the personality of the neighborhood suits you (not your friends). Here are some last tips to keep in mind:

- Visit the neighborhood during both day and night.
- Ask the people who live there—friends, acquaintances—what it's like.
- Do you need parking?
- Where's the nearest public transportation?
- Is there nightlife in the neighborhood?
- Will you like coming home to this neighborhood?

Other useful Web sites for Chicago neighborhood info:

www.cityofchicago.org

www.metromix.com

www.chicagoreader.com

It's a tall order, but don't be intimidated. The exciting part is that you get to experience all the diversity and cultural activity in the city, then choose where you will live. You make the choice!

Quotes from www.cityofchicago.org – BrainCandy 2001.

On the Road Again

The Chicagoland interstate highway system has honorary names that designate an entire interstate, or a portion of one, or a merged combination of two or more. Although they can be confusing, these names are important to master. Here is a definitive list.

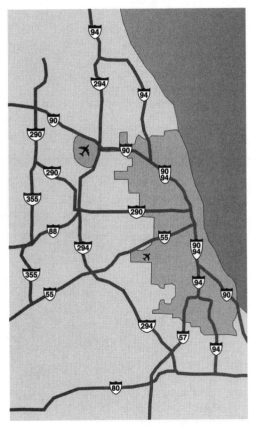

The Kennedy 90 from O'Hare airport to the Loop (including the 94 merge)

The Eisenhower 290

The Stevenson 55

The Edens 94 north of the 90/94 merge

The Dan Ryan 94 south of the Loop and part of 57

The Bishop Ford 94 south after the split with 57

The Kingery 94 south after merging with 294 and 80

The Skyway 90 south of the Loop after 90 and 94 separate

The Tri-State Tollway 294

The Northwest Tollway 90 west of O'Hare, leads to Northwest suburbs

The North-South Tollway 355

The East-West Tollway 88 (starts where 290 meets 294, leads to Western suburbs)

What the 'L' ?

Chicago has a great transit system that is anchored by the 'L'—an elevated and underground train system. There are nine color-coded routes that can transport you to almost any destination you desire in the city, including both major airports (O'Hare and Midway) and some select suburbs. The Chicago Transit Authority (CTA) operates both the train and bus system (which is also quite extensive and user-friendly). Fares are set at $1.50 per ride. You can transfer within a two hour timeframe twice for an additional 30 cents. Transfers from bus to 'L' or vice versa

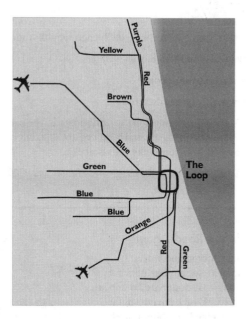

are accepted. While buses still accept paper and coin money, the primary way to get around is by fare card. CTA vending machines are located at all 'L' locations. For more information, visit www.transitchicago.com or call 1-888/YOUR-CTA.

Metra—A Chicago Commuter's Lifeline

The Metra rail system connects Chicago to almost all its surrounding suburbs, and commuters swear by it. For under $10, you can travel from the farthest reaches of suburbia, as well as parts of Indiana and Wisconsin.

For more about Metra, go to www.metrarail.com or call 312/322-6777. The regional transit authority also has a special hotline that can help you navigate how to get from any point A to any point B. Call 312/836-7000, in any area code, for customer service.

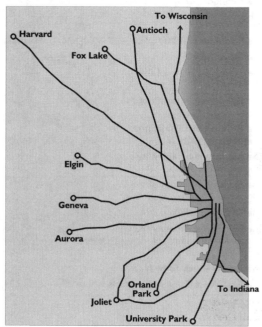

CTA 'L' Train System

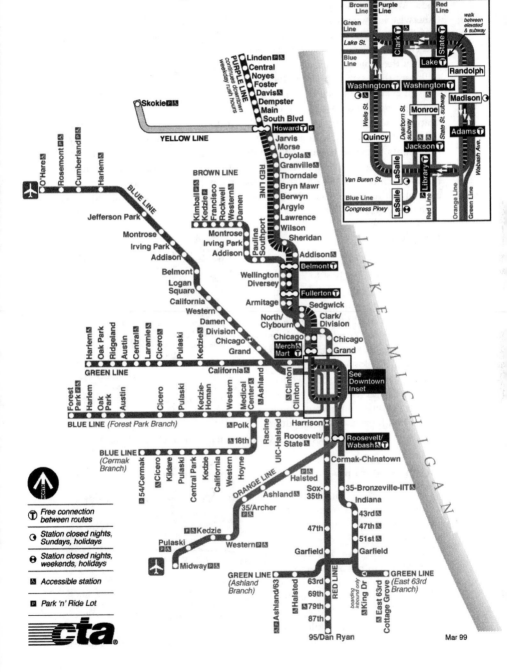

Downtown Inset

YELLOW LINE

PURPLE LINE

BROWN LINE

RED LINE

BLUE LINE

GREEN LINE

BLUE LINE (Forest Park Branch)

BLUE LINE (Cermak Branch)

ORANGE LINE

GREEN LINE (Ashland Branch)

GREEN LINE (East 63rd Branch)

Stations (Purple/Red Line): Linden, Central, Noyes, Foster, Davis, Dempster, Main, South Blvd, Howard, Jarvis, Morse, Loyola, Granville, Thorndale, Bryn Mawr, Berwyn, Argyle, Lawrence, Wilson, Sheridan, Addison, Belmont, Fullerton, Sedgwick, Clark/Division, Chicago, Grand

Skokie — Yellow Line

Brown Line stations: Kimball, Kedzie, Francisco, Rockwell, Western, Damen, Montrose, Irving Park, Addison, Paulina, Southport, Wellington, Diversey, Armitage, North/Clybourn

Blue Line: O'Hare, Rosemont, Cumberland, Harlem, Jefferson Park, Montrose, Irving Park, Addison, Belmont, Logan Square, California, Western, Damen, Division, Chicago, Grand

Green Line: Harlem, Oak Park, Ridgeland, Austin, Central, Laramie, Cicero, Pulaski, Kedzie, California, Damen, Ashland, Clinton

Forest Park, Harlem, Oak Park, Austin, Cicero, Pulaski, Kedzie-Homan, Western, Medical Center, Ashland, Clinton

Blue Line (Cermak Branch): 54/Cermak, Cicero, Kildare, Pulaski, Central Park, Kedzie, California, Western, Hoyne, Polk, 18th

Downtown/Red: Roosevelt/State, Roosevelt/Wabash, Harrison, UIC-Halsted, Racine, Halsted

Orange Line: Halsted, Ashland, 35/Archer, Kedzie, Pulaski, Western, Midway

Merch Mart, Chicago, Grand, See Downtown Inset

Cermak-Chinatown, Sox-35th, 35-Bronzeville-IIT, Indiana, 43rd, 47th, 51st, Garfield, 47th, 63rd, 69th, 79th, 87th, 95/Dan Ryan

Green Line: Ashland/63, Halsted, 63rd, King Dr, East 63rd, Cottage Grove

Pulaski, Kedzie, Western, Garfield

Downtown Inset labels: Brown Line, Purple Line, Green Line, Blue Line, Red Line, Lake St., Clark, State, Lake, Randolph, Washington, Madison, Monroe, Adams, Quincy, Jackson, Van Buren St., Wells St., Dearborn St. subway, State St. subway, Wabash Ave., Library, Congress Pkwy, Van Buren St., LaSalle, Orange Line, Green Line, Red Line, *walk between elevated & subway*

LAKE MICHIGAN

⊤ Free connection between routes

◐ Station closed nights, Sundays, holidays

⊖ Station closed nights, weekends, holidays

🅂 Accessible station

🅿 Park 'n' Ride Lot

Mar 99

Andersonville

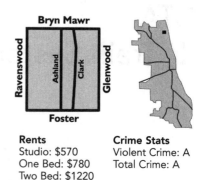

If you're looking for a cozy-but-in-a-hip-and-active-sort-of-way neighborhood, Andersonville's your spot. Otherwise known as Girl's Town, it's a popular stomping ground for lesbians and chilled-out gay men who can't keep up with the frantic pace of Boy's Town to the south. A family-oriented locale with an even mix of single-family homes, condos and apartments, the

Rents
Studio: $570
One Bed: $780
Two Bed: $1220

Crime Stats
Violent Crime: A
Total Crime: A

heart of Andersonville runs along Clark Street starting at Foster Ave. It has an old neighborhood feel with a slew of mom-and-pop and antique shops, tasty restaurants, bars and theatres (Neo-Futurists, Red Hen, Griffin, to name a few). Historically Scandinavian, diversity is a hallmark of this tight-knit neighborhood, which houses large Asian and Hispanic populations. Also, actor bars abound in this area; check out Simon's and Konak's to get a good introduction to the local scene.

Bucktown

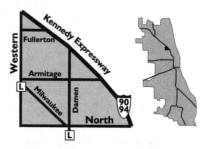

This is just your flat-out "cool" neighborhood with a touch of Bohemian flair. Over the years, Bucktown has transformed from an industrial corridor to a neighborhood alive with art, industry and commerce. Alongside Wicker Park, its sister-neighborhood-in-hipness, Bucktown is populated with cool clubs, night spots, coffee shops, bars and restaurants, and is a popular destination for young professionals and hipsters alike. Trapdoor

Rents
Studio: $600
One Bed: $850
Two Bed: $1340

Crime Stats
Violent Crime: B
Total Crime: B

Theatre, which also has a casting agency branch, is located in this area.

Buena Park

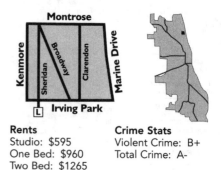

It's close to Wrigley Field, but without the traffic. However, due to its proximity to the ballpark and large numbers of high-rises along the lake, parking can be a nightmare. Although not as attractive or lively as Lakeview, Buena Park still has reasonable rents and is public-transportation-friendly. Also, a handful of theatre companies reside

Rents
Studio: $595
One Bed: $960
Two Bed: $1265

Crime Stats
Violent Crime: B+
Total Crime: A-

in this area, including National Pastime, Mary-Arrchie, Strawdog and Profiles.

Edgewater

Originally, Edgewater was settled by German, Swedish and Irish immigrants who carved out a posh residential subdivision for some of Chicago's most prosperous families and entrepreneurs. Today, it's a richly diverse community of working class families. It also attracts actors and artists with its low rents and easy access to public transportation. A car is okay in this neighborhood, but not necessary. Parking and driving can be bothersome, especially along the eastern edge of the neighborhood. Check out the Artists in Residence building. Raven Theatre's beautiful new space is located on the northwestern edge of the neighborhood.

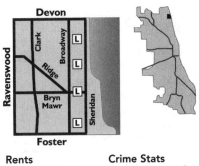

Rents
Studio: $530
One Bed: $750
Two Bed: $1095

Crime Stats
Violent Crime: C
Total Crime: B

Evanston

Just north of the city, Evanston is home to Northwestern University, which has cultivated a lot of Chicago talent and theatre companies. While some areas are very exclusive with mansion districts, the rents around the university and west of Ridge Street are quite reasonable. Overall, living here is generally more expensive than the city— and if you're the buying mood, the taxes can total more than your mortgage payment. Piven, Next Theatre and the Actor's Gymnasium are all located in this area.

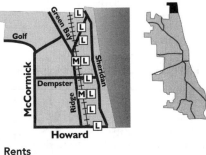

Rents
Studio: $700
One Bed: $870
Two Bed: $1190

Forest Park

Forest Park is a fairly accessible suburb, both by public transportation and car. The blue line stops here, and the Eisenhower Expressway (290) runs right through it. It's a culturally diverse suburban area, and home to Circle Theatre. Parking is not a problem, as the majority of residences are single-family homes. (Note: This western suburb should not be confused with another to the south, the similarly named Park Forest.)

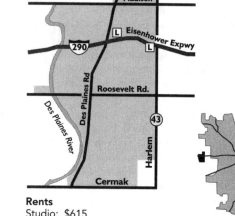

Rents
Studio: $615
One Bed: $700
Two Bed: $875

Humboldt Park

This largely Puerto Rican area is named for the beautiful park located in the middle of the neighborhood. The park itself is part of an intricate and vast boulevard system designed to link all of Chicago's parks from the north to the south sides.

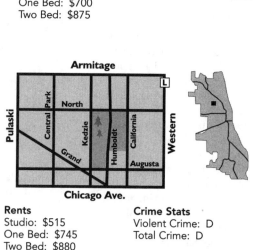

Rents
Studio: $515
One Bed: $745
Two Bed: $880

Crime Stats
Violent Crime: D
Total Crime: D

The park serves as a meeting and gathering place for events and recreation. Division Street, running through the southern end of the neighborhood, is known to the locals as "Paseo Boricua." It's a great neighborhood with vivid ethnic sights, smells and tastes; however, Humboldt Park still has problems associated with gang activity.

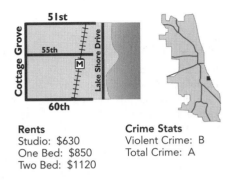

Hyde Park

Hyde Park flourished as a neighborhood beginning in 1892, corresponding with the founding of the University of Chicago. The World's Columbian Exposition in 1893 further boosted development. The area is reminiscent of a quiet, yet busy New England college town and reflects the diverse lifestyles of the students, professors and professionals who make this their home. Streets are lined with old, shady trees, while block after block displays an incredible array of 19th and 20th century residential architecture—some of the most beautiful in the city. While the university serves as the anchor of the neighborhood, other sites and attractions are equally accessible, including the South Shore Cultural Center, the DuSable Museum of African American History and the Museum of Science and Industry. And who could forget the Court Theatre? Once you've taken in the cultural ambiance, you can slip a bit northwest for a down and dirty ball game over at Comiskey Park—make that US Cellular Field. If the game isn't excitement enough, then maybe the fireworks afterwards will satisfy your entertainment needs.

Rents
Studio: $630
One Bed: $850
Two Bed: $1120

Crime Stats
Violent Crime: B
Total Crime: A

Lakeview

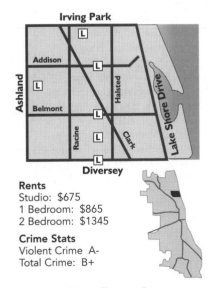

There's always something to do here—day or night. Late (and late-late) night bars, 24-hour eateries, Wrigley Field, diverse restaurants, coffee shops, vintage stores and a bevy of theatres are just a few reasons this area is so vibrant. Lakeview is a mix of young professionals, college grads and families. The rents definitely tend to be pricey; however, the saying "location, location, location" is very applicable here. Besides, it's always good to go where the boys are, and Chicago's definitive gay neighborhood—coined Boy's Town—is right here, running along Halsted between Belmont and Grace.

Rents
Studio: $675
1 Bedroom: $865
2 Bedroom: $1345

Crime Stats
Violent Crime A-
Total Crime: B+

Lakeview also serves as the central nervous system of the off-Loop theatre scene, with a slew of resident companies and shows in its vicinity, including Bailiwick, TimeLine, WNEP, Stage Left, ComedySportz, ImprovOlympic, The Theatre Building and Blue Man Group. Still, keep in mind that because of all this wonderful activity, parking and traffic are generally HORRIFIC. Permit parking is in full regulation here, but public transportation, thankfully, is plentiful and always accessible.

Lincoln Park

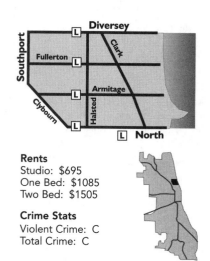

Lincoln Park boasts one of the most desirable zip codes in the City of Chicago. That claim is arguable—depending on taste and yuppie endurance—but the area definitely seems to have population issues, as residents spill over into surrounding neighborhoods with cheaper rents. The area is a mixture of residential and commercial zones, and is chock full of shopping, restaurants, bars and lots of single, beautiful people. It's also the home of DePaul University, Lincoln Park Zoo and lots of theatre, including Victory Gardens, Steppenwolf, The Royal George, Athenaeum and the Apollo.

Rents
Studio: $695
One Bed: $1085
Two Bed: $1505

Crime Stats
Violent Crime: C
Total Crime: C

Lincoln Square

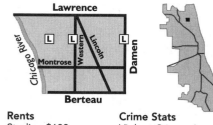

Lincoln Square is a homey German neighborhood that has become increasingly popular over the past several years. Overall, it's a diverse mix of Latino, Asian and Caucasian families; however, gentrification is hitting this area hard, making the formerly hidden gem increasingly crowded and expensive. Nevertheless, public transportation is good, and car parking is reasonable (for now). The Old Town School of Folk Music, TinFish Theatre and Phoenix Ascending are located here.

Rents
Studio: $680
One Bed: $735
Two Bed: $1010

Crime Stats
Violent Crime: A
Total Crime: B

Logan/Palmer Square

This ethnically diverse neighborhood was originally settled in the early 1900s by poor immigrant tradesmen who gradually built prosperous businesses in the area. These "nouveau riche" also erected huge mansions in a mishmash of architectural styles, many of which still complement the neighborhood. Following in the eclectic heritage of the area, Logan/Palmer Square is extremely popular with artists. Gentrification is now driving up the price of living in some parts of the neighborhood. Still, it has retained an artsy feel and is very accessible by car and public transportation.

Rents
Studio: $640
One Bed: $720
Two Bed: $1170

Crime Stats
Violent Crime: C-
Total Crime: C-

Northbrook

This northern suburb is easily accessible by car and the Metra train. However, you need to factor in traffic when estimating travel time, which tends to grow exponentially during and around rush hour. Rents are a bit high because the area is home to primarily high-income, single-family residents.

Rents
One Bed: $835
Two Bed: $1045

15

Oak Park

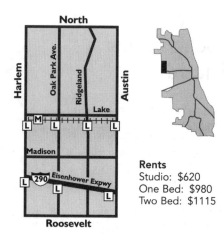

This diverse community has a historic, yet progressive, feel—like many college towns. It has a prominent place in history, being famous for the architecture of Frank Lloyd Wright and as the home (although not birthplace) of Ernest Hemingway. Because of its close proximity to the city, easy parking and available public transportation, Oak Park is attractive to many artists and actors. Rents, however, tend to

Rents
Studio: $620
One Bed: $980
Two Bed: $1115

be high. Oak Park even has its own downtown area, which gives it a warm, hometown feel. Additionally, there is a large gay population residing in Oak Park; this suburb is one of the few communities in the country that gives domestic partnership benefits to gay spouses of city employees.

Old Town

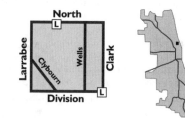

Sandwiched between the Gold Coast and Lincoln Park, the historic neighborhood of Old Town is a treasure trove of pricey restaurants, upscale shops and bars. Originally settled by German immigrants in the 1850s, the area was virtually destroyed by the Great Chicago Fire of 1871. The buildings that survived—

Rents
Studio: $850
One Bed: $1195
Two Bed: $1630

Crime Stats
Violent Crime: C+
Total Crime: C-

Victorian framed wood cottages and Queen Anne style homes—make up what is today known as the Old Town Triangle. The heart of Old Town (near Wells and North Ave.) lies close to the lake and adjoining parks, and it forms the theatrical epicenter of the neighborhood. Here stands the world famous Second City, A Red Orchid Theatre, Zanies Comedy Club and the never-ending run of Tony 'n' Tina's Wedding at Piper's Alley Theatre.

Park Forest

This southern suburb is located off Route 57. Park Forest previously boasted one of the original "regional shopping malls," acting as the prototype for such malls as Old Orchard and Water Tower Place. The community is a mix of both working class and professionals and has a comparatively low crime rate. Rents are reasonable, but public transportation is scarce—residents who venture into the city will have to fight traffic. The equity theatre Illinois Theatre Center (ITC), as well as the Tall Grass Arts Association Art Gallery and School, reside here.

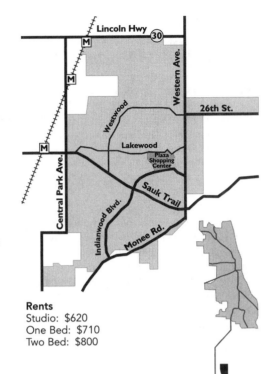

Rents
Studio: $620
One Bed: $710
Two Bed: $800

Pilsen

Pilsen is truly an immigrant's neighborhood. Formerly the entryway for the Polish, Irish and Czech, Pilsen is now home to the largest Mexican community in the United States. According to Citysearch.com, the heart of the Mexican business community primarily runs along 18th Street, where taquerias, fruiterias and other small, family-owned businesses operate. The area attracts many artists with its rustic old warehouse and loft spaces; add to this tradition of activism and social reform, and a hotbed for artistic creativity is born. The Duncan YMCA Chernin Center for the Arts is located in here. Somewhat accessible by 'L' and car, Pilsen is anchored by the University of Illinois at Chicago on the north side. Crime can be a concern, with gang activity still reported in this area.

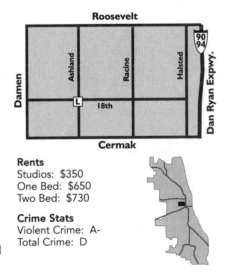

Rents
Studios: $350
One Bed: $650
Two Bed: $730

Crime Stats
Violent Crime: A-
Total Crime: D

Printer's Row/South Loop

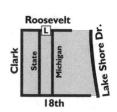

Like many Chicago's neighborhoods, Printer's Row started out as a bustling industrial area. It fell into ruin and neglect for a period of time before its current era of revitalization. This neighborhood is close to everything; it's very popular with young professionals working in the Loop, and the neighborhood

Rents
Studio: $845
One Bed: $1130
Two Bed: $1750

Crime Stats
Violent Crime: A-
Total Crime: B

reflects the tastes of those residents. Additionally, students attending nearby Columbia College and Roosevelt University live in the area. In fact, a large joint-dorm for the surrounding colleges is under construction. Easy access to the area is provided by public transportation, as well as by car via Lake Shore Drive and nearby expressways. Culture is close—just a short jaunt to the Adler Planetarium, the Shedd Aquarium, the Field Museum of Natural History and the Art Institute. For sports fans and outdoors enthusiasts, Soldier Field and Grant Park are at your doorstep. Big houses like the Goodman, Chicago Theatre, Gallery 37's Storefront Theatre, the Shubert and Noble Fool all reside in the nearby Loop area.

Ravenswood

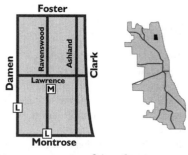

In personality, Ravenswood has a similar feel to Lincoln Square. Originally settled by German immigrants, the area historically has been working class, although recently it has become a haven for increasing numbers of young professionals fleeing the crowds and high prices of trendier neighborhoods to the south. Still, Ravenswood maintains a family feel ensconced within tree-lined streets. Public transportation is

Rents
Studio: $595
One Bed: $790
Two Bed: $1005

Crime Stats
Violent Crime: A
Total Crime: B

easy and parking isn't a complete nightmare, so going out and about in this neighborhood is not prohibitive. Lastly, the rents are fairly affordable, but are rising with gentrification. Defiant and a few other theatres have their rehearsal and office space housed in the warehouses of this area.

River West

This neighborhood is aptly named, as it is situated just west of the Chicago River. Formerly an industrial area, River West is home to many artists attracted to the large loft spaces, close proximity to downtown, easy public transportation and great night life. Those lofts not taken by artists, however, befell the fate of similar properties in other neighborhoods: Developers gobbled them up for new condominium residences or luxury town homes. As a result, this former center of blue-collar industrial enterprise has risen from the depths of working-class sweat to become one of the trendiest, most sought after neighborhoods in the city. Chicago Dramatists is located here, which fosters many new playwrights and work.

Rents
Studio: $705
One Bed: $950
Two Bed: $1290

Crime Stats
Violent Crime: B
Total Crime: B

Rogers Park

This northernmost neighborhood is popular among actors and artists for so many reasons: It's close to the lake, public transportation is readily available and the rents are still low. Loyola University sits on the eastern edge of the community and is surrounded by the standard collegiate fare—coffee shops, bookstores, restaurants, etc. There's lots of theatre in the area, as Lifeline, Curious Theatre Branch and Boxer Rebellion are local residents. This is an area where the neighborhood changes from block to block and safety varies, especially at night. Be sure to walk or visit the area during both day and night to test levels of comfort.

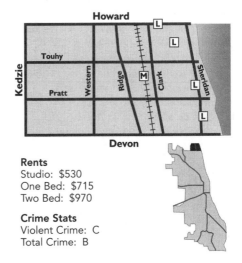

Rents
Studio: $530
One Bed: $715
Two Bed: $970

Crime Stats
Violent Crime: C
Total Crime: B

Roscoe Village

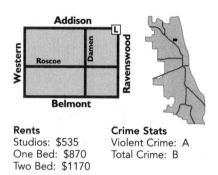

This funky little community situated directly west of Lakeview might soon make Chicago's most endangered neighborhood list. Rent is on the rise—but still reasonable—as Lincoln Parkers continue to spread north and west. Roscoe Village maintains a mellow cafe atmosphere that is rich with bars, restaurants and small shops. It also

Rents
Studios: $535
One Bed: $870
Two Bed: $1170

Crime Stats
Violent Crime: A
Total Crime: B

houses one of Chicago's oldest antique districts. The area is heavy on artists but light on theatres—except for the Viaduct, which is situated just west of this area, as well as Four Moon Tavern, an actor's bar run by actors.

St. Ben's

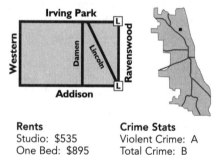

Similar in feel to Roscoe Village, St. Ben's is named for the Catholic parish of the area, Saint Benedict's. This neighborhood is primarily residential, with a lot of single-family homes and some apartment buildings. Due to this neighborhood design, parking is decent. Rents are a bit high, but there are lots of things to do along Lincoln Avenue.

Rents
Studio: $535
One Bed: $895
Two Bed: $1125

Crime Stats
Violent Crime: A
Total Crime: B

American Theatre Company and Breadline Theatre Group are based in the area.

Skokie

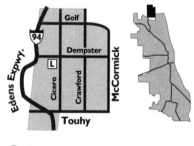

Skokie is home to one of the largest Jewish populations in the area. The suburb is diverse, however, containing large communities of Asians and Latinos as well. Skokie is a great option for actors and artists with families; the schools are good, and the area is close to the city. Skokie even has an 'L' extension train called the "Skokie Swift," or the Yellow Line, making public transportation into the city readily avail-

Rents
Studio: $600
One Bed: $810
Two Bed: $1000

able. Skokie is home to Northlight Theatre, which is housed in the Northshore Center for the Performing Arts.

Ukrainian Village

Contrary to its name, Ukrainian Village is really quite diverse, housing large communities of Latinos, Italians and, of course, Ukrainians. It's a cultural hotbed that makes the environment ripe for creative endeavor. While public transportation is available only by bus, parking isn't too bad in spots. The rents remain low, but it is yet another neighborhood feeling the pangs of gentrification. One distinctive Ukrainian Village trait is a real obligation between neighbors to look out for each other. There are many longtime residents who seem to know everything about everybody. This vigilance can be a relief or a hassle, depending on your point of view.

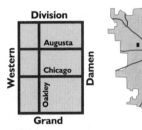

Division
Augusta
Western
Chicago
Oakley
Damen
Grand

Rents
Studio: $545
One Bed: $820
Two Bed: $1035

Crime Stats
Violent Crime: B
Total Crime: B

Uptown

Over the past year, the Uptown area has entered a phase of incredible revitalization. This historic neighborhood was in its heyday in the 1920s, then a bustling center of commerce and culture. The heart of this vitality was located at the corner of Lawrence and Broadway, which attracted entertainment seekers and big shots like Al Capone and Charlie Chaplin. Over the years, however, the neighborhood fell victim to disrepair and neglect and became known by the locals as "skid row," with its many homeless and vagrants taking up residence in the low-rent area. But local community groups formed to resurrect the neighborhood, making gentrification an issue. The Uptown Theatre is scheduled for a complete renovation, and developers have become interested in the inexpensive real estate. Frankie J's is also located here.

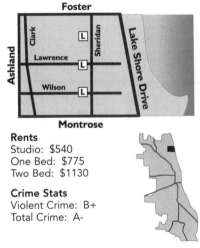

Foster
Ashland
Clark
Lawrence
Sheridan
Wilson
Lake Shore Drive
Montrose

Rents
Studio: $540
One Bed: $775
Two Bed: $1130

Crime Stats
Violent Crime: B+
Total Crime: A-

Wrigleyville

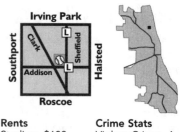

Irving Park

Aptly named, Wrigleyville—a neighborhood within the larger Lakeview community—lies directly around the ballpark. While strolling through the neighborhood, there can be no doubt where you are, as you are constantly bombarded with Cubs memorabilia. Great eats and watering holes abound—although most cater to the sports/frat crowd. Theatres are also nearby, including ImprovOlympic and Live Bait. Living by the ballpark provides endless social opportunities, but the very thing that makes the neighborhood breaks it too. Parking is terrible. Streets are crowded, and rents are high. Public transportation, however, is excellent.

Rents
Studios: $680
One Bed: $1000
Two Bed: $1325

Crime Stats
Violent Crime: A
Total Crime: B

West Loop/ Greektown

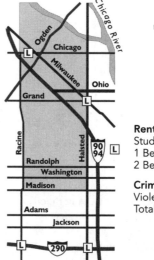

Just west of the Loop is a neighborhood with lots to offer any resident. True to its name, Greektown offers loads of Greek cuisine and culture. There are shops and clubs emphasizing the roots of this rich heritage. Very accessible by both public transportation and car, this former meat market area has been transformed into expensive real estate, with new developments and rehabbed condos popping up everywhere. Harpo Studios and Lou Conte Dance Studio are housed here.

Rents
Studio: $715
1 Bedroom: $1190
2 Bedroom: $1745

Crime Stats
Violent Crime: B
Total Crime: B

Wicker Park

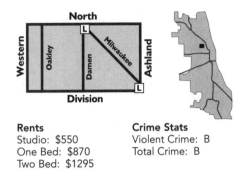

While gentrification needles at this neighborhood, the residents of Wicker Park try to buck it at every turn. The most recent and public display of defiance happened in 2001, when MTV's "The Real World" decided to set up shop on North Ave. Many residents raised their voices, concerned

Rents
Studio: $550
One Bed: $870
Two Bed: $1295

Crime Stats
Violent Crime: B
Total Crime: B

about the commercialization of the area and the potential impact on parking. This, however, did not shut down the production. Young, hip and trendy—individuality is golden here. The park itself is just north of the intersection of Damen, North and Milwaukee—the heart of the Wicker Park neighborhood and a hotbed for late-night activity. Public transportation is readily available, and a great help with troublesome parking. The rents are still relatively affordable, and safety has improved significantly over the last few years. Chopin Theatre and Roadworks are located here.

Apartment Services

Apartment Source
2638 N. Halsted
Chicago, IL 60614
Phone: 773/404-9900
Fax: 773/404-0669

Cagan Management
3856 W. Oakton
Skokie, IL 60076
Phone: 847/679-5512
Fax: 847/679-5516

Century 21 Amquest
2853 N. Halsted
Chicago, IL 60657
Phone: 773/404-2100 ext. 111
www.century21amquest.com

City Living Apartment Rentals
1300 W. Belmont
Chicago, IL 60657
Phone: 773/525-6161

Oak Park Regional Housing
1041 South Blvd.
Oak Park, IL 60302
www.apartmentsoakpark.org

Realty & Mortgage
928 W. Diversey
Chicago, IL 60614
Phone: 773/549-8300
www.aptrentals.com

Relocation Central
21 W. Elm, 2nd Flr.
Chicago, IL 60610
Phone: 312/255-9920
Fax: 312/255-9928
www.relocationcentral.com

The Apartment People
3121 N. Broadway
Chicago, IL 60657
Phone: 773/248-8800
Fax: 773/248-1007
www.apartmentpeople.com

Urban Equities R.E.C.
1602 W. Granville
Chicago, IL 60660
Phone: 773/743-4141
Fax: 773/465-4672

Housing

Artist in Residence
6165 N. Winthrop
Chicago, IL 60660
Phone: 800/LIVE-ART
Alt. Phone: 773/743-8259
www.artistinresidence.com

Sovereign Apartments
1040 W. Granville
Chicago, IL 60660
Phone: 773/274-8000
Fax: 773/274-1321

Three Arts Club (for women in the arts)
1300 N. Dearborn
Chicago, IL 60610
Phone: 312/944-6250
Fax: 312/944-6284
www.threearts.org

**Under the Ginko Tree
(Bed and Breakfast)**
Gloria Onischuk
300 N. Kenilworth
Oak Park, IL 60302
Phone: 708/524-2327
Fax: 708/524-2729

*Under the Ginko Tree Bed and Breakfast
Home: The Bed and Breakfast home in
the historic district of Oak Park.*

*A spacious home ideally used for filming,
photo shoots, etc.*

Temp Agencies

A Personnel Commitment
208 N. LaSalle, Ste. 189
Chicago, IL 60604-1003
Phone: 888/GET-A-JOB
Fax: 312/251-5154

Active Temporary Services
25 E. Washington, Ste. 1717
Chicago, IL 60602
Phone: 312/726-5771
Fax: 312/726-3273

Active Temporary Services
3145 N. Lincoln - Main Level
Chicago, IL 60657
Phone: 773/404-5700
Fax: 773/404-9635

Advanced Personnel
225 W. Washington, Ste. 500
Chicago, IL 60606
Phone: 312/422-9333
Fax: 312/422-9310
Alt. Phone: 312/335-9111
(Michigan Ave.)
www.advpersonnel.com

*Advanced Personnel is a staffing firm
supplying office support employees to
major financial, healthcare and Fortune
500 corporations in Chicagoland. Our
flexible scheduling helps match actors
with temporary and full-time positions.
Corporate positions: executive assistants,
customer service professionals, production specialists, desktop publishers and
administrative assistants. Contact us at
312/422-9333.*

See our ad on page 24.

Appropriate Temporaries
79 W. Monroe, Ste. 819
Chicago, IL 60603
Phone: 312/782-7215
Fax: 312/704-4195

BPS Staffing, Inc.
200 N. LaSalle, Ste. 1900
Chicago, IL 60601
Phone: 312/920-6710
Fax: 312/920-6744

City Staffing
2 N. LaSalle, Ste. 630
Chicago, IL 60602
Phone: 312/346-3400
Fax: 312/346-5200

See our ad on page 23.

Dunhill Staffing Services
211 W. Wacker, Ste. 1150
Chicago, IL 60606
Phone: 312/346-0933
Fax: 312/346-0837
www.dunhillstaff.com

Kelly Services
20 N. Martingale Rd., Ste. 140
Schaumburg, IL 60173
Phone: 847/995-9350
Fax: 847/995-9366
www.kellyservices.com

Coming to Chicago

25

Loftus & O'Meara
166 E. Superior, Ste. 410
Chicago, IL 60611
Phone: 312/944-2102
Fax: 312/944-7009

Mack & Associates Personnel, Ltd.
Lana Iceberg
100 N. LaSalle, Ste. 2110
Chicago, IL 60602
Phone: 312/368-0677
Fax: 312/368-1868

Manpower Temporary Services
Phone: 312/648-4555
www.manpowerchicago.com

Paige Temporary, Inc.
5215 Old Orchard Rd., Ste. 500
Skokie, IL 60077
Phone: 847/966-0111
Fax: 847/966-8479
www.paigepersonnel.com

Prestige Employment Service
19624 Governors Hwy.
Flossmoor, IL 60422
Phone: 708/798-7666
Fax: 708/798-9099

Pro Staff Personnel Services
10 S. Wacker, Ste. 2250
Chicago, IL 60606
Phone: 312/575-2120
Fax: 312/641-0224

Proven Performers
180 N. LaSalle, Ste. 3820
Chicago, IL 60601
Phone: 312/917-1111
Fax: 312/917-0474
www.provensolutions.biz

Right Employment Center
53 W. Jackson
Chicago, IL 60604
Phone: 312/427-3136
Fax: 312/427-3145
www.rightservices.com

Select Staffing
208 S. LaSalle, Ste. 1244
Chicago, IL 60604
Phone: 312/849-2229
Fax: 312/849-2234

Seville Staffing
180 N. Michigan, Ste. 1510
Chicago, IL 60601
Phone: 312/368-1272
Fax: 312/368-0207

Seville Staffing has been providing Chicago-area talent with temporary Office Support jobs such as: Administrative Assistant, Word Processor, Reception, Data Entry and Customer Service Clerk positions since 1979. We also offer weekly pay, vacation pay, health insurance, and respect for the work you do. Call 312/368-1272 for an appointment.

Smart Staffing
29 S. LaSalle, Ste. 635
Chicago, IL 60603
Phone: 312/696-5306
Fax: 312/696-0317
www.smartstaffing.com

Spherion
11 S. LaSalle, Ste. 2155
Chicago, IL 60603
Phone: 312/781-7220
www.spherion.com

Temporary Opportunities
53 W. Jackson, Ste. 215
Chicago, IL 60604
Phone: 312/922-5400
Fax: 312/347-1206
www.opgroup.com

The Choice for Staffing
123 W. Madison, Ste. 1600
Chicago, IL 60602
Phone: 312/372-4500
Fax: 312/853-4068
www.choicestaff.com

The Larko Group
11 S. LaSalle, Ste. 1720
Chicago, IL 60603
Phone: 312/857-2300
Fax: 312/857-2355
www.thelarkogroup.com
See our ad on page 26.

Today's Office Staffing
1900 E. Golf Rd., Ste. L10
Schaumburg, IL 60173
Phone: 847/240-6550
Fax: 847/240-6560

Unique Office Services
203 N. Wabash, Ste. 608
Chicago, IL 60601
Phone: 312/332-4183
Fax: 312/332-2688

Venturi Staffing Partners
222 N. LaSalle, Ste. 450
Chicago, IL 60601
Phone: 312/541-4141
Fax: 312/641-1762

Watson Dwyer Staffing
25 E. Washington, Ste. 707
Chicago, IL 60602
Phone: 312/899-8030
Fax: 312/899-8036

Wordspeed
200 N. Dearborn, Ste. 807
Chicago, IL 60601
Phone: 312/201-1171
Fax: 312/201-1279

Helpful Phone Numbers

AT&T
Phone: 800/222-0300
www.att.com

ComEd (Electric)
P.O. Box 805379
Chicago, IL 60680-5379
Phone: 1/800-Edison-1
Alt. Phone: 1/800-334-7661
www.ceco.com/comed/overview/
ecr_overview.shtml

MCI
Phone: 800/444-3333—Long Distance
Alt. Phone: 888/624-5622—Local Service
www.mci.com

Peoples Energy (Gas)
130 E. Randolph
Chicago, IL 60601
Phone: 866/556-6004—Toll-Free
Alt. Phone: 866/556-6001—Toll-Free
www.peoplesenergy.com

Police (EMERGENCY)
Phone: 911

Police (NON-EMERGENCY)
Phone: 311

Sprint
Phone: 800/877-4646—Long Distance
Alt. Phone: 888/723-8010—Local Service
www.sprint.com

Photo: Aaron Gang

CHAPTER 2
TRAINING

The Neutrino Project
FuzzyCo

Improv Training Gives Actors a Leg Up

By Becky Brett

As actors immersed in the vast sea of Chicago talent, anything that can give you an edge is worth exploring. And most working professionals and casting directors—especially in regards to TV and film—will tell you that there is a very high demand for actors who have improvisational experience.

"In anything from auditioning to reworking a script, actors who have improv training tend to float higher above everyone else," says Beth Kligerman, senior associate producer at The Second City.

Even in the most rigid performance situation, such as in opera where the music strictly dictates how fast you go or what note you hit, "you're still working with another person who may present something different for you to respond to," says Lyric Opera singer Alicia Berneche.

Yes, even Lyric Opera believes in the importance of improv study within their professional training program, incorporating classes with Sheldon Patinkin, stage director and co-founder of The Second City, into their work on operas such as *The Marriage of Figaro* and *Die Fledermaus.*

In fact, according to Kligerman, "The world of acting, theatre and film is turning itself much more to the world of improv, so the ability to improvise is paramount."

When improv training is layered with acting technique "it makes for more consciousness and flow," notes Jonathan Pitts, executive producer of the Chicago Improv Festival (CIF). "You don't see the gears grinding so much."

Patinkin agrees and incorporates improv into all of his training sessions. "Improv exercises and games help enormously in building an ensemble. They help enormously with playing your character's wants and inner life, and they teach you how to play with others."

Actress Edie McClurg (*Ferris Bueller's Day Off*, "WKRP in Cincinnati") uses improv in every job, whether comedic or serious, film or television or even animation. To every scene she says, "I will add the noise of life, which comes from improvisation." Whether in *Natural Born Killers* or *Planes, Trains & Automobiles*, McClurg turns to her improv training to help her "do the next logical thing. When the writer is sitting behind a desk, he's not in the room where the character has to live," says McClurg, so improv helps her round out the scene.

Many stage directors and casting directors now look for actors with improv training, knowing that these actors will be more responsive to each moment on stage. Casting director Claire Simon says that she is "absolutely" more likely to call someone in with improv experience. With all the last minute script changes common to filming commercials, Simon notes, "improv training is especially helpful, and it helps an actor get out of his head."

"You can throw a take on a scene at them, and they'll just run with it," says Bob Mason, casting director for Chicago Shakespeare Theatre and occasional casting consultant for other theatres such as the Goodman. Adding that improv training is "incredibly valuable," he finds actors with improv training have the edge when it comes to parts like the Mechanical roles in *A Midsummer Night's Dream,* where there may not be many lines, but he would cast based on how an actor improvises the character.

Now that you see how useful it is, where can you go for improv classes? Chicago, being the birthplace of modern improvisation for the theatre, is home to many schools specifically geared towards improvisers. Pitts, as executive producer of CIF, recommends that students check out all the different schools and techniques. "Audit classes to see what feels most interesting and exciting to you, and follow your instincts about what feels right," he says. "Improv training is about learning to listen to and use and trust your intuition."

The Second City, ImprovOlympic, The Noble Fool Theatre and many others offer extensive improv training programs. Additionally, annual events such as CIF and the Funny Women Festival provide opportunities to take workshops with teachers from around the globe. For more information on the various schools of thought, also look at yesand.com—the online meeting place for many improvisers—where you can learn about teachers and training centers from the people who have been there.

Knowing that, as an actor, you can make something (a character) from nothing (the suggestion of a whiffle ball) should give you the confidence to make strong acting choices and help you soar from audition to curtain call.

Classes - Acting

Act One Studios, Inc.
640 N. LaSalle, Ste. 535
Chicago, IL 60610
Phone: 312/787-9384
Fax: 312/787-3234
www.actone.com

Commercial Technique I - Get "camera-ready" for all types of commercial auditions.

Industrial Film & Ear Prompter - Learn to analyze and perform technical scripts and use an ear prompter.

TV & Film I, II & Workshop - Learn the "ins and outs" of the film and television world.

Fundamentals I, II & Scene & Monologue Workshop - Learn to make efffective choices from the script.

Acting Instinctively - Flexibility, creativity, and imaginative freedom are explored.

Meisner Technique I, II & Workshop - Leads to a very truthful moment-to-moment style of acting.

Monologue Workshop - Prepare two to four monologues for auditions.

Audition Technique I & II - Learn the art of cold reading theatre auditions.

Shakespeare Beg. & Adv. - Approaches based on the work of Shakespeare & Co.

Masters Class - An ongoing scene study class taught by Steve Scott.

Voice-Over I & II - Learn what it takes to be successful in the voice-over market.

Movement Scene Study - Learn to bring a physical life to your character.

Actors' Center of Chicago
3047 N. Lincoln, Ste. 390
Chicago, IL 60657
Phone: 773/549-3303
Fax: 773/549-0749

Beginning Meisner Technique

Advanced Meisner Repetition

Advanced Meisner Technique

Master Meisner Technique

Movement (based on Williamson technique, adapted to Meisner)

Audition Skills (monologues, cold reading, audition technique)

Beginning Scene Study

Advanced Scene Study

Technique on Camera

TV/Film on Camera

Training

**The Actors Gymnasium
& Performing Arts School**
Noyes Cultural Arts Center
927 Noyes
Evanston, IL 60201
Phone: 847/328-2795
Fax: 847/328-3495
www.actorsgymnasium.com

*Acro-Dance, Clown Theatre, Dance 101,
Drum Performance, Gymnastics , Mime
101, The Lookingglass Workshops,
Pilates-Based Workshop, Viewpoints,
Circus Arts*

Actors Workshop
1044 N. Bryn Mawr
Chicago, IL 60660
Phone: 312/622-1136
www.actorsworkshop.org

*Unlimited classes for a flat fee of $150
per month. The Weekly Grid/Professional
Pathway is a comprehensive and affordable professional training program taking
the actor through the levels of Beginning
to Advanced to Professional. We have an
open door policy. Visitors are always
welcome.*

See our ad on page 33.

The Artistic Home
1420 W. Irving Park
Chicago, IL 60613
Phone: 773/404-1100
Fax: 708/387-7286
Theartistichome@aol.com
www.theartistichome.org

Technique 1, 2, 3

Scene Study

Acting for Film 1 and 2

Voice for the Actor

Playwrights Up and Moving

*The Artistic Home's curriculum is a
Meisner-based technique augmented by
LA and Chicago working experience that
emphasizes living moment to moment,
making strong choices and developing
emotional freedom. Playwrights and
directors are offered hands-on experience in scene study, showcases and workshops of new scripts. Instructors: Kathy
Scambiatterra, John Mossman, Mary Ann
Thebus, CeCe Klinger, Patrick Thornton,
Gillian Kelly.*

The Audition Studio
Rachael Patterson
20 W. Hubbard, Ste. 2E
Chicago, IL 60660
Phone: 312/527-4566
Fax: 312/527-9085
info@theauditionstudio.com
www.theauditionstudio.com

The Audition Studio is committed to training actors in a challenging, supportive professional environment. Our teaching is based upon the "12 Guideposts" of Michael Shurtleff, well-known teacher, casting director and author of the "Actor's Bible," "Audition." Mastery of these prinicples complements instinct and talent with a practical set of skills. This clear-cut technique demystifies the actor's process and offers a path of creative discovery through action.

Classes offered include: Intro to Shurtleff, Cold Reading, Monologue, Scene Study, On-Camera, Voice-Over, Voice, Shakespeare and Workshops.

See our ad on page 34.

Breadline Theatre Group
1802 W. Berenice
Chicago, IL 60613
Phone: 773/327-6096
breadline@breadline.org
www.breadline.org

For our complete range of current classes, please see our Web site.

Chicago Actors Studio
1567 N. Milwaukee
Chicago, IL 60622
Phone: 773/645-0222
Fax: 773/767-4151
chiactorsstudio@aol.com
www.actors-studio.net

Centrally located in Chicago with classes for beginners to working professionals. A training faculty with over 60 years of combined experience that understands each student's individualized needs, creating supportive and encouraging environments. Classes include scene study, character development, film, commercials, stage, voice/diction, auditioning, marketing, student showcase productions, etc. The school has its own theatre, TV station and boot camp.

Chicago Center for the Performing Arts Training Center
777 N. Green
Chicago, IL 60622
Phone: 312/327-2040
Fax: 312/327-2046
www.theaterland.com

Duncan YMCA
Chernins Center for the Arts
1001 W. Roosevelt
Chicago, IL 60608
Phone: 312/738-7980
Fax: 312/738-1420

ETA Creative Arts
7558 S. South Chicago
Chicago, IL 60619-2644
Phone: 773/752-3955
Fax: 773/752-8727
www.etacreativearts.org

Adult Acting - Beginning and Advanced Sound, Lighting, Stage Management How to Audition for Commercials

Illinois Theatre Center
P.O. Box 397
Park Forest, IL 60466
Phone: 708/481-3510
Fax: 708/481-3693
ilthctr@bigplanet.com
www.ilthctr.org

ITC offers classes for children (7 yrs. and older), teens and adults (beginning and advanced levels), and private coaching for auditions and college theatre programs. All courses offer instruction in movement, voice and diction, character developmet, scene study, improv, and use of the imagination. Fall, Winter, Spring (10-week sessions).

The Improv Playhouse
David Stuart
116 W. Lake
Libertyville, IL 60048
Phone: 847/968-4529
Fax: 847/968-4530
www.improvplayhouse.com

The Improv Playhouse, Libertyville. Foundational through advanced improvisation, story theatre, radio drama, beginning through advanced dramatic arts classes for adults and youth. Staff are arts professionals from premier improv and drama programs. Chicago Area Keith Johnstone's Theater Sports Licensee. Several north suburban locations. Contact David Stuart.

Training

35

The Neo-Futurists
5153 N. Ashland
Chicago, IL 60640
Phone: 773/878-4557
Fax: 773/878-4514
NEOFUT@aol.com
www.neofuturists.org

The Neo-Futurists Performance Workshop and Advanced Neo-Futurist Performance Workshop - Both classes are studies in writing, directing and performing your own work.

New American Theatre
118 N. Main
Rockford, IL 61101-1102
Phone: 815/963-9454
www.newamericantheater.com

New American Theatre offers a variety of classes for students ages 5 yrs. to adult. Please call or email for current brochure.

Piven Theatre Workshop
927 Noyes
Evanston, IL 60201
Phone: 847/866-6597
Fax: 847/866-6614
www.piventheatreworkshop.com

This renowned training center offers

beginning, intermediate and professional level classes in improvisation, theatre games, story theatre, and scene study. Submit H/R for intermediate and advanced scene study.

Come learn to play again at the theatre school that launched John & Joan Cusack, Aidan Quinn, Lili Taylor, Jeremy Piven and many more! Classes for young people from 4th grade through high school. Call for current class information.

See our ad on below.

Brenda Pickleman
535 N. Michigan, Ste. 2914
Chicago, IL 60611
Phone: 630/887-0529

Using intensive on-camera scene study and a variety of teaching methods, this workshop is designed to train serious actors to successfully compete in the LA market for film and television. Workshops are held on Tuesday evenings in the heart of Chicago.

Brenda Pickleman - 630/887-0529.

Plasticene
2122 N. Winchester, Ste. 1F
Chicago, IL 60614
Phone: 312/409-0400
www.plasticene.com

Summer Physical Theatre Intensive

Ongoing Workshops

See our ad on below.

Sarantos Studios
2857 N. Halsted
Chicago, IL 60657
Phone: 773/528-7114

Feature Film Acting

Scene Study

Monologue Preparation

On-Camera Auditioning

Basic Acting Technique

The School at Steppenwolf
758 W. North, 4th Flr.
Chicago, IL 60610
Phone: 312/335-1888 ext. 5608
Fax: 312/335-0808
jberry@steppenwolf.org
www.steppenwolf.org

Founded in 1998, The School at

Steppenwolf immerses gifted actors in the ensemble traditions, values and methods that make Steppenwolf unique. Our previous faculty and staff have been unanimous in praise of the environment that the School creates for actors to practice the craft they love as they learn more about the power of working together.

Studio 2
1802 W. Berenice
Chicago, IL 60613
Phone: 773/271-4889
www.studio2chicago.org

At Studio2 we offer Meisner-based training featuring:

Small Classes

Personal Attention

Award Winning Instructors

RESULTS!

The Studio of The Moving Dock
The Fine Arts Building
410 S. Michigan, Ste. 720
Chicago, IL 60605
www.movingdock.org

Training

Victory Gardens Theatre
2257 N. Lincoln
Chicago, IL 60614
Phone: 773/549-5788
Fax: 773/549-2779
trainingcenter@victorygardens.org
www.victorygardens.org

Basic Acting, Musical Theater, Introduction to Scenes & Monologues, Speech & Movement, Dialects, Building a Character, Monologues, Scene Study, Comedy Styles, Directing, Training, Improv

Classes - Improv

The Annoyance
2941 N. Greenview, Ste. 3
Chicago, IL 60611
Phone: 773/929-6200
www.annoyanceproductions.com

ComedySportz
2851 N. Halsted
Chicago, IL 60657
www.comedysportzchicago.com
Phone: 773/549-8080

The Improv Playhouse
116 W. Lake
Libertyville, IL 60048
Phone: 847/968-4529
Fax: 847/968-4530
www.improvplayhouse.com

ImprovOlympic
3541 N. Clark
Chicago, IL 60657
www.improvolymp.com
Phone: 773/880-0199
Fax: 773/880-9979

See our ad on below.

Old Town School of Folk Music
4544 N. Lincoln Ave.
Chicago, IL 60625
Phone: 773/728-6000
Fax: 773/728-6999
www.oldtownschool.org

The Playground
3341 N. Lincoln
Chicago, IL 60657
Phone: 773/871-3793
mastersseries@the-playground.com
www.the-playground.com

Second City
1616 N. Wells
Chicago, IL 60614
www.secondcity.com
Phone: 312/664-3959
Fax: 312/664-9837

See our ad on page 39.

Classes - Dance

The Academy of Dance Arts
1524 Center Circle
Downers Grove, IL 60515
Phone: 630/495-4940
www.theacademy-ibt.com

Ballet (ages 3 to adult), Point, Jazz (ages 3 to adult), Hip-Hop, Tap (ages 3 to adult), Lyrical, Professional Ballet Program

American Dance Center Ballet Co.
10464 W. 163rd Pl.
Orland Park, IL 60467
Phone: 708/747-4969
Fax: 708/747-0424

Ballet, Point, Jazz, Hip-Hop, Modern, Tap, Swing

Authentic Mid East Belly Dance
P.O. Box 56037
Chicago, IL 60656-0037
Phone: 773/693-6300
Fax: 773/693-6302
www.jasminjahal.com

Traditional Middle Eastern
& Classical Egyptian Dance

Ballet Chicago
218 S. Wabash, 3rd Flr.
Chicago, IL 60604
Phone: 312/251-8838
Fax: 312/251-8840
www.balletchicago.org

Ballet (ages 2 1/2-adult); Preparatory,
Student, Professional Training, and
Open/Adult Fitness Divisions; Arts
industry class card discounts available

Beverly Art Center
2407 W. 111th
Chicago, IL 60655
Phone: 773/445-3838
Fax: 773/445-0386

Ballet, Jazz, Modern, Tap, Stretch and
Strength, African

Boitsov Classical Ballet
410 S. Michigan, Ste. 300
Chicago, IL 60605
Phone: 312/663-0844
Fax: 312/939-2094

Ballet - Vaganova Technique (Moscow
Bolshoi Theatre system of training)

Chicago Multicultural Dance Center
806 S. Plymouth Ct.
Chicago, IL 60605
Phone: 312/461-0030
Fax: 312/461-1184
www.cmdcschool.com

Ballet, Jazz, Tap, Latin, Modern, Hip-Hop

Chicago National Association of
Dance Masters
5411 E. State, Ste. 202
Rockford, IL 61108
Phone: 815/397-6052
Fax: 815/397-6799
www.cnadm.com

Workshops only; no ongoing classes

Dance Center Evanston
610 Davis
Evanston, IL 60201
Phone: 847/328-6683
Fax: 847/328-6656
www.dancecenterevanston.com

Ballet, Jazz, Tap, Ballroom, Modern

Dance Dimensions
595B N. Pinecrest
Bolingbrook, IL 60440
Phone: 630/739-1195

Ballet, Jazz, Tap, Ballroom, Swing, Tumbling, Salsa

Dance Therapy Center
Fine Arts Building
410 S. Michigan
Chicago, IL 60605
Phone: 312/461-9826
Fax: 312/461-9843

Ballet, Modern

Dancecenter North
540 N. Milwaukee
Libertyville, IL 60048
Phone: 847/367-7970
Fax: 847/367-7905
www.dancecenterNorth.com

Classical Ballet, Point, Jazz, Tap, Irish Step Dance, Social Dance, Jazz, Funk, Pilates and Extensive Pre-School Program

Discovery Center
2940 N. Lincoln
Chicago, IL 60657
Phone: 773/348-8120
Fax: 773/880-6164
www.discoverycenter.cc

Ballet, Jazz, Modern, Tap, Ballroom, Belly Dance, Contemporary Latin, Hip-Hop, Salsa, Social Dance, Swing, Tango, Kardio Kickboxing

Evanston School of Ballet Foundation
1933 Central
Evanston, IL 60201
Phone: 847/475-9225

Classical Ballet

Golden's School of Dance
1548 Burgundy Pkwy.
Streamwood, IL 60107
Phone: 630/540-0996
Fax: 630/540-9650

Ballet, Jazz, Tap, Ballroom, Clogging, Lyrical, Hip-Hop, Swing, Poms, Acting

Gus Giordano Dance Center
614 Davis
Evanston, IL 60201
Phone: 847/866-9442
Fax: 847/866-9228
www.giordanojazzdance.com

Ballet, Jazz, Modern, Tap, Hip-Hop, Ballroom, Pilates, Children's programs

Hedwig Dances
2936 N. Southport, Ste. 210
Administrative Offices
Chicago, IL 60657
Phone: 773/871-0872
Fax: 773/296-0968
www.hedwigdances.com

Modern, African, Yoga, Hip-Hop, Tai Chi, Company Class, Beginning Ballet, Children's Classes

Joel Hall Dance Center
1511 W. Berwyn
Chicago, IL 60640
Phone: 773/293-0900
Fax: 773/293-1130
www.joelhall.org

Ballet, Jazz, Modern, Tap, Hip-Hop, Egyptian, Pilates

Jo's Footwork Studio
1500 Walker
Western Springs, IL 60558
Phone: 708/246-7868

Ballet, Jazz, Modern, Tap, Hip-Hop

Lou Conte Dance Studio
1147 W. Jackson
Chicago, IL 60607
Phone: 312/850-9766
Fax: 312/455-8240
www.hubbardstreetdance.com

Home of Hubbard Street Dance Chicago

Ballet, Jazz, Modern, Tap, Dance Fitness, Hip-Hop, African

See our ad on page 152.

Milwaukee Ballet
504 National
Milwaukee, WI 53204
Phone: 414/643-7677
Fax: 414/649-4066
www.milwaukeeballet.com

Ballet, Jazz, Modern

Muntu Dance Theatre of Chicago
6800 S. Wentworth, Ste. 3E96
Chicago, IL 60621
Phone: 773/602-1135
Fax: 773/602-1134
www.muntu.com

*African and African-American Dance,
Music and Folklore*

North Shore School of Dance
107 Highwood
Highwood, IL 60040
Phone: 847/432-2060
Fax: 847/432-4037
www.northshoredance.com

*Ballet, Jazz, Modern, Tap, Hip-Hop,
Irish, Yoga*

Old Town School of Folk Music
4544 N. Lincoln
Chicago, IL 60625
Phone: 773/728-6000
Fax: 773/728-6999
www.oldtownschool.org

*Ballet, Jazz, Tap, African, Aztec, Belly,
Breakdance, Flamenco, Flat-Foot, Hip-
Hop, Hula, Indian, Irish, Latin, Mexican,
Swing, Tango, Brazilian, Capoeira*

Patterson School of Ballroom Dance
1240 Sunset Rd.
Winnetka, IL 60093
Phone: 847/501-2523

Ballroom Dance

Rockford Dance Company
711 N. Main
Rockford, IL 61103
Phone: 815/963-3341
Fax: 815/963-3541
www.rockforddancecompany.com

*Ballet, Jazz, Modern, Tap, Ballroom,
Tango Argentino, Irish, Folk*

Ruth Page School of Dance
1016 N. Dearborn
Chicago, IL 60610
Phone: 312/337-6543
Fax: 312/337-6542
www.ruthpage.org

Ballet, Jazz, Tap, Pilates

School of Performing Arts
200 E. 5th, Ste. 132
Naperville, IL 60563
Phone: 630/717-6622
Fax: 630/717-5131
www.schoolofperformingarts.com

*Ballet, Jazz, Modern, Tap, Hip-Hop, Fine
Arts Adventures (Preschool)*

**Shelley's School of Dance
and Modeling, Ltd.**
450 Peterson
Libertyville, IL 60048
Phone: 847/816-1711
Fax: 847/816-1717

*Ballet, Jazz, Modern, Tap, Hip-Hop,
Lyrical, Point*

Teresa Cullen
702 Waukegan, Ste. 5A
Wilmette, IL 60091
Phone: 847/832-0584
Fax: 847/832-0586

Flamenco, Ballet

Von Heidecke School of Ballet
1239 S. Naper
Naperville, IL 60540
Phone: 630/527-1052
Fax: 630/527-0488
Alt. Phone: 815/577-7011

Ballet

Classes - Kids

About Face Youth Theater
Brian Goodman
1222 W. Wilson, 2nd Flr. West
Chicago, IL 60640
Phone: 773/784-8565 ext.104
Fax: 773/784-8557
afyt@aboutfacetheatre.com
http://www.aboutfaceyouththeatre.com

*This six-month performance workshop
explores storytelling, interviewing and
performance techniques, as well as
lectures and discussion with artists,
activists and community leaders. The
workshop culminates in a five-week run
of a newly developed play.*

Act One
Steve Merle
640 N. LaSalle, Ste. 535
Chicago, IL 60610
Phone: 312/787-9384
Fax: 312/787-3234
Actone@actone.com
www.Actone.com

*Beginning and advanced on-camera
classes, meet for nine weeks.*

Training

Actors Center of Chicago
3047 N. Lincoln, Ste. 390
Chicago, IL 60657
Phone: 773/549-3303
Fax: 773/549-0749
www.actorscenterchicago.com

Classes offered encompass movement, performance, musical theatre and more.

Actors Gymnasium
Noyes Cultural Arts Center
927 Noyes St.
Evanston, IL 60201
Phone: 847/328-2795
Fax: 847/328-3495
www.actorsgymnasuim.com

Offers a variety of physical theatre and circus arts classes. Offers a variety of movement classes based on gymnastics, tumbling and dance for kids and parents

Beverly Arts Center
Christine Addachi
2153 W. 111th St.
Chicago, IL 60643
Phone: 773/445-3838
Fax: 773/445-0386
vmackmore@ameritech.net
www.beverlyartcenter.org

Four week dance camp: This camp combines creative movement and pre-ballet games and exercises.

Centerlight Theatre
Katherine Bus
3444 Dundee Rd.
Northbrook, IL 60062
Phone: 847/559-0110 ext. 237
Voice: 847/559-9493 TTY
Fax: 847/559-8199
info@icodaarts.org
http://www.icodaarts.org/centerlight.html

This organization offers theatre classes for a mixed group of deaf, hearing and hard of hearing kids.

Chicago Center for the Performing Arts
Siobhan Sullivan
777 N. Green
Chicago, IL 60622
Phone: 312/327-2040
http://www.theaterland.com/training.htm

Offers a variety of classes for teenaged actors including acting for stage and screen, improv, musical and on-camera technique.

Chicago Kids Company
Jesus Perez
3812 W. Montrose
Chicago, IL 60618
Phone: 773/539-0455
Fax: 773/539-0452
www.chicagokidscompany.com

CKC's summer musical camp focuses on staging an orginal musical.

Chicago Moving Company
3035 N. Hoyne, 2nd Flr.
Chicago, IL 60618
Phone: 773/880-5402
Fax: 773/880-5402
www.chicagomovingcompany.org

Offers a creative movement class available through the "Arts Partners in Residence" program with the Chicago Park District. For ages 10 and up, the Cultural Arts Camp focuses on jazz and modern dance, drumming and visual arts. It's free through the Chicago Park District.

Chicago Theatre Company
Luther Goins
500 E. 67th
Chicago, IL 60637
Phone: 773/493-0901
Fax: 773/493-0360
www.chicagotheatrecompany.com

This weekly drama class meets for five months and covers everything from mime, improv, performance to audition skills.

DePaul University School of Music
Community Music Division
804 W. Belden, Ste. 328
Chicago, IL 60614-3296
Phone: 773/325-7262
Fax: 773/325-7264
www.music.depaul.edu/MusicWeb/CMD/CmPre.htm

The Musical Theatre Workshop for Teens focuses on acting, movement and vocal technique

Duncan YMCA
Chernins Center for the Arts
Pam Dickler
1001 W. Roosevelt
Chicago, IL 60608
Phone: 312/738-7980
Fax: 312/738-1420

Currently working on developing classes for younger students. During the year they offer theatre classes focusing on a variety of topics from scene study and improv to character work. Kids also have the opportunity to work with video and recording equipment.

Eileen Boevers Performing Arts Workshop
595 Elm Pl., Suite 210
Highland Park, IL 60035
Phone: 847/432-8223
Fax: 847/432-5214

Acting, singing and dancing classes

ETA Creative Arts
7558 S. South Chicago Ave.
Chicago, IL 60619-2644
Phone: 773/752-3955
Fax: 773/752-8727
http://www.etacreativearts.org/classes.html

September through June, eta offers classes focusing on drama, music and dance.

Free Street Programs
David Schein
1419 W. Blackhawk
Chicago, IL 60622
Phone: 773/772-7248
www.freestreet.org

Pang is Free Street's teen company, which produces performance exchanges with other visionary artists. Teenstreet is a multi-tiered jobs program designed to employ low-income teens to create and perform free shows for children throughout the city.

Teenstreet offers a summer-only compo-nent of their performance jobs for teens program.

Gallery 37 Center for the Arts
66 E. Randolph
Chicago, IL 60601
Phone: 312/744-8925
Fax: 312/744-9249
info@gallery37.org
www.gallery37.org

This eight-week summer training course provides apprentice artists the opportu-nity to work with professional artists in theatre, music, writing and visual arts.

Illinois Theatre Center
Etel Billig
P.O. Box 397
Park Forest, IL 60466
Phone: 708/481-3510
Fax: 708/481-3693
ilthctr@bigplanet.com
www.ilthctr.org

The theatre offers a summer arts day camp that encompasses music, dance, creative writing, theatre and art.

Improv Playhouse
David Stuart
116 W. Lake
Libertyville, IL 60048
Phone: 847/968-4529
Fax: 847/968-4530
info@improvplayhouse.com
www.improvplayhouse.com

Offers a variety of improv classes for young performers, including theatre games and creative drama.

Lookingglass
2936 N. Southport, 3rd Flr.
Chicago, IL 60657
Phone: 773/477-9257 ext 193
studio@lookingglasstheatre.org
lookingglasstheatre.org

These classes explore theatre at a deeper level, looking at specific skills and tequniques from theatre design to performance styles.

Northlight Theatre
Brad Larson
9501 N. Skokie Blvd.
Skokie, IL 60077
Phone: 847/679-9501 ext 3301
www.northlight.org

This summer camp covers a wide array of topics and skills including improv, musicals and TV/film. The camp is offered at both the Northshore Center for the Performing Arts and Evanston Township High School.

Old Town School of Folk Music
4544 N. Lincoln
Chicago, IL 60657
Phone: 773/728-6000
Fax: 773/728-6999
www.oldtownschool.org

The school offers introductory classes to theatre for young children, which can be continued in special classes that create new musicals such as "Bored Silly" and "The Magic Zoo".

Training

43

Piven Theatre Workshop
Dianne Leavitt
927 Noyes
Evanston, IL 60201
Phone: 847/866-6597
Fax: 847/866-6614
www.piventheatreworkshop.com/

Come learn to play again at the theatre school that launched John & Joan Cusack, Aidan Quinn, Lili Taylor, Jeremy Piven and many more! Classes for young people from 4th grade through high school. Call for current class information.

School of Performing Arts
200 E. 5th Ave., Ste 132
Naperville, IL 60563
Phone: 630/717-6622
Fax: 630/717-5131
www.schoolofperformingarts.com

The school offers a variety of theatre classes including Improv, Audition Workshop and a Musical Theater Dance Workshop.

Second City, The
Rob Chambers
1616 N. Wells
Chicago, IL 60614
Phone: 312/664-4032
Fax: 312/664-9837
www.secondcity.com

Second City offers a set of classes for the novice and more experienced teen improvisor.

Steppenwolf Theatre Company
Lois Atkins
1650 N. Halsted
Chicago, IL 60614
Phone: 312/335-1888 ext. 5639
Fax: 312/335-0808
latkins@steppenwolf.org
steppenwolf.org

This two-semester program is led by resident artists and focuses on the creation of a new piece of work incorporating text, music, movement and visual arts.

The Audition Studio North
Rachel Patterson
20 W. Hubbard
Chicago, IL 60610
Phone: 312/527-4566
Fax: 312/527-9085
theauditionstudio.com

*A full slate of classes including
monolgues and scene work.*

Classes - Scriptwriting

Breadline Theatre Group
1802 W. Berenice
Chicago, IL 60613
Phone: 773/327-6096
breadline@breadline.org
www.breadline.org

*For our complete range of current
classes, please see our Web site.*

Chicago Alliance for Playwrights
Phone: 773/929-7367 ext. 60
www.chicagoallianceforplaywrights.org
june@chicagoallianceforplaywrights.org

Chicago Dramatists
1105 W. Chicago Ave.
Chicago, IL 60622
Phone: 312/633-0630
Fax: 312/633-0610
www.chicagodramatists.org

The Neo-Futurists
5153 N. Ashland
Chicago, IL 60640
Phone: 773/878-4557
Fax: 773/878-4514
NEOFUT@aol.com
www.neofuturists.org

*The Neo-Futurists Performance
Workshop*

*Advanced Neo-Futurist Performance
Workshop - Both classes are studies in
writing, directing and performing your
own work.*

New Tuners Theatre
1225 W. Belmont
Chicago, IL 60657
Phone: 773/929-7367

Workshops in Writing for Musical Theatre

Victory Gardens Theatre
2257 N. Lincoln
Chicago, IL 60614
Phone: 773/549-5788
Fax: 773/549-2779
trainingcenter@victorygardens.org
www.victorygardens.org

Classes - Stage Combat

**The Actors Gymnasium
& Performing Arts School**
Noyes Cultural Arts Center
927 Noyes
Evanston, IL 60201
Phone: 847/328-2795
Fax: 847/328-3495
www.actorsgymnasium.com

Fencing 2000
328 S. Jefferson
Chicago, IL 60606
Phone: 312/879-0430

Forte Stage Combat
859 Chancel Circle
Glen Ellyn, IL 60137
Phone: 630/942-9102
fortestage@aol.com

Raoul Johnson
6525 N. Sheridan
Chicago, IL 60626
Phone: 773/508-3841

New American Theatre
118 N. Main
Rockford, IL 61101-1102
Phone: 815/963-9454
www.newamericantheater.com

Rachel Pergl
6658 N. Rockwell, Ste. 1
Chicago, IL 60645
Phone: 773/973-1073

R & D Choreography
7443 N. Hoyne, Ste. 1N
Chicago, IL 60645
Phone: 847/333-1494
info@fightshop.org
www.fightshop.org

Training

Coaches - Acting

Bud Beyer
1979 S. Campus
Evanston, IL 60208
Phone: 847/491-3372

Belinda Bremner
Phone: 773/871-3710

An audition is a job interview using someone else's words. The key to a successful audition is finding an author who tells your story in your words. Your choice of audition material speaks volumes. Decide what that message is and then craft your audition. Ideally suited for the well-trained actor looking for an edge.

Dexter Bullard
2122 N. Winchester
Chicago, IL 60614
Phone: 773/227-6487

Dexter Bullard is a Jefferson-Cited Chicago director, Artistic Director of Plasticene Physical Theater, and a director for The Second City. Dexter has taught acting, improvisation, and audition technique for over six years at University of Illinois, Columbia College, The Actors' Center, The Audition Studio, and at The Second City Training Center. Gain immediate results for auditions or breakthroughs in acting over a few sessions. Very affordable sliding scale.

Dale Calandra
Phone: 773/508-0397

"Personal Training for the Total Actor"

Your Monologue is a SHOWCASE of your talent. ACT TO WIN! Contemporary to classic, one-person shows, cold reading, on-camera, and callbacks. Over 500 actors privately coached since 1983. Creative Director, The Fourth Wall Training Center; Artistic Director, Oak Park Festival Theatre.

Linda Gillum
Phone: 773/878-3077

Kevin Heckman
1716 W. Albion, Ste. 3A
Chicago, IL 60626
Phone: 312/562-3748

Lori Klinka
916 Rainbow
Glenwood, IL 60425
Phone: 708/709-0880
Fax: 708/709-0881

Ruth Landis
5054 N. Hamlin
Chicago, IL 60625
Phone: 773/732-3183
Fax: 773/463-3683

Build inner safety so that creativity flows naturally and spontaneously while preparing the actor technically for auditions (monologues, on-camera, cold-reading) and performance experience. As a longtime acting coach and certified body-psychotherapist and hypnotherapist, we explore mind/body/emotion awareness around performance anxiety, blocks, creating ease with self, using work rooted in Alexander, Feldenkrais, and Gestalt therapy. Ruth coaches actors, is in private practice, and has taught at Victory Gardens, Northwestern, Columbia and Roosevelt University.

See our ad on page 44.

Janet Louer
312/543-5297

See our ad on page 52

Richard Marlatt
Phone: 773/338-8755

Michael Menendian
6157 N. Clark
Chicago, IL 60660
Phone: 773/338-2177
Fax: 773/508-9794
www.raventheatre.com

Janet B. Milstein
Phone: 773/465-5804

Award-winning acting instructor, Janet has trained hundreds of actors, beginners to professionals. Her students continually get cast in Chicago theatre and have been signed by agents in Chicago, NY, and LA. Janet offers affordable private coaching in monologues and cold reading that will teach you the skills to audition powerfully and with confidence. Author of "111 One-Minute Monologues," "Cool Characters for Kids," and two forensics books due out this year.

Syd Moore
Phone: 773/259-4275

Kurt Naebig
20 W. Hubbard
Chicago, IL 60610
Phone: 630/495-7188

Kathryn Nash
Phone: 312/943-0167

Cecilie O'Reilly
2023 N. Damen
Chicago, IL 60647
Phone: 773/486-3649
Fax: 312/344-8077

Monica Payne
Phone: 773/404-2782

Fredric Stone
5040 N. Marine, Ste. 3A
Chicago, IL 60640
Phone: 773/334-4196

A working professional actor/director with over 25 years experience (New York and Chicago, including Chicago Shakespeare, Northlight and The Goodman), Fredric coaches actors in monologue and scene preparation for auditions — both contemporary and classical. He created and taught The Audition Workshop at Organic Theatre and currently teaches an 8-week Performing Shakespeare class at Victory Gardens Theatre, Chicago Shakespeare, Northlight, and The Goodman.

Karen Vaccaro
Phone: 773/201-0951

Coaches - Movement

Chicago Center for the Alexander Technique
1252 W. Catalpa, Ste. 4605
Chicago, IL 60640
Phone: 773/728-3235
www.ateducationresearch.com

Courtney Brown
3723 N. Southport
Chicago, IL 60613
Phone: 773/878-3865

Marina Gilman
5701 S. Dorchester
Chicago, IL 60637
Phone: 773/955-0016
Fax: 773/955-0016

Marina Gilman is a certified Feldenkrais® Practitioner, licensed Speech and Language Pathologist, and holds an MM in Voice. She specializes in prevention and rehabilitation of voice professionals including singers, actors, and broadcast

journalists. Her approach to teaching is a combination of somatic education and traditional voice training.

T. Daniel and Laurie Willets
6619 N. Campbell
Chicago, IL 60645
Phone: 773/743-0277
www.tdanielcreations.com

Coaches - Voice-over

Act One Studios, Inc.
640 N. LaSalle, Ste. 535
Chicago, IL 60610
Phone: 312/787-9384
Fax: 312/787-3234
www.actone.com

The Audition Studio
Rachael Patterson
20 W. Hubbard, Ste. 2E
Chicago, IL 60660
Phone: 312/527-4566
Fax: 312/527-9085
info@theauditionstudio.com
www.theauditionstudio.com

Helen Cutting
445 E. Ohio, Ste. 1914
Chicago, IL 60611
Phone: 312/527-1809
helen@voicepowr.com

Private Voice-Over Coaching sessions for Radio/Television Commericals, Speech Technique, Script Analysis and Demo Tape production.

With over 25 years' experience as a professional Voice-Over Talent and Coach, Helen provides in-depth training at all levels for Commercials, Narrations, Animation, Promos and all aspects of the Voice-Over Business.

Call for private consultation.

Marina Gilman
5701 S. Dorchester
Chicago, IL 60637
Phone: 773/955-0016
Fax: 773/955-0016

Marina Gilman is a certified Feldenkrais® Practitioner, licensed Speech and Language Pathologist, and holds an MM in Voice. She specializes in prevention and rehabilitation of voice professionals including singers, actors, and broadcast journalists. Her approach to teaching is a combination of somatic education and traditional voice training.

Sound Advice
2028 W. Potomac, Ste. 2&3
Chicago, IL 60622
Phone: 773/772-9539
www.voiceoverdemos.com

Get trained by two of Chicago's top former agents, Gina Mazza (CED) and Tyrone Dockery (Stewart), and Kate McClanaghan, producer at top ad agency (DDB Worldwide). Training includes the following: commercial technique, cold reading, vocal technique, audition technique, in studio voice-over workshop, and mastering the business of being a working talent.

Voice Over U
Phone: 773/774-9886
www.sherriberger.voicedemo.com

Voice Over U is one of the most recommended and highly regarded voice-over training programs in the Midwest with a complete "roadmap" into the business, a variety of valuable recording workshops and honest evaluations. Private coaching: Sherri Berger pinpoints a performer's strengths and weaknesses, keeps them abreast of trends and helps them discover more interesting vocal nuances, style and range capabilities.

Voices Unlimited
541 N. Fairbanks Ct.
Chicago, IL 60611
Phone: 312/832-1113
www.voicesunlimited.com

Coaches - Voice and Speech

Chicago Actors Studio
1567 N. Milwaukee
Chicago, IL 60622
Phone: 773/645-0222
Fax: 773/767-4151
chiactorsstudio@aol.com
www.actors-studio.net

Lia Corinth
Phone: 847/328-4202

Kate DeVore, MA
4451 N. Hamilton
Chicago, IL 60625
Phone: 773/334-7203
www.KateDeVore.com

Over thirteen years experience as voice, speech and dialect coach; certified voice/speech pathologist specializing in performers' voice. Voice enhancement, exploration and development. Training in vocal projection, resonance, power, flexibility, ease and range. Vocal extremes (shouting and screaming) without injury. Vocal health and maintenance. Holistic approach to voice enhancement also available, incorporating energy and complementary healing techniques to free and strengthen the voice.

Marina Gilman
5701 S. Dorchester
Chicago, IL 60637
Phone: 773/955-0016
Fax: 773/955-0016

Marina Gilman is a certified Feldenkrais® Practitioner, licensed Speech and Language Pathologist, and holds an MM in Voice. She specializes in prevention and rehabilitation of voice professionals including singers, actors, and broadcast journalists. Her approach to teaching is a combination of somatic education and traditional voice training.

Deb Kowalczyk, MA
Phone: 773/255-8024
Fax: 773/878-0503
deb@clearspeak.net
www.clearspeak.net

Strongly influenced and by using techniques gleaned from Patsy Rodenburg and Kristin Linklater, Deb uses a four-fold approach to finding and freeing your true voice. Changes can be heard in the first session. The following areas are addressed: Projection, Pitch Range, Diction, Freeing Vocal Tensions.

- Special expertise in modifying foreign accents and regional dialects.
- Dialect acquisition for the stage.

Over 20 years experience. Individual and small group sessions are available.

Richard Marriott
410 S. Michigan, Ste. 920
Chicago, IL 60605
Phone: 312/360-1728

Professionally Speaking
2818 N. Ashland
Chicago, IL 60657
Phone: 773/218-9183

Ann Wakefield
1500 N. LaSalle, Ste. 3C
Chicago, IL 60610
Phone: 312/751-9348

William Rush Voice Consultants
410 S. Michigan, Ste. 920
Chicago, IL 60604
Phone: 312/360-1039
Fax: 630/620-1271

Coaches - Dialect

Martin Aistrope
3011 W. George
Chicago, IL 60618
Phone: 773/286-2862

Claudia Anderson
Phone: 773/296-6929

*25 years teaching and coaching experi-
ence. Dialect coaching for production.
Designated Linklater voice teacher.
"Freeing the Natural Voice" approach to
improving your voice. One-on-one
coaching for the individual. Coaching for
heightened text, monologues, and songs.*

Belinda Bremner
Phone: 773/871-3710

Kate DeVore
4451 N. Hamilton
Chicago, IL 60625
Phone: 773/334-7203
www.KateDeVore.com

*Character-based dialect acquisition and
coaching. The way we speak is an
integral part of who we are; this principle
informs technical coaching for sound
changes, voice placement (resonance),
and musicality of a dialect. Non role-
specific dialect training also available, as
is coaching in Standard American (accent
reduction). Materials and personalized
coaching tapes provided.*

Cecilie O'Reilly
2023 N. Damen
Chicago, IL 60647
Phone: 773/486-3649
Fax: 312/344-8077

Coaches - Singing

Tamara Anderson
1023 Barberry
Round Lake Beach, IL 60073
Phone: 847/546-5548
Fax: 847/546-5717
voxdoc@sbcglobal.net

*Learn the technique that many Grammy
Award winners use. Personalized instruc-*

*tion. Breath support, range, pitch, vocal
freedom, control, confidence.
Performance coaching, overcoming stage
fright. Help for damaged voices, learn
state of the art vocal techniques.
Beginners to professionals. Specializing in
contemporary styles of music.*

Bridget Becker
Phone: 773/381-9358

Mark Burnell
2008 W. Potomac
Chicago, IL 60622
Phone: 773/862-2665
Fax: 773/862-2655
markburnell.com

Mark Burnell 773/862-COOL

*Cabaret, Jazz, Broadway, Pop, R&B. Get
your show together: repertoire, arrange-
ments. Prepare your audition: style,
phrasing, transposition, rehearsal tapes.
Work your chops: technique, flexibility,
improvisation, ornamentation. MFA and
10 years with Carnegie Mellon Music
Theatre Department. markburnell.com*

The Center For Voice
410 S. Michigan, Ste. 635
Chicago, IL 60605
Phone: 312/360-1111

Dr. Ronald Combs
917 W. Castlewood
Chicago, IL 60640
Phone: 773/271-8425
Fax: 773/271-0364

Lia Corinth
Phone: 847/328-4202

David H. Edelfelt
1243 W. Foster
Chicago, IL 60640
Phone: 773/878-SING

See our ad on page 30.

Matthew Ellenwood
4318 N. Sheridan
Chicago, IL 60613
Phone: 773/404-2739

*My studio practice focuses on solid vocal
technique paired with artistic interpretation and sensitive coaching which results
in creating moving, captivating and
memorable performances/auditions.
60 minute lesson for $40.00.*

Training

Marina Gilman
5701 S. Dorchester
Chicago, IL 60637
Phone: 773/955-0016
Fax: 773/955-0016

*Marina Gilman is a certified Feldenkrais®
Practitioner, licensed Speech and
Language Pathologist, and holds an MM
in Voice. She specializes in prevention
and rehabilitation of voice professionals
including singers, actors, and broadcast
journalists. Her approach to teaching is a
combination of somatic education and
traditional voice training.*

Gillian Kelly
Phone: 773/764-0867
www.voicequestinc.com

Vincent Lonergan
Phone: 773/761-0262

Richard Marriott
410 S. Michigan, Ste. 920
Chicago, IL 60605
Phone: 312/360-1728

Northwestern University
711 Elgin
Evanston, IL 60208
Phone: 847/491-7485
Fax: 847/491-5260

Old Town School of Folk Music
4544 N. Lincoln
Chicago, IL 60625
Phone: 773/728-6000
Fax: 773/728-6999
www.oldtownschool.org

Rebecca Patterson
Phone: 773/736-6431
xchroid@core.com.

*Rebecca Patterson Voice Studio offers
technique for the singer and singing
actor, audition and performance preparation, and support for the beginning
singer. Students experience expanded
range and dynamics, clearer tone, and
increased breath management through
this motion-based technique. As skills
develop, singers achieve greater expression and depth of performance. Chicago
and Oak Park, 25 yrs experience.*

Patricia Rusk
1263 W. Foster
Chicago, IL 60640
Phone: 773/784-7875

Sherwood Conservatory of Music
1312 S. Michigan
Chicago, IL 60605
Phone: 312/427-6267
Fax: 312/427-6677

Peggy Smith-Skarry
1347 W. Winona
Chicago, IL 60640
Phone: 773/728-5240

Michael Thorn
400 E. Randolph, Ste. 2927
Chicago, IL 60601
Phone: 312/565-0862

The Voice Works
Near North
Chicago, IL
Phone: 312/944-3867

Frank Winkler
1765 George Ct.
Glenview, IL 60025
Phone: 847/729-1893

**What a Voice Productions
(The Vocal Studio)**
P.O. Box 558188
Chicago, IL 60655
Phone: 708/388-5585
www.whatavoice.com

William Rush Voice Consultants
410 S. Michigan, Ste. 920
Chicago, IL 60604
Phone: 312/360-1039
Fax: 630/620-1271

Wilmette Voice & Piano Studio
Wilmette, IL
Phone: 847/251-7449

Coaches - Instrument

**DePaul University -
Community Music Division**
804 W. Belden
Chicago, IL 60614-3296
Phone: 773/325-7262
Fax: 773/325-4935
music.depaul.edu

*A workshop program in musical theatre is
offered. It is an intensive, performance-
oriented program. Class sessions include
vocal and physical warm-ups, theatre
games, song preparation, interpretation
of text, character analysis, and stage
movement. Each student performs in*

group numbers and at least one solo or scene. Participants take an active role in the developmental process, working as an ensemble toward the final end-of-session performance.

Old Town School of Folk Music
4544 N. Lincoln
Chicago, IL 60625
Phone: 773/728-6000
Fax: 773/728-6999
www.oldtownschool.org

Sherwood Conservatory of Music
1312 S. Michigan
Chicago, IL 60605
Phone: 312/427-6267
Fax: 312/427-6677

Speech Therapy

Center for Stuttering Therapy
9933 Lawler
Skokie, IL 60077
Phone: 847/677-7473
Fax: 847/677-7493
www.cfst.com

Kate DeVore, MA, CCC-SLP
4451 N. Hamilton
Chicago, IL 60625
Phone: 773/334-7203
www.KateDeVore.com

As a voice, speech and dialect trainer as well as a speech pathologist specialized in professional voice, Kate has created a unique combination of artistic and scientifically based techniques for vocal rehabilitation and speech training. She also specializes in working with people who stutter, using similar principles to facilitate a feeling of ease and control in speech.

Deb Kowalczyk, MA, CCC-SLP
Phone: 773/255-8024
Fax: 773/878-0503
deb@clearspeak.net
www.clearspeak.net

Having spent 25 years as a licensed Speech Pathologist, Deb has successfully treated all types of Speech/Language problems. These have included, but are not limited to: Voice disorders from vocal nodules, gender related vocal differences, stuttering, diction problems, language problems from stroke or head injury.

Expertise with adults and children. Member of ASHA.

Krause Speech & Language Services
233 E. Erie, Ste. 815
Chicago, IL 60611
Phone: 312/943-1927
Fax: 312/943-2692

Kathleen E. Long
11142 S. Campbell
Chicago, IL 60655
Phone: 773/239-8089

Professionally Speaking
2818 N. Ashland
Chicago, IL 60657
Phone: 773/218-9183

Bonnie Smith, PhD, CCC-SLP
1855 W. Taylor
Chicago, IL 60612
Phone: 312/996-6520
Fax: 312/996-8106
www.otol.uic.edu/speech.htm

Ear Prompter Coaches

Rick Plastina
1117 N. Taylor
Oak Park, IL 60302
Phone: 708/386-8270

Local Universities

Columbia College
600 S. Michigan
Chicago, IL 60605
Phone: 312/663-1600
www.colum.edu

MFAs offered in 10 disciplines focusing on the arts, media, education, and communication.

DePaul University
The Theatre School
2135 N. Kenmore
Chicago, IL 60614
Phone: 773/325-7999
http://theatreschool.depaul.edu

MFAs offered in Acting, Directing, Costume Design, Lighting Design and Set Design.

Training

Illinois State University
School of Theatre
Campus Box 5700
Normal, IL 61761
Phone: 309/438-8783
Fax: 309/438-7214
www.orat.ilstu.edu/theatre

MFAs offered in Acting, Directing and Design.

Indiana University
Theatre 200
1211 E. Seventh St.
Bloomington, IN 47405
Phone: 812/855-4503
Fax: 812/855-4704
www.fa.indiana.edu/~thtr

MFAs offered in Acting, Directing, Playwriting, Costume Design, Lighting Design, Set Design and Theatre Tech.

Loyola University Chicago
Granada Centre 450
6525 N. Sheridan Road
Chicago, IL 60626
Phone: 773/508-3396
Fax: 773/508-2460
www.luc.edu

Michigan State University
149 Auditorium Building
East Lansing, MI 48824
Phone: 517/355-6690
Fax: 517/355-1698
http://pilot.msu/theatre/unit

MFAs offered in Acting and Production Design.

Northern Illinois University
School of Theatre Arts
DeKalb, IL 60115
Phone: 815/753-1335
Fax: 815/753-8415

MFAs offered in Acting, Directing, and Design/Tech.

Northwestern University
1979 S. Campus
Evanston, IL 60208
Phone: 847/491-3170
Fax: 847/467-2019
http://www.communications.north-western.edu/theatre

MFAs offered in Directing and Stage Design.

Roosevelt University
430 S. Michigan
Chicago, IL 60605-1394
Phone: 312/341-3719
Fax: 312/341-3814
www.roosevelt.edu

MFAs in Directing/Dramaturgy, Musical Theatre and Performance-Acting.

School of the Art Institute
37 S. Wabash
Chicago, IL 60603
Phone: 312/899-5100
www.artic.edu

MFAs offered in Performance, Film, Video and New Media.

Southern Illinois University
Department of Theatre
Carbondale, IL 62901-6608
Phone: 618/453-5741
Fax: 618/453-7582
www.siu.edu/~mccleod/

MFAs offered in Directing, Playwriting, and Design.

University of Illinois at Chicago
Department of Performing Arts
1040 West Harrison St. MC 255
EPASW Building, Room L042
Chicago, IL 60607-7130
Phone: 312/996-2977
Email: dpa@uic.edu

University of Illinois, Urbana-Champaign
4-122 Krannert Center
500 S. Goodwin
Urbana, IL 61801
Phone: 217/333-2371
Fax: 217/244-1861
www.theatre.uiuc.edu/theatre/

MFAs offered in Acting and Design/Management/Tech.

Western Illinois University
Browne Hall
Macomb, IL 61455
Phone: 309/298-1543
www.wiu.edu

MFAs offered in Acting, Directing and Design.

Photo: Dean La Prairie

CHAPTER 3
ACTOR'S TOOLS

Golden Boy
Raven Theatre

Knowing the Lingo—
A Valuable Tool

By Mechelle Moe

Each industry has its own vocabulary, and the acting world—on-camera or on-stage—is no exception. Below is a short list of terms you will run across while out in the field.

Actors' Equity Association Stage actors and stage managers labor union (see Unions & Legal Resources)

AFTRA American Federation of Television and Radio Artists (see Unions & Legal Resources)

Bite and Smile A very literal term for a type of commercial that is generally MOS (Mit Out Sound) and advertising food products. Think of that extra fresh stick of gum you've been craving, pop it in your mouth and give a sparkling smile to show how much you enjoy it.

Booking A booking means that you've been hired for a job, and usually refers to on-camera work.

Breakdowns A listing given to agents which details production company projects and cast requirements such as type, age range, audition/callback date, shoot date, casting director, etc.

Buyout A buyout is a contractual agreement that states a set fee the talent will receive if they agree to opt out of all rights to future money, i.e. residuals.

Callback Basically, you've made the first cut in the audition process and are invited back to the second or final round of auditions.

Cold Reading An actor auditions with script in hand—not memorized or partially-memorized—without a lot of prep time.

Composite/Comp Card A comp card is a composite of several photographs that exhibit different looks or styles and reflect various aspects of your personality. Generally, this is required if you are being submitted for print or modeling work.

Copy The script for a commercial audition, sometimes only one or two lines in length.

Actor's Tools

Craft Service The job of craft service is to feed the cast and crew during a shoot. They provide breakfast, lunch and dinner as well as snacks. Mandatory on a union set, but not always provided for non-union gigs.

Dailies This refers to the film shot—usually the day before—that is developed and viewed on a daily basis during an ongoing shoot as a means of quality control.

Earprompter This is an earpiece connected to a small tape recorder that actors wear during taping in order to help them navigate long, technical scripts quickly. Industrials or any type of live narration event typically require actors to be earprompter proficient.

Exclusivity A contractual agreement between an actor and talent agency that prohibits the talent to list with or solicit work from other competing agencies. In Chicago, actors tend to be multi-listed with agencies rather than going exclusive.

Extra An actor hired to play a minor part or serve as background to a scene. These parts typically have few or no lines. It definitely is grunt work that garners little respect; but if you want to familiarize yourself with the process, this is your opportunity to be a fly on the wall.

Headshot & Resume A professional 8x10 photo of yourself with your resume attached to the back. The resume lists previous work experience on-camera or onstage, along with any training or special skills.

Iced Slang used to refer to talent who have been put on hold for a project—there is potential for booking, but also a high chance of cancellation.

Industrial Training and educational films made for corporations.

Live Industrial Live performances about products or services which are held for corporations.

LookSee It's just what it sounds like—you are invited down so casting directors and clients can take a quick look, along with a Polaroid, to see if you're the type they're looking for.

Monologue A memorized selection of text (usually from a play) performed at an audition. Auditors will generally set requirements for length (one to three minutes is pretty normal) and type (i.e., classical or contemporary).

MOS Mit Out Sound are moments on screen where there is no dialogue, but there are reaction shots or visuals.

Must Join You're considered to have must join status if you book a union job after 30 days from which you booked your first union job. You do not have to join the union if you do not book another union job after this time period.

On-Camera Refers to anything on-camera such as TV, film, commercials and industrials.

On Hold The casting director will put an actor on hold if the client wants them for a job but has not formally hired them yet. The actor may not book any other jobs during this period which conflict with the first job's production dates.

Open Call/"Cattle Call" A mass audition held to find new or inexperienced talent. This usually means dealing with hundreds of people, long lines and long waiting periods on the chance of being discovered.

Pilot A mock-up of a new television show that producers try to sell to the networks; if the show is "picked up," it usually receives a trial run of 13 episodes.

Pilot Season Production companies start casting next season's shows during late winter to early spring. Breakdowns are distributed nationwide, but casting preference is giving to Los Angeles actors.

Print Work Print photography—open to both actors and models—used in the advertisement of a product. Think magazines, billboards or the product container itself.

Reel Usually three to five minutes in length, the reel (usually shot on digital beta cam or high 8, so that it dubs well to VHS later without losing definition) is comprised of brief clips highlighting your best work on-camera, and can also include stage video. Investing in a good reel is not essential for working in Chicago, but it is a required marketing tool for LA and New York.

Residuals A payment made to the talent for each additional showing of a recorded television show, commercial, print job, voice-over, etc.

SAG Screen Actors Guild (see Unions & Legal Resources)

Sides Usually one to two pages of the script made available to the actor for the audition. Memorization isn't generally required, but you should be extremely familiar and comfortable with the text.

Slate Casting directors will ask you to "slate" your name and sometimes your agency for an on-camera audition.

Stand-In An individual who matches certain characteristics (height, weight, skin tone) of the talent and stands in position while the crew is lighting the scene and setting up for the shot.

Taft-Hartley Also known as the National Labor Relations Act, Taft-Hartley is a term used by unions to define a potential new member's status. The act allows non-union talent to work one or more union jobs within a 30-day time period

Actor's Tools

of the first booking without having to join the union. Talent must join after that period in order to book any future union job.

Tear Sheet A hard copy example of print work that has been ripped out of a magazine or product's package.

Teleprompter A monitor set at camera level that displays the script for the actor to read.

Type A generic classification that actors are broken down into in terms of their look and personality. To figure out your type, ask yourself: What's my realistic age range? Am I more like the kid just out of college, or the young mom or dad? What ethnic types do I pass for? What's my level of education? Annual income? Sense of humor—loud and gregarious or sarcastic and dry, etc. Also look at the basic stereotypes offered on television and see which way you lean or who you most look like.

Voice-Over The voice of an unseen actor in TV, film and radio spots, etc. Voice-over work can be anything from a radio commercial to a book-on-tape to your favorite cartoon character.

Photographers

John Abbott
4015 N. Whipple
Chicago, IL 60618
Phone: 773/583-3823

Joseph Amenta Photography
555 W. Madison, Ste. 3802
Chicago, IL 60661
Phone: 773/248-2488

Linda Balhorn
55 E. Washington, Ste. 1300
Chicago, IL 60601
Phone: 312/263-3513

Jamie Banasiak
Phone: 773/793-1084

Brad Baskin
850 N. Milwaukee
Chicago, IL 60622
Phone: 312/733-0932
www.bradbaskin.com

Bauwerks Progressive Photography
2475 N. Clybourn
Chicago, IL 60614
Phone: 773/529-4199
Fax: 773/326-0796
www.bauwerks.com

Sandra Bever
1521 Dearborn St.
Joliet, IL 60435
Phone: 815/723-3051
Fax: 815/727-1687
www.sandrabever.com

Peter Bosy Photography, Inc.
6435 Indian Head Trail
Indian Head Park, IL 60525
Phone: 708/246-3778
Fax: 708/246-1080
peterbosy@aol.com
www.peterbosy.com/faces.html

Michael Brosilow Photography
1370 N. Milwaukee
Chicago, IL 60622
Phone: 773/235-4696
Fax: 773/235-4698
See our ad on page 62.

Daniel Byrnes Photography
113 W. North Ave.
Chicago, IL 60610
Phone: 312/337-1174

Wayne Cable Photography
312 N. Carpenter
Chicago, IL 60607
Phone: 312/226-0303
Fax: 312/226-6995
infor@waynecable.com
www.waynecable.com

Camera 1
3946 N. Monticello
Chicago, IL 60618
Phone: 773/539-1119

Mike Canale Photography
614 Davis St.
Evanston, IL 60201
Phone: 847/864-0146

Guy Cardarelli
119 W. Hubbard, 3rd flr.
Chicago, IL 60610
Phone: 312/321-0694

Patty Carroll
2505 W. Chicago Ave.
Chicago, IL 60622
Phone: 773/342-0707
Alt. Phone: 773/342-0797
www.elimpersonators.com

Classic Photography, Inc.
John Karl Breun
38 S. Main, Ste. 2A
Mount Prospect, IL 60056
Phone: 847/259-8373
Fax: 847/259-8474
www.classicphoto.com
See our ad on page 64.

Keith Claunch
2540 W. Eastwood
Chicago, IL 60625
Phone: 312/285-6074

Andrew Collings
1550 N. Damen
Chicago, IL 60622
Phone: 773/384-2200
www.andrewcollings.com

Cat Conrad Photography
510 W. Belmont, Ste. 1810
Chicago, IL 60657-4600
Phone: 773/459-3571
Fax: 773/755-0612
catconrad@aol.com
www.catconradphoto.com

HEADSHOTS - Quality New York photographer now in Chicago. You'll be relaxed and look your best. Top makeup/hair available.
See our ad on page 60.

Actor's Tools

61

Costume Images
3634 W. Fullerton
Chicago, IL 60647
Phone: 773/276-8971
Fax: 773/276-0717
www.costume-images.com

Joel DeGrand Photography
2950 W. Carroll
Chicago, IL 60612
Phone: 312/515-1515
www.degrand.com

Digipix Photography
Phone: 312/539-6189

Dan DuVerney
1937 W. Division, 1st flr.
Chicago, IL 60622
Phone: 773/252-6639

Edda Taylor Photographie
Courthouse Square, Ste. 304
Crown Point, IN 46307
Phone: 219/662-9500
www.eddataylor.com

Elan Photography
5120 Belmont, Ste. A
Downers Grove, IL 60515
Phone: 630/960-1400
Fax: 630/969-1972
www.elanphotography.com

Dale Fahey
Phone: 773/973-5757

Aaron Gang Photography
1016 N. Ashland
Chicago, IL 60622
Phone: 773/782-4363
www.aarongang.com
See our ad on page 67.

Gerber/Scarpelli Photography
1144 W. Fulton Market
Chicago, IL 60607
Phone: 312/455-1144
Fax: 312/455-1544

Jennifer Girard
1455 W. Roscoe
Chicago, IL 60657
Phone: 773/929-3730
Fax: 773/871-2308
www.jennifergirard.com

Steve Greiner
1437 W. Thomas
Chicago, IL 60622
Phone: 773/227-4375
Fax: 773/227-4379

IronHorse Productions
3310 S. Aberdeen, Ste. 1-A
Chicago, IL 60608
Phone: 773/890-4355
Fax: 773/890-4345

Deon Jahnke
228 S. 1st
Milwaukee, WI 53204
Phone: 414/224-8360
Fax: 414/224-8356
www.execpc.com\~deon

JLB Photography
350 N. Ogden
Chicago, IL 60607
Phone: 312/339-3909

Gary Jochim
1470 W. Huron, Ste. 2F
Chicago, IL 60622
Phone: 312/738-3204
Fax: 312/738-3204

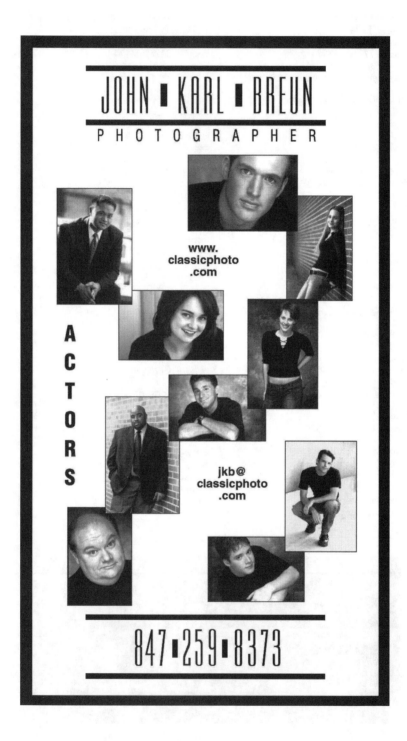

JOHN ■ KARL ■ BREUN
P H O T O G R A P H E R

www.
classicphoto
.com

A
C
T
O
R
S

jkb@
classicphoto
.com

847 ■ 259 ■ 8373

Michael J. Kardas Studio
2635 N. Albany
Chicago, IL 60647
Phone: 773/227-7925

Art Ketchum Studios
2215 S. Michigan
Chicago, IL 60616
Phone: 312/842-1406
Fax: 312/842-6546

Jeremy Kruse
Phone: 312/664-7598
krusephoto@comcast.net
www.krusephoto.com

See our ad below.

Larry Lapidus Photography
2650 W. Belden, Ste. 304
Chicago, IL 60647
Phone: 773/235-3333
www.lapidusphoto.com

*I am considered by many to be the most
reputable "headshot" photographer in
Chicago. My directorial technique sets me
apart from other photographers. The
rapport we develop is the most essential
tool in capturing your true individuality.
We will express your character in a
fashion that is perfect for commercial
purposes in theatre, television, or film.
Recommended by top talent agents,
casting directors, and acting teachers.
Satisfaction guaranteed. Photographic
fees: $425 includes 45 minute consulta-
tion, three rolls, and two 8x10 custom
prints. Credit cards accepted.*

Sara Levinson
1142 S. Michigan
Chicago, IL 60607
Phone: 312/583-0338
www.saralevinsonphoto.com

Laurie Locke
4018 S. Oak Park Ave.
Stickney, IL 60402
Phone: 708/749-2444

Ken Manthey
kmanthey@wneptheater.org
www.wneptheater.org/Manthey/_html/w
elcome.html

Max Photography
P.O. Box 14620
Chicago, IL 60614
Phone: 773/477-6548

Michael McCafrey Photography
109 W. Hubbard
Chicago, IL 60610
Phone: 312/222-9776

Brian McConkey
312 N. May, Ste. 6J
Chicago, IL 60607
Phone: 312/563-1357
Fax: 312/563-1615
www.gratefulheads.net

Rick Mitchell, Inc.
652 W. Grand
Chicago, IL 60610
Phone: 312/829-1700

Moore Photographic
Phone: 773/276-0249

Allan Murray
1717 N. Hudson
Chicago, IL 60614
Phone: 312/337-0286

Joseph A. Nicita
1500 W. Ohio
Chicago, IL 60622
Phone: 312/666-2443

Piccolo Theatre Talent clockwise from top left: Courtney Hester, Deborah Craft, Ken Raabe

©REP3.com

Working Actors Agree
Don't Panic

get shot right
get shot by REP3.com

26 years of experience serving the Theatre Community
Mondays dedicated to the Theatre Industry
Copyright protection credit for your safety
Theatrical Promotional Photography
My name is my guarantee of quality
Privacy guarantee in writing
The best reprints available
Digital design services
Marketing campaigns
Digital retouching
Composites
Headshots
Portfolios
Postcards

Robert Erving Potter III

REP3

www.REP3.com
312-226-2060
Potter@REP3.com

Photographer ASMP/EP

Papadakis Photography
17 Lexington Rd.
South Barrington, IL 60010
Phone: 847/428-4400
Fax: 847/428-4403
www.papadakisphotography.com

REP3.com aka Robert Erving Potter III
2056 W. Superior
Chicago, IL
Phone: 312/226-2060
www.REP3.com

"I recommend Rob (REP3.com) highly; his photographs, input and suggestions result in excellent, professional marketing devises for the Actor."-Joyce Sloane Producer Emeritus, The Second City. REP3 dedicates Mondays to the Theatre Industry. Please make an appointment: discuss your photographic & marketing needs, view REP3's portfolio & schedule a shoot.

See our ad on page 66

Pret-a-Poser Photography
100 E. Hillside Ave.
Barrington, IL 60010
Phone: 847/382-2211
Fax: 847/304-9419

See our ad on page 68.

David Puffer Studio
Phone: 773/267-6500

Isabel Raci
Phone: 773/486-1980
isabelraci@core.com

Mary Rouleau Photography
1030 Forest Ave.
Evanston, IL 60202
Phone: 847/328-0219

Rubinic Photography
319 N. Western
Chicago, IL 60612
Phone: 312/733-8901
Fax: 312/733-8902
www.rubinic.com

Paul Sherman Photography
955 W. Fulton, 3rd Flr.
Chicago, IL 60607
Phone: 312/633-0848
Fax: 312/666-1498
www.paulshermanphotos.com

Sima Imaging
1821 W. Hubbard, Ste. 301
Chicago, IL 60622
Phone: 312/733-1788
Fax: 312/733-6890

Actor's Tools

Aaron Gang
PHOTOGRAPHY
1016 N. Ashland Chicago IL 60622
www.aarongang.com
773 - 782 - 4363

More. Better. Headshots

Kenneth Simmons
3026 E. 80th
Chicago, IL 60617
Phone: 773/684-7232

Pete Stenberg Photography
1048 W. Fulton Market
Chicago, IL 60607
Phone: 312/421-8850
Fax: 312/421-8830
www.petestenberg.qpg.com

*Photographing people at their best!
Specializing in headshots for actors and
composites for models. Renowned
Chicago photographer for over 20 years.
Children and Adults. Agency recom-
mended. Free consultation. Make-up
artist/hair stylist available. Rush service.
Credit cards accepted. Located in
Chicago's West Loop area, near several
agencies. Relaxed, fun atmosphere.*

Suzanne Plunkett Photographs
3047 N. Lincoln, Ste. 300
Chicago, IL 60657
Phone: 773/477-3775
Fax: 773/477-4640
www.suzanneplunkettphotographs.com

Gary Trantafil
312 N. May, Ste. 100
Chicago, IL 60607
Phone: 312/666-1029
Fax: 312/666-1259

Tyrone Taylor Photography
1143 E. 81st
Chicago, IL 60619
Phone: 773/978-1505

Vic Bider Photography
1142 W. Taylor
Chicago, IL 60607
Phone: 312/829-5540

Michael Vollan
800 W. Huron, 3rd Flr.
Chicago, IL 60622
Phone: 312/997-2347

G. Thomas Ward Photography
1949 W. Leland, Ste. 1
Chicago, IL 60640
Phone: 773/271-6813
www.thepeoplephotographer.com

Actor's Tools

Sharon White Photography
2941 W. Belmont
Chicago, IL 60618
Phone: 773/539-0870
Fax: 312/539-0434

Jean Whiteside
6410 N. Glenwood, Ste. 1S
Chicago, IL 60626
Phone: 773/274-5545

Winkelman Photography
P.O. Box 531
Oak Park, IL 60303-0531
Phone: 312/953-2141

Yamashiro Studio
2643 N. Clybourn
Chicago, IL 60614
Phone: 773/883-0440
Fax: 773/883-0453
www.yamashirostudio.com

Photo Reproductions

A&B Photography
650 W. Lake, 2nd Flr.
Chicago, IL 60661
Phone: 312/454-4554
Fax: 312/454-1634
www.a-bphoto.com
See our ad on page 62.

ABC Pictures
1867 E. Florida
Springfield, MO 65803
Phone: 417/869-3456
Fax: 417/869-9185
www.abcpictures.com
See our ad on page 69.

Acme Copy Corp.
218 S. Wabash, 4th Flr.
Chicago, IL 60604
Phone: 312/922-6975
Fax: 312/922-6976

Anderson Graphics, Inc.
Phone: 800/262-6114
Fax: 818/909-9105
www.andersongraphics.com
See our ad on page 75.

Bodhis Photo Service
112 W. Grand
Chicago, IL 60610
Phone: 312/321-1141
Fax: 312/321-3610

Minuteman Press
445 W. Erie
Chicago, IL 60610
Phone: 312/368-0577
Fax: 312/368-4989

National Photo Service
114 W. Illinois
Chicago, IL 60610
Phone: 312/644-5211
Fax: 312/644-6285
www.nationalphoto.com
See our ad on page 71.

Photoscan
646 Bryn Mawr
Orlando, FL 32804
Phone: 800/352-6367
www.ggphotoscan.com

Triangle Studio
3445 N. Broadway
Chicago, IL 60657
Phone: 773/472-1015
Fax: 773/472-2201
www.trianglecamera.com

Quantity Photo
119 W. Hubbard, 2nd Flr.
Chicago, IL 60610
Phone: 312/644-8290
Fax: 312/644-8299
www.quantityphoto.com

Photo Retouching

John Bresnahan
3320 N. Clifton
Chicago, IL 60657
Phone: 773/248-7211

Bob Faetz Retouching
203 N. Wabash, Ste. 1320
Chicago, IL 60601
Phone: 312/759-0933
Fax: 312/759-0944

Irene Levy Retouching Studios
Marina Towers
300 N. State, Ste. 3431
Chicago, IL 60610
Phone: 312/464-0504
Fax: 312/464-1665

G. Mycio Digital Imaging
333 N. Michigan, Ste. 715
Chicago, IL 60601
Phone: 312/782-1472
Fax: 312/782-9874

David Renar Studio
320 N. Damen
Chicago, IL 60612
Phone: 312/226-0001

Makeup Artists

Andrea Nichols
Phone: 312/851-6754

Cathy Durkin
1749 N. Wells, Ste. 1106
Chicago, IL 60614
Phone: 312/787-0848

Che Sguardo Makeup Studio
500 N. Wells
Chicago, IL 60610
Phone: 312/527-0821

Darcy McGrath
Phone: 312/337-1353

Denise Milito
Phone: 773/465-1134
tortoisedm@aol.com

Gina McIver
Phone: 708/268-4536

Jenna Garagiola
Phone: 773/447-6550

Krissy Bailey
Phone: 219/864-7822
Fax: 219/781-5755—Cell
Liplash@aol.com

Marianne Strokirk Salon
361 W. Chestnut
Chicago, IL 60610
Phone: 312/944-4428
Fax: 312/944-4429
www.mariannestrokirk.com

Marilyn Miglin Institute
112 E. Oak
Chicago, IL 60611
Phone: 800/662-1120
Fax: 312/943-1184
www.marilyn-miglin.com

Media Hair & Makeup Group
Phone: 708/848-8400

Nancy P. Stanley
Phone: 773/871-1396

Nouvelle Femme
1151 Wilmette Ave.
Wilmette, IL 60091
Phone: 847/251-6698

Actor's Tools

Sandy Morris
Phone: 773/549-4951

Sharleen Acciari
1007 W. Webster
Chicago, IL 60614
Phone: 773/248-1273

Shelly Rolf
Phone: 630/262-1142
Fax: 630/262-0461

Stephanie Spero
Phone: 708/404-7449—Cell
Alt Phone: 708/425-7449
chirpspero@hotmail.com

Suzi Ostos
Phone: 773/868-1738

Tammy McEwen
Phone: 630/226-9092

Transformations by Rori
146 N. Oak Park Ave.
Oak Park, IL 60301
Phone: 708/383-8338
Fax: 708/383-6796

Transformations by Rori
110 S. Arlington Heights Rd.
Arlington Heights, IL 60005
Phone: 847/454-0600

Resume Services

Act One Bookstore
2540 N. Lincoln
Chicago, IL 60614
Phone: 773/348-6757
Fax: 773/348-5561
See our ad on page 56.

Bob Behr
4738 N. LaPorte
Chicago, IL 60630
Phone: 773/685-7721
Fax: 773/283-9839

Chicago Actor Help
5045 N. Damen, Ste. 1E
Chicago, IL 60625
Phone: 773/334-1709
www.cah.freeservers.com

Ink Well
112 W. Illinois
Chicago, IL 60610
Phone: 312/644-4700
Fax: 312/644-4703

Trade Papers

Act One Reports
640 N. LaSalle, Ste. 535
Chicago, IL 60610
Phone: 312/787-9384
Fax: 312/787-3234
www.actone.com
Updated listings of agencies, casting directors, photographers, and industry-related information.

American Theatre Magazine
355 Lexington Ave.
New York, NY 10017
Phone: 212/697-5230
Fax: 212/557-5817
www.tcg.org
See our ad on page 166.

Audition News
P.O. Box 250
Bloomingdale, IL 60108
Phone: 630/894-2278
Fax: 630/894-8364

Backstage
770 Broadway, 6th Flr.
New York, NY 10003
Phone: 646/654-5700
www.backstage.com

Backstage West
5055 Wilshire Blvd., 5th Flr.
Los Angeles, CA 90036
Phone: 323/525-2356
Fax: 323/525-2354
www.backstagewest.com

Breakdown Services, Ltd.
1120 S. Robertson, 3rd Flr.
Los Angeles, CA 90035
Phone: 310/276-9166
Fax: 310/276-8829
www.breakdownservices.com

Callboard
870 Market, Ste. 375
San Francisco, CA 94102
Phone: 415/430-1140
Fax: 415/430-1145
www.theatrebayarea.org

Equity News
165 W. 46th
New York, NY 10036
Phone: 212/719-9570
Fax: 212/921-8454

Hollywood Reporter
5055 Wilshire Blvd.
Los Angeles, CA 90036-4396
Phone: 323/525-2150
www.hollywoodreporter.com

PerformInk
3223 N. Sheffield, 3rd Flr.
Chicago, IL 60657
Phone: 773/296-4600
Fax: 773/296-4621
www.performink.com

The Chicago Area's most comprehensive source for audition notices, training information, and Chicago Theatre and Film information.

Ross Reports Television and Film
770 Broadway
New York, NY 10003-9595
Phone: 646/654-5863
www.backstage.com/rossreports

Screen Magazine
16 W. Erie
Chicago, IL 60610
Phone: 312/664-5236
Fax: 312/664-8425
www.screenmag.com

The Chicago Creative Directory
333 N. Michigan, Ste. 810
Chicago, IL 60601
Phone: 312/236-7337
Fax: 312/236-6078
www.creativedir.com

Theatre Directories
P.O. Box 510
Dorset, VT 05251
Phone: 802/867-2223
Fax: 802/867-0144
www.theatredirectories.com

Variety
P.O. Box 15878
North Hollywood, CA 91615
Phone: 800/552-3632—Subscriptions
www.variety.com

Answering Services

Burke Communications
P.O. Box 4152
Oak Park, IL 60303-4152
Phone: 708/383-8580
Fax: 708/386-1336
www.burkecommsystems.com
See our ad on page 73.

Stage Weapons

The Armoury American Fencers Supply
1180 Folsom St.
San Francisco, CA 94103
Phone: 415/863-7911
Fax: 415/431-4931
www.amfence.com

Arms and Armor
1101 Stinson Blvd. NE
Minneapolis, MN 55413
Phone: 612/331-6473
www.armor.com

Center Firearms Co.
10 W. 37th St.
New York, NY 10018
Phone: 212/244-4040
Fax: 212/947-1233

IAR Arms
33171 Camino Capistrano
San Juan Capistrano, CA 92675
Phone: 877/722-1873
sales@iar-arms.com
www.iar-arms.com
www.swordsdirect.com

Actor's Tools

Sheet Music

Act One Bookstore
2540 N. Lincoln
Chicago, IL 60614
Phone: 773/348-6757
Fax: 773/348-5561

Carl Fisher Music
333 S. State
Chicago, IL 60604
Phone: 312/427-6652
Fax: 312/427-6653

Lighting Rental

Chicago Spotlight, Inc.
1658 W. Carroll
Chicago, IL 60612
Phone: 312/455-1171
Fax: 312/455-1744
www.chicagospotlight.com

Designlab
328 N. Albany
Chicago, IL 60612
Phone: 773/265-1100
Fax: 773/265-0800
www.designlab-chicago.com
See our ad on page 167.

Grand Stage Lighting Company
630 W. Lake
Chicago, IL 60661
Phone: 312/332-5611
Fax: 312/258-0056
www.grandstage.com

Dance Supplies

Big 'N' Little Shoes
3142 W. 111th
Chicago, IL 60655
Phone: 773/239-6066

Dance & Mime Shop
643 W. Grand
Chicago, IL 60610
Phone: 312/666-4406
www.danceandmimeshop.com

Illinois Theatrical
P.O. Box 34284
Chicago, IL 60634
Phone: 773/745-7777
Fax: 800/877-6027
www.illinoistheatrical.com

Leo's Dancewear Inc.
1900 N. Narragansett
Chicago, IL 60639
Phone: 773/889-7700
Fax: 800/736-5330
info@leosdancewear.com
www.leosdancewear.com

Motion Unlimited
218 S. Wabash, 8th Flr.
Chicago, IL 60604
Phone: 312/922-3330
Fax: 312/922-7770

Organizers

Holdon Log™
ww.holdonlog.com
See our ad on page 79.

Actor's Tools

Costume Shops & Makeup Supplies

A Magical Mystery Tour
6010 W. Dempster
Morton Grove, IL 60053
Phone: 847/966-5090
Fax: 847/966-7280

All Dressed Up Costumes
150 S. Water
Batavia, IL 60510
Phone: 630/879-5130
Fax: 630/879-3374
www.alldressedupcostumes.com

Beatnix
3400 N. Halsted
Chicago, IL 60657
Phone: 773/281-6933
Fax: 773/281-0929

Broadway Costumes, Inc.
1100 W. Cermak
Chicago, IL 60608
Phone: 312/829-6400
Fax: 312/829-8621
www.broadwaycostumes.com

Center Stage
497 Rt. 59
Aurora, IL 60504
Phone: 630/851-9191

Chicago Costume Company
1120 W. Fullerton
Chicago, IL 60614
Phone: 773/528-1264
Fax: 773/935-4197
www.chicagocostume.com

Chicago Hair Group
734 N. LaSalle
Chicago, IL 60610
Phone: 312/337-4247

Facemakers, Inc.
140 Fifth St.
Savannah, IL 61074
Phone: 815/273-3944
Fax: 815/273-3966
www.facemakersinc.com

Fantasy Costumes Headquarters
4065 N. Milwaukee
Chicago, IL 60641
Phone: 773/777-0222
Fax: 773/777-4228
www.fantasycostumes.com

Flashy Trash
3524 N. Halsted
Chicago, IL 60657
Phone: 773/327-6900
Fax: 773/327-9736

Josie O'Kain Costume & Theatre Shop
2419B W. Jefferson
Joliet, IL 60435
Phone: 815/741-9303
Fax: 815/741-9316
www.josieokain.com

Kryolan
132 Ninth St.
San Francisco, CA 94103
Phone: 800/KRY-OLAN
Fax: 415/863-9059
info-usa@kryolan.com
www.kryolan.com
See our ad on page 74.

MAC
40 E. Oak
Chicago, IL 60611
Phone: 312/951-7310
www.maccosmetics.com

Razzle Dazzle Costumes
1038 Lake St.
Oak Park, IL 60301
Phone: 708/383-5962
Fax: 708/383-0069
www.razzledazzlecostumes.com

Show Off
1472 Elmhurst Rd.
Elk Grove Village, IL 60007
Phone: 847/439-0206
Fax: 847/439-0219
www.showoffinc.com

Task Force Military
2341 W. Belmont
Chicago, IL 60618
Phone: 773/477-7096

Demo Tapes/CDs

Audio One, Inc.
325 W. Huron, Ste. 512
Chicago, IL 60610
Phone: 312/337-5111
Fax: 312/337-5125

Bobby Schiff Music Productions
363 Longcommon
Riverside, IL 60546
Phone: 708/442-3168
Fax: 708/447-3719

Bosco Productions
160 E. Grand, 6th Flr.
Chicago, IL 60611
Phone: 312/644-8300

See our ad on page 80.

C. R. Rainbow Recording
Michael Carlson
Buddy Reeder
Phone: 773/761-7246
crRainbow@aol.com

See our ad on page 74.

Rainbow Bridge Recording
117 W. Rockland
Libertyville, IL 60048
Phone: 847/362-4060
Fax: 847/362-4653

Sound Advice
2028 W. Potomac, Ste. 2&3
Chicago, IL 60622
Phone: 773/772-9539
www.voiceoverdemos.com

Sound Advice is the most complete, start-to-finish voiceover demo production service. We maintain no one does what you do. The copy is written/selected specifically fo you by Professional Producers. Our mailing list and marketing plan is unparalleled. We coach, direct and produce you to get you completely poised to work. Get trained and produced by two of Chicago's top former Talent Agents, Gina Mazza (CED) and Tyrone Dockery (Stewart) and Kate McClanaghan Producer at top Ad Agency (DDB Worldwide).

See our ad on page 76.

Sound/Video Impressions
110 S. River Rd.
Des Plaines, IL 60016
Phone: 847/297-4360
Fax: 847/297-6870

Reels

Absolute Video Services, Inc.
715 S. Euclid
Oak Park, IL 60302
Phone: 708/386-7550
Fax: 708/386-2322
www.absolutevideoservices.com

Allied Vaughn
1200 Thorndale
Elk Grove Village, IL 60007
Phone: 847/595-2900
Fax: 847/595-8677
www.alliedvaughn.com

Cinema Video Center
211 E. Grand
Chicago, IL 60611
Phone: 312/644-0861
Fax: 312/644-2096
www.networkcentury.com

ELB's Entertainment, Inc.
2501 N. Lincoln, Ste. 198
Chicago, IL 60614-2313
Phone: 800/656-1585
Fax: 800/957-3527
www.elbsentertainment.com

Golan Productions
1501 N. Magnolia
Chicago, IL 60622
Phone: 773/274-3456
Fax: 312/642-7441
www.atomicimaging.com

Master Images Video Duplication
112 Carpenter
Wheeling, IL 60090
Phone: 847/541-4440

Broadview Media
142 E. Ontario
Chicago, IL 60611
Phone: 312/337-6000
Fax: 312/337-0500
www.broadviewmedia.com

Nxtrm (pronounced Nextroom)
230 E. Ontario, Ste. 302
Chicago, IL 60611
Phone: 312/335-3620
Fax: 312/335-3622
www.nxtrm.com

Video Replay, Inc.
118 W. Grand
Chicago, IL 60610
Phone: 312/467-0425
Fax: 312/467-1045
www.videoreplaychicago.com

Ear Prompters

Credible Communication, Inc.
155 Little John Trail NE
Atlanta, GA 30309
Phone: 404/892-0660
www.ear-prompter.com

Sargon Yonan
67 E. Madison, Ste. 1415
Chicago, IL 60603
Phone: 312/782-7007
Fax: 312/782-7529

Actor's Tools

CHAPTER 4
FILM & TV

The Price
Writers' Theatre

A Fresh Start For Visual Media In Illinois

By Bob Labate

Not so long ago, the outlook for professionally-produced visual media in Illinois was as gray as a February day in Chicago. And, as with a cold, cloudy day, everyone complained, but few did anything positive about it—preferring instead to fight over the remaining scraps of commercial and indie film production work. But this outlook is beginning to change, and we may begin to reverse years of runaway productions.

The Decline of Illinois Film Production

The decline of the Illinois film industry is well documented. Direct expenditures for film production in Illinois cratered by 42 percent between 1999 and 2001 and, according to Chicago Film Office estimates, commercial location shooting time (a good indicator of commercial production) fell by about one-third in the past five years, from 297 days in 1997 to 197 days in 2001. And, while the Midwest continues to fascinate filmmakers and remains a popular backdrop for telling a story, our slice of the production pie continues to shrink. For example, the film *My Big Fat Greek Wedding,* though set in Chicago, was shot in Toronto, used no Chicago-based talent and produced no revenue for the state of Illinois.

There are many reasons for the migration of the film business, and Canada—with its potent mixture of tax credits, rebates, incentives and buying power—is often cast as the villain-in-chief in such "Runaway Productions" for the migration of the film business. Yes, producing a film in Canada can reduce costs by 20 to 30 percent, but Canada is not the only country to offer incentives for film production. In today's global economy, any country or region with a competitive advantage will gain market share, and Canada is proof that if you offer state-of-the-art infrastructure and skilled professional individuals at a competitive price, then production will follow.

The problem is not that Canada is stealing film productions that otherwise would be shot in Illinois. The truth is that, despite an excellent technical infrastructure, a strong commercial base and a wealth of trained professionals, Illinois is not even close to being financially competitive with other states, let alone Canada.

Following the Canadian example, many states offer cost-savings packages that include waivers of sales and use taxes, rebates and incentives. For example, New York State waives sales and use taxes for machinery, equipment and services used in the production or postproduction of feature films, TV programs, music videos and commercials. In addition, New York City provides free access to public locations and parking on public lands and parks, and there is often no charge for police services when such are required. Two dozen other states have similar forms of tax waivers or refunds for spending on production equipment and services. For producers that spend at least $300,000 annually, Louisiana has both an employment tax credit for below-the-line Louisiana workers and an expanded investor tax credit for Louisiana businesses. New Mexico goes further by partnering with resident venture capital firms to make as much as $7.5 million in private equity funds available per project. In contrast, until the passage of the Film Production Services Tax Credit Act (which becomes effective on Jan. 1, 2004), Illinois has one of the highest sales taxes in the country and relatively few tax credits.

To address the problem of runaway production, a small group of knowledgeable, Chicago-based media professionals met often over the past year to discuss various first steps towards making Illinois more competitive.

A first step was the preparation of a 40-page white paper titled "Creating Visual Media in Illinois: A Plan for Sustained Growth, 2003 and Beyond." A copy of the white paper is available at www.illinoisproduction.org. It is one of the best reports of its kind in the country and, among other things, it: (i) reviews the changing nature of the media and entertainment industries; (ii) describes the economic impact and root causes of runaway production in Illinois; (iii) offers strategies for stemming the flow of productions and jobs, which include a package of tax incentives, rebates and measures similar to those adopted in a number of other states and Canada; and (iv) attempts to provide a single voice and vision for what has been an important but fractious Chicago industry. It is "must reading" for anyone involved in media or the visual arts in Illinois.

A second step was the formation of a nonprofit company, **The Illinois Production Alliance (IPA),** devoted to unifying the Illinois media community and to developing (and advocating) legislative proposals consistent with that unified vision. The goal was ambitious, but the collective efforts of the IPA and a broad range of industry professionals resulted in the creation and passage of new legislation this year, The Illinois Production Services Tax Credit Act. Essentially, the new act creates a 25 percent wage-based tax incentive for film, video or television production, after Jan. 1, 2004, that has been certified by the Illinois Department of Commerce and Community Affairs. The act is not easy to read and there are a number of qualifications, but it is an excellent beginning.

Film-Friendly Environment

Despite years of decreasing film and television production, Chicago has retained its character as a film-friendly place. There is only space to skim the surface, but now that there is new financial incentive for visual media, producers should take advantage of the many organizations that support visual media. Here are a few:

Columbia College has the largest film department outside of Los Angeles and, through its courses and seminars, is a focal point for teaching the creative, technical and business end of the industry. Bruce Sheridan, the head of Columbia's film school, has enormous experience as an award-winning producer who

Film & TV

understands the business as well as the art of film. The film school also has an excellent documentary film department that seems to have a hand in most of the broadcast-quality documentaries produced in Chicago.

The Independent Feature Project (www.ifp.org) has long been the leading nonprofit organization for nurturing indie film in Chicago. Among other events, the IFP sponsors the IFP/Chicago Production Fund, the Flyover Zone Short Film Festival and the IFP/Chicago Annual Filmmakers' Conference, as well as monthly forums on various aspects of filmmaking.

A new institutional resource is The School of The Art Institute, which operates the **Gene Siskel Film Center** (www.artic.edu/webspaces/siskelfilmcenter). Under its new executive director, Randy Adamsick, it is the premiere screening location for indie film in Chicago. The Siskel Center has a full schedule of rarely screened films and retrospectives that show the depth of past and current independent films.

Chicago-based film festivals such as the **Chicago Underground Film Festival** (www.cuff.org) and the **Chicago International Film Festival** (www.chicagofilmfestival.com) have never been stronger in the films they screen, nor better attended. On a monthly basis, **The Chicago Community Cinema** (www.chicagocommunitycinema.com) screens shorts, indie film trailers, student work and feature films, and sponsors events at which those involved in the Chicago film/video community can meet and network.

Filmmakers on a budget usually can find help at **Lawyers for the Creative Arts** (312/649-4111), the foremost source of legal information and assistance for artists and arts organizations in Chicago, and at **The Nonprofit Financial Center** (www.nonprofitfinancial.org), which is a gold-mine of information for those interested in raising funds from foundations and creating and maintaining nonprofit corporations.

Finally, two other valuable organizations are the **Chicago Film Office** (www.cityofchicago.org/filmoffice) and the **Illinois Film Office** (www.illinoisbiz.biz/film). Both offices provide information on the rules and regulations governing film in Illinois and are resources for finding equipment and skilled people. The Illinois Film Office also distributes (for free) the PRODUCTION GUIDE, which lists just about everything and everyone you'll need to make your film.

Collaborative Professionals

When I ask clients why they make movies in Chicago, they normally refer to the collaborative nature of the people who work here. The film community is relatively small, people know each other and they are usually willing to help with recommendations and advice, whether on a technical, creative or business issue. A quick look at any of the available creative or film directories (such as SCREEN MAGAZINE'S "Chicago Production Bible" or this book) should produce dozens, if not hundreds, of names of individuals who can act, direct, edit, art direct, line produce, provide graphic support or a musical soundtrack—all at a reasonable cost. Egos are generally kept in check, and the sense of competition found on both coasts is far less apparent.

"Collaborative" also means that commercial companies that supply goods and services to the film industry are generally willing to accommodate and work with indie filmmakers so that it all fits within the budget or the production schedule. At local seminars, producers who have enjoyed some artistic or commercial success are usually willing to spend some time with those who are new to the field or who have questions on technical or creative issues.

Financing and Distribution

These are the two weakest areas of the Chicago indie film infrastructure. While the State of Illinois has made some effort to provide funding (primarily through the Illinois Development Finance Authority), the most common form of financing remains equity (investment) financing for for-profit companies and through foundation and government grants for those making films through or in conjunction with a nonprofit company. Film distribution, both locally and nationally, is also limited, but inroads exist and distribution sources appear to be increasing if you are willing to look and are persistent enough to ask. But it is not for the shy or the faint of heart.

Film Organizations

Film & TV

Chicago Film Office
Richard Moskal, Director
One N. LaSalle Street, Ste. 2165
Chicago, IL 60602
Phone: 312/744-6415
Fax: 312/744-1378
filmoffice@cityofchicago.org
www.ci.chi.il.us/FilmOffice

The Illinois Film Office
Brenda Sexton, Director
100 W. Randolph, 3rd Fl.
Chicago, IL 60601
Phone: 312/814-3600
Fax: 312/814-8874
http://www.illinoisbiz.biz/film

The Illinois Production Alliance
Mark Egmon, Board President
One E. Erie, Ste. 605
Chicago, IL 60626
Phone: 312-867-5504
info@illinoisproduction.org
www.illinoisproduction.org

**The Independent Film Project
(IFP/Chicago)**
Rebekah Cowing, Executive Director
33 East Congress Parkway, Rm. 505
Chicago, IL 60605
Phone: 312/435-1825
Fax: 312/435-1828
rcowing@ifp.org
www.ifp.org

Understanding the On-Camera Industry Food Chain & Your Relationship to the other Fish (& Sharks)

By Rachael Patterson, Director of The Audition Studio

Becoming a working actor is a monumental achievement. More than in most industries, navigating the acting biz requires strong right brain (the creative side) and strong left brain (the pragmatic side) skills. It is essential—in order to get started, promote yourself and ultimately work—that you balance your talent and training with business savvy and a realistic understanding of the business.

In order to understand where you fit in the process of commercial and film production, let's begin by looking at how a commercial is cast.

The Client is the product—i.e. Cheerios, Budweiser or Volkswagen. When the client decides to make a commercial or develop a new advertising campaign, they hire an advertising agency to create the concept.

Ad Agencies employ right brain types (the creatives: copy writers, art directors) to create the spot, and left brain people (the producers, account reps) to take care of the business and numbers side. Once the spot is approved by the client, the ad agency hires a production company to produce the spot.

Production Companies hire right brain creatives (the director, production designer, props people) and left brain pragmatics (the producer). If there are people in the spot, the production company also hires a casting director.

Casting Directors must run a business (left brain), as well as understand the tastes of the director and work well with actors (right brain). The casting director is paid by the producers for prepping and running auditions. Casting directors don't actually cast; instead, they present a variety of actors that they think might be appropriate for the job. As Rachel Tenner of Tenner, Paskal & Rudnicke Casting (TPR) says, "We are like personal shoppers for the director; they expect us to understand the tone of the script and the kinds of actors that they will respond to." The casting director, when casting a spot, will fax specs of the job (the types i.e., models 18-25 or professional looking ethnic women 40-55) to agents and ask for submissions (headshots and resumes of actors that fit the bill).

Agents then pull actors' headshots/resumes from their files that fit the specs of the job and messenger them to the casting director.

It is your job to get into the agent files and become an actor that that they think of first when the specs arrive. You must understand your type, and make sure your agent sees you in the same way, so that you will get called for the "right" jobs. As an actor, you may resist the concept, but typecasting is a reality of the biz. Typecasting is industry lingo used by directors of film, television and commercials for casting according to the actor's personality or physical appearance to convey an immediate message to the audience. For example, if the pizza delivery guy looks like a grad student at the University of Chicago, it's a different statement than if he looks like a high school dropout. It's crucial that actors know their type in order to market themselves appropriately. If your picture is more glamorous than you are, and your agent doesn't really know your work, then you will never be submitted for the quirky, goofy, nerdy gal that you really are and that you will be cast as.

This discussion leads to the question of how an actor establishes a friendly, working relationship with an agent. What should the expectations of the actor/agent relationship be? What are dos and don'ts when meeting an agent or casting director for the first time?

When Mickey Grossman of Linda Jack Talent goes through new actor submissions, he looks for "types that the agency doesn't currently have on file, union actors who are already working and actors of ethnicity." He says that they are also always looking for young talent. "I try hard not to look at talent as clones. I want to see who they are," says Grossman. "If I've brought you in, I already think you've got something…I want to see who you are, your personality and confidence. If you're a dead fish until you open your mouth or they say 'action,' you're dead in the water." Grossman works hard to educate young actors, and advises: "I don't care how much of an artist you are—you need to treat this as your own personal business, you are running your own business. Young actors don't need to know everything, but they need to know the basics, ask questions, be proactive. It may be cliché, but remember the agent only gets 10 percent."

Bob Schroeder, TV/film director of Aria Model and Talent, says, "An actor determines his or her relationship with the agent. Most actors are so happy to have an agent—someone who likes them—that they often don't expect enough of the relationship. They should expect their agent to give advice on headshots, resumes, your look, your type, etc."

Shroeder suggests asking your potential agent how they view you, where they think you fit in the business and where they see you in the future. "If you are afraid to call your agent to ask for advice or ask a question—then start looking for a new agent," he says. "That's not the relationship you should have with someone who works for you." Schroeder points out that many actors think once they get representation, their work is done, when truthfully their work is just beginning.

Actors need to be on stage in Chicago (either theatre or improv) and be involved with training. This gives your agent something to work with—other than your talent—in order to sell you and get you into the casting director's office.

Film & TV

"The amount of effort that the actor puts into his own career will dictate how hard the agent will work," adds Sam Samuelson of the Stewart Agency.

"If I had just one thing to say to actors," says Mickie Paskal of TPR Casting, "it would be to empower yourselves. If we have responded to your agent's submission or your work on stage by the time we call you in, it is because we have responded to something that is intrinsic to who you are, and that's why we want to see you—that's what we are expected to show our clients and that will be what ultimately gets you cast."

And Jen Rudnicke reminds actors "to bring yourself to the role and not waste time worrying about what the client might or might not want."

Samuelson reiterates what the other industry folk say by encouraging actors to "be yourself and have a good time. Talent being equal, it's the person that is most comfortable with themselves that will ultimately get the job."

So keep your power in the process, your nose to the grindstone, your sense of humor and don't forget—you can handle the sharks.

McBlaine

& associates INC

Leader in Non-Union Agencies

**805 W. Touhy Ave.
Park Ridge, IL 60068
(847) 823-3877**

See our listing on page 94.

Getting Paid

By Becky Brett

Art and commerce—it is difficult to combine the two, which is probably why most artistic organizations are non-profit. No one says they want to be an actor for the money (Jim Carrey's *a priori* $20M check aside). We do it for the love of it, the passion and the rush of creation.

And then there's voice-over work. Or industrials. Or commercials. These we do to pay the rent that keeps us in our Lakeview or Andersonville apartment near the theatres that house our creative rush.

What happens when these jobs—and they are jobs—don't pay the rent? What if an actor literally does not get paid for work done? And if you are lucky enough to make a living in the theatre, what happens when the theatre hits the skids and your show gets cancelled?

In many ways, it is a backward system. The actor is expected to perform on a certain date, having prepared for several days or even weeks beforehand, while the producer can wait almost as long as they want to pay.

If the work is through a union agency, you have many options to collect your check. Companies that hire union talent are required to pay a bond to the union to cover professional fees. In theory, even if the company goes belly-up, you should still get paid. As an added incentive, unions can charge clients with late fees to ensure timely payment.

Kathryn Lamkey, central regional director for the Actors' Equity Association, said that for theatre work, Equity requires that theatres place a bond equivalent to two weeks salary. This will generally cover the actors in the event of a sudden closing notice. If the theatre repeatedly has problems with checks bouncing, they may ask the theatre to pay their actors in cash.

Lamkey says that, fortunately, she has not heard many complaints lately from the Equity companies, nor about the non-union theatres; but "in these economic times, actors working non-union should be careful because they are operating without union protection."

Writer, actor, teacher and PERFORMINK contributor Belinda Bremner echoes Lamkey, saying, "The one way to guarantee getting paid is to make sure you have a union-franchised agent." However, not everyone has made it to the rarefied air of unionhood. The good news is union agents do hire non-union talent for jobs—everyone has to start somewhere. "Not even the Barrymores came out of the womb with a union card," says Bremner.

If you are not working with a union agent, it is harder, but you can still protect yourself. Actors are not powerless. Asserting yourself or making sure all terms are clear up front is not being high-maintenance, it is being responsible. Here are some proactive steps actors can take before getting into a bad financial situation.

Film & TV

Check references. You ask your friends to recommend a good doctor, a quiet restaurant or a funny movie. Why not a reliable agency? For example, if someone were to ask today if they should work with a certain voice-over agency, many Chicago actors would tell them to run.

Cultivate a relationship with your agent. Many actors comment that they feel pimped out by their agents. Even though the agent works for the actor and is paid because of the actor's work, there is an air of expectation, even of entitlement—that the agent is due unconditional respect. However, actors with good relationships and open communication with their agents may feel more empowered to address these financial issues as they come up.

Read the fine print. You may be getting screwed because you actually did sign on for it. We can't emphasize enough the importance of reading your contract carefully. If you are not under a union-negotiated agreement, your risk of being taken advantage of is higher. Are there provisions for overtime pay? Does it set a limit on the number of hours you may work and what will happen if you go over those hours? The devil is in the details—exorcise it.

Even if you work without a contract, make it clear in your first conversation, in a very businesslike tone when you expect to be paid. Sometimes "paperwork" is the excuse for not cutting a check in a timely manner. Avoid this by having them send paperwork to you in advance to fill out.

If, in spite of all this good advice, you go more than 30-90 days without getting paid, you do have options. (30 days is something of an industry standard, unless your contract specifically states a different time period for payment.) If it is a union gig, go immediately to your union. You've paid your dues—literally—so let them work for you.

If this was a non-union job and you're on your own to collect payment, try calling the agency first. Be polite but firm, and try to figure out where your check is. Hey, these guys are busy too. It could be that your check is sitting on someone's desk waiting for you to come pick it up. Or it could even be filed away somewhere. On the first call, it's nice to give your agent the benefit of the doubt.

It's the second, third and fourth calls that might get a little more contentious. If you find you're getting the runaround from the agency and you can't afford a lawyer, try going through the Illinois Department of Labor (IDOL). Just be prepared to wait. If you file a Wage Payment and Collection complaint, they can take 60 days or even as long as a year to process it.

Illinois Department of Labor
160 N. LaSalle Ste. C-1300
Chicago, IL 60601
Phone: 312/793-2808

Also go through their Web site at www.state.il.us/agency/idol, where you can download labor laws and complaint forms. The phone number for wage payment and collection information is 312/793-2808.

Ultimately, you are responsible for how you are treated and under what conditions you work. If you have problems because you did not read your contract carefully, you have only yourself to blame. For many of us, this is how we learn.

However, if you have been diligent and are still not getting what you rightly earned, you are not powerless. "Somebody has to bell the cat," says Bremner. In other words, someone needs to let other actors know this is an agency they should be careful of. Actors are only blacklisted if they behave unethically, not if they are looking out for their well-being.

In an effort to preempt any potential problems, Bremner offered these Seven Early Warning Signs You're Getting Screwed:

- Your agent is also a casting director.

- An agent "discovers" you on the street or in a bar.

- They say they're a manager. ("Unless you're a rock star or a wrestler, you don't need a manager in Chicago," says Bremner.)

- They only want to meet you somewhere other than in a downtown office— like a coffee shop or the train station.

- They require a "listing fee" from you.

- They push you to do something you're uncomfortable with.

- They won't tell you when you're being paid.

- The agent is not in this book or in Act One Reports.

Film & TV

Talent Agencies - Union Franchised

Ambassador Talent
333 N. Michigan, Ste. 910
Chicago, IL 60601

Aria Model and Talent Management
1017 W. Washington, Ste. 2C
Chicago, IL 60607
Phone: 312/243-9400
www.ariamodel.com

Actors/models must submit resume headshot/composite by mail. Agency will contact you, if interested. No voice-over. SAG/AFTRA/Equity franchised.

Robert Schroeder—on-camera

Raye Ruff— TV, film

Janice Rodriguez —commercial print

Sebastian McWilliams—men's fashion, fashion director

Emily Bartolime—women's fashion

Katherine Tenerowicz—women's fashion, plus size

Nancy Tennicott—runway

Arlene Wilson Talent
430 W. Erie, #210
Chicago, IL 60610
Phone: 312/573-0200
www.arlenewilson.com

Catherine Hagen, C.O.O.

Submit headshot and resume by mail first. The agency will contact you, if interested. AFTRA/SAG/Equity franchised.

Anna Oliveira—agency director

Peter Forster—acting division

Sarah Wilson—women fashion

Erika Larson —children, on-camera, commercial print

Ann Marie Lofgren—men's division

Baker & Rowley
1327 W. Washington, Ste. 5C
Chicago, IL 60607
Phone: 312/850-4700
Fax: 312/850-4300
bakerandrowley@attbi.com
www.bakerandrowleytalent.com

Send five headshot/resumes and two voice demos, Attn: New Faces. Agents will contact you, if interested. Multi-cultural representation. Open registration Tuesdays 12-2pm. No other drop-ins. Attn: New Faces.

AFTRA/SAG/Equity franchised.

Big Mouth Talent
935 W. Chestnut, Ste. 415
Chicago, IL 60622
Phone: 312/421-4400

Send headshot and resume with a SASE. Agency will call if interested. All ages.

Attn: Brooke Tonneman.

SAG/AFTRA/Equity franchised.

Encore Talent Agency, Inc.
700 N. Sacramento, Ste. 221
Chicago, IL 60612
Phone: 773/638-7300
Fax: 773/638-6770
www.encoretalentagency.com

Submit headshot and resume along with a SASE. No drop-ins.

SAG/AFTRA franchised

Susan Acuna —adults

Dawn Gray—theater, voice-over

Diana Varela—children

ETA, Inc.
7558 S. South Chicago Ave.
Chicago, IL 60619
Phone: 773/752-3955

Joan P. Brown, President

Mail composites and resumes to Joan P. Brown, who will contact you, if interested. SAG/AFTRA Franchised.

Ford Talent Group
641 W. Lake, Ste. 402
Chicago, IL 60661
Phone: 312/707-9000

Katie Ford, President

Actors, please submit pictures and resumes to Ford Talent Group, Attn: new talent.

AFTRA/SAG franchised.

Molly Reid & Linise Belford— on-camera

Geddes Agency
1633 N. Halsted, Ste. 300
Chicago, IL 60614
Phone: 312/787-8333

Elizabeth Geddes, Vice-President

Actors must submit headshot and resume by mail only. Agency will call, if interested. AFTRA/SAG/Equity franchised.

Elizabeth Geddes—film, TV, theatre

Emily Beste—voice-over

Chelsey Peterson—agent assistant, children

Lily's Talent Agency, Inc.
1301 W. Washington, Ste. B
Chicago, IL 60607
Phone: 312/601-2345
www.lilystalent.com
info@lilystalent.com

Lily Liu, President

Actors must submit two headshots and resumes and S.A.S.E. by mail. Include phone number and statistics. Agency will respond, if interested.

AFTRA/SAG/Equity franchised.

Lily liu—head agent

Jessica Thomas— on-camera, voice-over

Heidi Bauers— print

Erika Strickmaker— fashion, print, promotional

Linda Jack Talent
230 E. Ohio, Ste. 200
Chicago, IL 60611
Phone: 312/587-1155
www.lindajacktelent.com
info@lindajacktelent.com

Submit by mail. AFTRA/SAG/Equity franchised.

Linda Jack—voice-over

Vanessa Lanier—voice-over

Mickey Grossman—on-camera

Stacy Shafer—on-camera, new talent submissions

Debbie Cohen—on-camera, voice-over

Amie Richardson—children

Naked Voices, Inc.
865 N. Sangamon, Ste. 415
Chicago, IL 60622
Phone: 312/563-0136
www.nakedvoices.com

Debby Kotzen, Owner

Send in 2-minute, professionally made demo tape or CD by mail only.

Norman Schucart Enterprises (SB-North)
1417 Green Bay Rd.
Highland Park, IL 60035
Phone: 847/433-1113

Norman Schucart, President

New talent should first submit headshot/composite and resume with phone number by mail (include S.A.S.E. postcard). If interested, the agency will arrange to interview you in Chicago.

AFTRA/SAG franchised.

Norman Schucart—TV, industrial film, print, live shows

Nancy Elliott—TV, industrial film, print, live shows

Salazar & Navas, Inc.
700 N. Green, Ste. 503
Chicago, IL 60622
Phone: 312/666-1677
www.salazarnavas.com

Myrna Salazar, President

Trina Navas, Vice President

Hispanic/Latin types preferred, but all types considered and represented. New talent seen on Tuesdays, 12-4pm.

AFTRA/SAG franchised.

Myrna Salazar—on-camera, voice-over, film, commercial print, print adults

Shirley Hamilton, Inc.
333 E. Ontario, Ste. 302B
Chicago, IL 60611
Phone: 312/787-4700
www.shirleyhamilton.com

Shirley Hamilton, President

Lynne Hamilton, Vice President

Registration by mail only with S.A.S.E. Actors must submit headshot and resume. Agency will contact by mail, if interested.

AFTRA/SAG/Equity franchised.

Monica Campbell & Walker Brockington—on-camera, trade show, voice-over, TV, Film

Laurie Hamilton—print, marketing

Stewart Talent
58 W. Huron
Chicago, IL 60610
Phone: 312/943-3131
www.stewarttalent.com

Jane Stewart, President

Actors: Mail or drop-off two pictures and resumes between M-F 9am-5:30pm. The appropriate agent will contact you within six to eight weeks, if interested. No walk-ins.

AFTRA/SAG/Equity franchised.

Sam Samuelson—TV, stage, film

Nancy Kidder—industrial film

Joan Sparks—voice-over

Wade Childress—commercial print

Kathy Gardner—children, print

Sheila Dougherty—voice-over

Jenn Hall—children

Todd Turina—Film, TV

Jenny Wilson—Film, TV

Film & TV

93

Voices Unlimited, Inc
541 N. Fairbanks, Ste. 2735
Chicago, IL 60611
Phone: 312/832-1113

Talent Agencies - Non-Union

BMG Model and Talent
456 N. May
Chicago, IL 60622
Phone: 312/829-9100
Fax: 312/829-6698
www.bmgmodels.com

BMG represents Fashion and Commercial Print talent of all ages. Adult talent must be height and weight proportionate with women 5'8" to 5'11" and men 5'11 to 6'3". Open interviews are held on Thursdays from 2-4pm, except for holiday weeks.

Concept Model Management, Inc.
1301 S. Grove Ave., Ste. 160
Barrington, IL 60010
info@conceptmodels.com
www.conceptmodels.com

Models only, please. Exclusive and non-exclusive talent. 17-24 years in age. No walk-ins. Send photo & resume/composite card. Agency will call, if interested.

Karen Stavins Enterprises, Inc.
303 E. Wacker, Concourse Level
Chicago, IL 60601
Phone: 312/938-1140
www.stavinstalent.com

Submit picture and resume, composites or voice tapes. Attn: New Talent. Agency will contact you, if interested. Non-union talent booked for commercials, industrials, TV/film, voice-over, trade shows, live shows. 17 years and older.

McBlaine & Associates, Inc.
805 Touhy Ave.
Park Ridge, IL 60601
Phone: 847/823-3877

No drop-ins. Send a headshot and resume with a S.A.S.E.

Paige Ehlman, Brett Ehlman—print, voice-over, industrial, commercial, film, children, new faces, music video.

See our ad on page 88.

Nouvelle Talent
P.O. Box 578100
Chicago, IL 60657
Phone: 312/944-1133
Ann Toni Sipka, President
Send picture and resume. Agency will contact you, if interested.
Ann Toni Sipka—(New York) trade show
Carlotta Young—(Chicago) trade show

Talent Group, Inc.
1228 W. Wilson
Chicago, IL 60640
Phone: 773/561-8814
talentgrp@aol.com
No drop-ins. Send a headshot and resume or voice-over tape Attn: Juliet Wilson. Ages 18 and older.

Talent Agencies - Milwaukee

Arlene Wilson Talent, Inc.
807 N. Jefferson, Ste. 200
Milwaukee, WI 53202
Phone: 414/283-5600
www.arlenewilson.com
info.milwaukee@arlenewilson.com
Catherine Hagen, Agency COO
Open call for actors Wed. 1:30-3pm. Must have current headshots and resumes or voice demo. May also send materials.
AFTRA franchised.
Carol Rathe—voice-over, on-camera, broadcast dir.

Jennifer's Talent Unlimited, Inc.
740 N. Plankinton, Ste. 300
Milwaukee, WI 53203
Phone: 414/277-9440
www.jenniferstalent.com
Jennifer L. Berg, President
Actors must submit a headshot and resume Attn: Marna.
Agency will contact you, if interested.
AFTRA franchised.

Lori Lins, Ltd.
7611 W. Holmes
Milwaukee, WI 53220
Phone: 414/282-3500
Lori Lins, President
Actors must submit headshot, resume and cover letter. Agency will respond, if interested.
AFTRA/SAG franchised and non-union.
Lori Lins, Betty Antholine—bookers

Convention and Tradeshow

Best Faces
1152 N. LaSalle, Ste. F
Chicago, IL 60610
Phone: 312/944-3009
bestfaceschicago@aol.com
www.bestfacesofchicago.com
Send materials Attn: Judy Mudd. Agency will contact you, if interested.

Corporate Presenters (A Division of Karen Stavins Enterprises)
303 E. Wacker, Concourse Level
Chicago, IL 60601
Phone: 312/938-1140
www.stavinstalent.com
Submit composite or headshot attn: New Talent. Agency will contact, if interested. Narrators, hosts/hostesses and models booked for trade shows, conventions, special promotions and variety acts. 17 years and older.

The Group, Ltd.
10120 S. Eastern Ave.
Henderson, NV 89052
Phone: 702/895-8926
Mail materials. No drop-ins. No talent under 21. Agency represents females (21-40)/males (21-50). Trade show talent only. Interested in all talent including narration, foreign languages, and prefers audio prompter. Contact: Mary Troxel, Talent Coordinator.

Casting Directors

All City Casting (Union, Non-Union)
P.O. Box 577640
Chicago, IL 60657-7640
Phone: 773/588-6062
Attn: June Pyskacek

Big House Casting & Audio
944 N. Noble, Ste. 1
Chicago, IL 60622
Phone: 773/772-9539
www.bighousecasting.com
Attn: Kourtney Vahle & Kate McClanaghan
Send one demo/resume.
SAG/AFTRA franchised.

Chicago Casting Center
777 N. Green St.
Chicago, IL 60622
Phone: 312/327-1904
Attn: Janet Louer, Tina O'Brien, Siobhan Sullivan

Claire Simon Casting
1512 N. Fremont, Ste. 202
Chicago, IL 60622
Phone: 312/202-0124
Attn: Claire Simon

David O'Connor Casting
1017 W. Washington, Ste. 2A
Chicago, IL 60607
Phone: 312/226-9112
www.oconnorcasting.com
Attn: David O'Connor

E'Sa-Rah Casting
700 N. Green St., Ste. C20
Chicago, IL 60622
Phone: 312/455-8383
esarahcasting@aol.com
Attn: Elizabeth Hill, Jacquelyn Conard

Jane Alderman Casting
c/o Act One Studios
640 N. LaSalle, Ste. 535
Chicago, IL 60610
Phone: 312/397-1182
Attn: Jane Alderman—Casting Director

Don Kaufman
PO Box 401
Orland Park, IL 60462
See our ad on page 91.

K.T.'s
P.O. Box 577039
Chicago, IL 60657-7039
Phone: 773/525-1126
non-union casting
See our ad blah.

Reginacast
8491 Sunset Blvd., Ste. 372
West Hollywood, CA 90069
Phone: 312/409-5521—Talent Hotline
reginacast@aol.com
www.reginacast.com
Send a current photo with your age and height, phone numbers and email address to both locations. If possible, please email and call hotline number for specific requirements before mailing.

Film & TV

Segal Studio
1040 W. Huron
Chicago, IL 60622
Phone: 312/563-9368
Attn: Jeffery Lyle Segal

Tenner, Paskal, Rudnicke Casting
20 W. Hubbard, Ste. 2E
Chicago, IL 60611
Phone: 312/527-0665
Fax: 312-527-9085
www.tprcasting.com
Attn: Rachel Tenner, Mickie Paskal, Jennifer Rudnicke

Trapdoor Casting
1655 W. Cortland
Chicago, IL 60622
Phone: 773/384-0494
www.trapdoortheater.com
Attn: Beata Pilch & Nicole Wiesner

Umlaut Casting
612 N. Taylor Ave.
Oak Park, IL 60302
Phone: 312/342-0111
www.umlautcasting.com
Attn: Peter Oestreich

Extras Casting

K.T.'s
P.O. Box 577039
Chicago, IL 60657-7039
Phone: 773/525-1126

Send 6 pictures or composites and resumes. Include phone number, address, social security number, height, weight, hair and eye color, age (or age range), car color and make.

Reginacast
8491 Sunset Blvd., Suite 372
West Hollywood, CA 90069
Phone: 312/409-5521 Talent Hotline
reginacast@aol.com
www.reginacast.com

Send a current photo with your age and height, phone numbers and email address to both locations. If possible, please email and call hotline number for specific requirements before mailing.

Windy City Films
Phone: 773/205-1212
www.windycitycasting.com
See our ad below.

CHAPTER 5
UNIONS & LEGAL RESOURCES

Pacific Overtures
Chicago Shakespeare Theatre

Actors' Equity Association

By Kevin Heckman

Actors' Equity Association (AEA, or simply Equity), like many labor unions, came into existence in the early part of the 20th century. Their constitution was drafted in 1913, and the American Federation of Labor (which would go on to become the AFL-CIO) accepted them in 1919. Early on, they initiated a performer's strike that led to producers' acceptance of AEA as a bargaining entity, and thus began the gradual reformation of the conditions under which performers' labored.

The mission of Equity is to "secure and protect the rights of members in their business relations with employers, to govern members democratically, and to foster and stimulate theatre," according to their pamphlet "About Equity."

Equity is the stage actors and stage managers union. Similar unions exist in Canada and the United Kingdom, but they are not directly affiliated in any way, though reciprocal agreements exist to cover certain situations. Primarily, Equity negotiates contracts with producers to set certain minimum wages, working conditions and to protect performers. Additionally, they provide other benefits to members including insurance, pension, casting information and more. Finally, Equity is affiliated with several charitable or support organizations including Broadway Cares/Equity Fights Aids, The Actors' Fund of America, and the Actors' Federal Credit Union.

So You Want To Join Equity?

You're an actor. It's your calling, your life, the food of your soul, and you want to make a living at it, too. So, it's time to give up that day job and join Equity.

Waiter? My reality check, please. Equity can be a great thing for some performers and the kiss of death for others, depending on a wide variety of factors (more on that later). But if you want to join, there are several ways.

The simple route: If a producer offers you an Equity contract and you sign it, POW! You're Equity. You still have to pay the appropriate fees and so forth, but this the simplest way to join the union.

Many Equity houses (though not all) also offer an Equity Membership Candidacy program (EMC). By working as a non-Equity actor at the theatre in question, you accumulate points (one point per week). After reaching 50 points, the next contract you sign with an Equity house must be as a member of the union. Joining EMC costs $100, which will be applied to your initiation fees (see below).

Members of the other 4-A unions (SAG and AFTRA are the most common) can join Equity directly by submitting proof of employment governed by that 4-A union.

In any case, a new member of Equity has to pay an initiation fee that's currently $1,000. Equity will allow you to deduct it from your wages, but the entire amount must be paid within two years of joining the union. Membership privileges don't begin until you've paid at least $300. As of April 1, 2004, the initiation fee rises to $1,100.

Once you're a member, you pay dues in two ways. Annual dues of $118 are due semi-annually. Work dues, consisting of two percent of your wages, are also deducted from each paycheck.

Now You're Equity!

So, by hook or crook, you've joined the Actors' Equity Association. What do you get for such privileged status?

First, the union now sets your minimum wages. Depending on the size of the producing theatre, this amount can range from a modest $152 to a more sizable $666 with a theatre operating under the most common Chicago Area Theatre (CAT) contract. This amount might be even greater for tours or larger, for-profit productions. Other theatres operate under LORT, TYA or a variety of other types of contracts. Most Chicago theatres, however, operate under CAT III or lower contracts, meaning your minimum weekly wage will more likely come in under $319.75. As you can see, most actors will not be able to depend solely on stage work to earn a living.

You also get benefits, including a pension and (for some) health insurance. Insurance is probably the most common reason for joining Equity, but it's not available to all. If you work 10 weeks in four consecutive quarters, you qualify for a year's worth of health coverage. This requirement must be satisfied again to gain another year of coverage, and so forth.

Equity also limits the number of hours you can be asked to work, sets the frequency with which you must receive breaks and days off, and requires certain standards of cleanliness and safety in your work environment. Finally, they require that producers give all Equity members the opportunity to audition at least once per year. Some theatres satisfy this requirement by holding a general call once a year; others hold auditions on a per-show basis. In either case, those auditions will be registered with Equity, and only union members may make appointments (though non-Equity performers can walk in, as time permits).

So Should I Join?

Equity does not enjoy the best reputation in Chicago for a variety of reasons, some good, some not. The biggest is always some variation on "I'll never work!".

The fact is that most parts cast in the Chicagoland area are cast with non-Equity actors. Though you might be surprised to see the number of companies listed in the Equity section of the theatre listings, most of them hire only one or two Equity actors. Frequently, those contracts go to ensemble members. To work regularly as an Equity actor, you'll probably have to commit to frequent travel to theatres in Indiana, Wisconsin, Missouri, and beyond. It will also help if you can sing and/or dance. Even then, the supply of actors far exceeds the demand, meaning that many performers will not work.

Unions & Legal Resources

One solution to this problem is to talk to producers. Are there theatres where you can expect to get regular consideration as an Equity performer? If yes, you might get the work to make the choice a good one. You probably still won't work as much as you did when you were non-union, but hopefully you'll work enough. Also, talk to folks at the Equity office here in town. They don't want you joining the union if you're not ready, and they may have suggestions.

They Don't Care About Their Members!

Of course, this is completely untrue. However, the roots of that complaint lie in some legitimate issues. First of all, Equity remains a New York-centric union. Most of the high-paying work begins there. Most of the governing board comes from there. Of course, Chicago and New York are thoroughly different markets, and the rules for one don't always make sense for the other. Secondly, most of Equity's membership isn't working at any given moment. As a result, the union's negotiating power with producers is weakened. Producers know Equity wants employment for its members, so the union occasionally agrees to less-than-ideal contracts or doesn't enforce its own rules as diligently as it could in order to preserve work for its actors. Finally, the bureaucracy of the union sometimes makes the answers to simple questions hard to come by.

So get involved. Go to meetings. Talk to the reps. Know the rules. It's not ideal organization, but what organization is? Involvement will help you understand the union, and maybe even help to change it in positive ways.

They're Elitist!

Equity doesn't always maintain the best public image to actors who haven't joined. Non-Equity walk-ins are often treated rudely. Some Equity employees won't take the time to return calls or answer questions to non-members. Even the rulebook refers to non-members as non-professionals, a description that many veterans of the off-Loop scene resent. However, actors should keep in mind that Equity exists for its members. Many of the union's business reps, in particular, will be quite helpful if approached respectfully.

The Great Mystery: Financial Core

Financial Core status essentially means that you, the actor, pay your union only the amount necessary to negotiate your contract and administer benefits (insurance, pension, etc.). Technically, you are not a union member and cannot vote or hold office. However, since you are not a member, you are also able to do non-union work without penalty. Arguably, Financial Core weakens the union by removing the incentive for a producer to produce as a union house. Still, many Equity members or potential members find the idea of Financial Core appealing. After all, the main concern with joining Equity is the lack of work. Through Financial Core, a performer can still do non-union work, apparently giving them the best of both worlds.

Things aren't that simple, of course. Unlike SAG and AFTRA, which, grudgingly, recognize Financial Core status, Equity refuses to acknowledge it. This may seem ridiculous, since Equity is essentially refusing to acknowledge a Supreme Court decision, but their stance will probably persist until someone takes them to court over it. In the meantime, Equity insists that Financial Core members have actually left the union. Furthermore, the status carries a stigma to some, since Financial Core continues to be a very divisive issue. There is no easy answer at this point, but it's not a decision to be made lightly. Sharequest Publishing produces a manual, "Financial Core Handbook," which is a bit didactic and very one-sided, but it sets out the argument for Financial Core.

And The Upshot Is...?

Every career is different, of course, and most actors who pursue theatre as a career will probably join Equity at some point. However, timing that point is very important, and it depends on your "type," experience and familiarity with Chicago theatre. It's also probable that, even if you join Equity, you'll still have to maintain other jobs to make ends meet, as few Equity theatres agree to pay more than the minimum (there's that supply/demand dynamic at work again). The union, in Chicago at least, has gradually been moving to make Equity more appealing to theatres, which should gradually open up more work to folks in town. All you can do is make an informed decision. Talk to union actors. Talk to producers. Talk to Equity itself. Like any major decision, the challenges and rewards are great. Otherwise, it wouldn't be a major decision, would it?

Unions & Legal Resources

AFTRA & SAG

By Christina Biggs

The American Federation of Television and Radio Artists (AFTRA) and the Screen Actors Guild (SAG) are the two non-stage performer unions. AFTRA and SAG are administered out of the same office under one executive director in Chicago. They are, like all unions, run by elected board members.

Whether or not a production is covered by AFTRA or SAG has always been complicated, but the advent of digital media and the buyout of smaller production companies by behemoths like AOL Time Warner, Disney and Viacom has increased jurisdictional competition. In June 2002, AFTRA gained contracts to nearly a dozen TV pilots—which in the past had been SAG's—setting the stage for the second merger attempt in five years.

The July 2003 consolidation referendum, however, was once again defeated, this time by a mere 2.2 percent margin. SAG's board of directors quickly voted to pass a resolution reaffirming the Principles of Consolidation and Affiliation with AFTRA, and many believe the merger will still come to pass. Presently, 35 percent of SAG and 60 percent of AFTRA members are dual cardholders.

While the two unions continue to remain separate, they're sticking to traditional jurisdictions. SAG covers all movies, most animation and prime time television, regardless of the medium. If a movie is shot on film, digital video or released only on TV, it's SAG's. AFTRA has made some in-roads on animation and covers all daytime television, plus specials like award shows. AFTRA also covers radio.

Union jurisdiction gets murky when it comes to commercials, industrials (workplace videos), basic cable and non-prime time programming or syndicated programming. Officially, it's up to the producer to decide which contract to use, and producers usually use the contract they're most comfortable with.

In cities where AFTRA and SAG are run out of the same office, the staff figures out some sort of equitable solution. In Chicago, for instance, jurisdiction over television commercials and industrials is determined by the medium used. Commercials and industrials in Chicago are SAG if they are shot on film and AFTRA if they are shot on video. The current battles between AFTRA and SAG focus on digital media, basic cable and entertainment content for the internet.

Membership

Joining AFTRA and SAG is fairly easy, though not cheap. Any person who has performed or intends to perform in AFTRA's jurisdiction is eligible for membership. New members must pay a one-time initiation fee of $1,200 plus $58 in first dues. After joining, a member's twice yearly dues are based on earnings in AFTRA's jurisdiction during the prior year.

For SAG, you first have to be cast under a SAG contract. Once you get the contract, you are eligible to join SAG, but you don't necessarily have to join right away. The Taft-Hartley Act (or the National Labor Relations Act) essentially says that a union can't require someone to join until 30 days after their first day of employment. For a steel worker, that's usually a month after they're hired. For an actor, it could be years after they get their first job.

Once you get that first SAG job, you generally have 30 days to take as much union work as you can before you must join the union. SAG does offer what's known as the OK 30 rule. What this means is that SAG is willing to offer a one-time, 30-day extension to work under union contract. But there is a catch. You absolutely must ask for permission before your 31st day of union work.

Whether on your 31st or 61st day of SAG work, the initiation fee currently is $1,356, calculated at two times the day rate of a movie. Minimum yearly dues are $100, paid in twice yearly installments—the first in addition to the initiation fee when you join. It would be wise to save the $1,406 necessary to join rather than finding your career on hold while sorting out the specifics.

SAG and AFTRA do offer payment plans and are willing to help, but you must have something to offer. Also, AFTRA accepts credit card payments. You cannot join either union over the phone.

Contracts

There are multiple SAG and AFTRA contracts for various aspects of the business. The last round of negotiations ensured that if you make a commercial for TV, you will be paid a $500 session fee (radio fees for commercials are $220). Above that, if your commercial runs on network TV—ABC, NBC, CBS, FOX—then you will get paid every time that commercial runs. If the commercial runs on cable, you will get paid a flat rate above the session fee for 13 weeks of use. Most commercials will have a combination of cable and network runs. More detailed information on rates can be found online.

Tracking ad residuals is a bit of a problem. SAG and AFTRA assert that they are being underpaid because some commercials that run aren't counted when checks are totaled. Under the 2000 commercials contract, the industry has set up a pool to develop an electronic monitoring system, but that has yet to be implemented. Commercial contracts are once again being negotiated, so visit www.performink.com for the most current information.

Benefits

AFTRA and SAG are unions and, therefore, give their members the same benefits as any union, including pension, retirement and health plans.

Currently, actors must earn at least $9,000 in SAG or $10,000 in AFTRA during a 12-month period to be eligible for health insurance. For AFTRA, that's going to remain the same. For SAG, the minimum earnings will increase each year until 2007, when an actor will have to make at least $11,000 to be eligible for health insurance.

On a set, AFTRA and SAG negotiate everything from meals to overtime. If you're on a shoot and something comes up that is questionable, tell the production manager that it's all right with you if it's all right with your union and your

Unions & Legal Resources

agent, then get on the phone and call either one. SAG has a toll-free number that will access a Guild office from anywhere nationwide and automatically forward the caller to the appropriate SAG branch (800/SAG-0767). Let them do the arguing for you—that's what you're paying them for.

Joining a union is not an easy decision. There are rules and regulations galore. Sometimes it might seem as if they get in the way. But all the rules are there to protect members, and actors need all the protection they can get.

Unions

Actors' Equity Association
125 S. Clark, Ste. 1500
Chicago, IL 60603
Phone: 312/641-0393
Fax: 312/641-6365
Audition Phone: 312/641-0418
www.actorsequity.org

**American Federation of
Television & Radio Artists**
1 E. Erie, Ste. 650
Chicago, IL 60611
Phone: 312/573-8081
Fax: 312/573-0318
chicago@aftra.com
www.aftra.org

Directors Guild of Chicago
Chicago Headquarters
400 N. Michigan, Ste. 307
Chicago, IL 60611
Phone: 312/644-5050
Alt. Phone: 888/600-6975
Fax: 312/644-5776
www.dga.org

Screen Actors Guild
Chicago— North Region Office
1 E. Erie, Ste. 650
Chicago, IL 60611
Phone: 312/573-8081
Fax: 800/599-1675
www.sag.org

Legal Resources

By Mechelle Moe

Oftentimes, actors are left to fend for themselves—particularly if they don't have union status. But never fear, there are a slew of government agencies set up to help you deal with disputes, claims and other legalities that may be out of your realm of knowledge. Below is a short list of key organizations you can contact for assistance.

EMPLOYMENT ISSUES

Illinois Department of Labor
160 N. LaSalle, Ste. C-1300
Chicago, IL 60601
312/793-2800
www.state.il.us/agency/idol

If you have a payment dispute with your employer, contact the Wage Claim Division of the Department of Labor. They'll step in if your employer has stiffed you on your wages. First, you'll need to file a complaint with the Wage Claim Division; next, they will send a letter to the employer on your behalf; after they have received a response, they will review the case and either dismiss the claim or move it to the next level—a hearing.

If the employer is found liable at the hearing, they are given a time period in which to make the payment. If they skip that, then the case is turned over to the Attorney General's office, where legal proceedings begin. It is important to stay in touch with the Department of Labor and keep them abreast of the situation and whether the claim has been resolved or not.

The Equal Employment Opportunity Commission

National Office
1801 L Street NW
Washington, DC 20507
202/663-4900
www.eeoc.gov

Chicago District Office
500 W. Madison, Ste. 2800
Chicago, IL 60661
312/353-2713

The Equal Employment Opportunity Commission (EEOC) protects individuals against discrimination—that includes race, color, sex, religion, national origin, age or disability—in the workplace, by a labor union, or by an employment agency when applying for a job. Charges may be filed through the EEOC office, but note that there are time restrictions. So, if you believe you were a victim of discrimination, you are advised to act promptly.

In cases of sexual discrimination, females can also contact the Women's Bureau (www.dol.gov/wb/). Although the bureau is not an enforcing agency, there are many resources and statistics available. They focus on empowering women in the workplace, enhancing the work environment and providing a support network.

Department of Human Rights
100 W. Randolph, Ste. 10-100
Chicago, IL 60601
312/814-6200
www.state.il.us/dhr/

The Department of Human Rights administers the Illinois Human Rights Act, which prohibits discrimination because of race, color, religion, sex, national origin, ancestry, citizenship status (with regard to employment), age 40 and over, marital status, physical or mental handicap, military service or unfavorable military discharge. A discrimination charge can be initiated by calling, writing or appearing in person at the department's Chicago or Springfield office within 180 days of the date the alleged discrimination took place in all cases except housing discrimination (one year filing deadline).

CONSUMER ISSUES

Office of Attorney General
Consumer Protection Bureau
500 S. 2nd St.
Springfield, IL 62706

Chicago Hotlines
800/386-5438
TTY: 800/964-3013
www.ag.state.il.us

The Attorney General serves as the chief consumer protection official in the State of Illinois and handles approximately 28,000 complaints annually. The Consumer Protection Division of the Attorney General's office protects consumers and businesses who have been victimized by fraud, deception or unfair competition. Complaint forms can be downloaded from the Web address listed above.

Better Business Bureau
BBB Chicago & N. Illinois
330 N. Wabash, Ste. 2006
Chicago, IL 60611
312/832-0500
feedback@chicago.bbb.org
www.chicago.bbb.org

The Better Business Bureau (BBB) handles anything that deals with contracts and obligations. They do not take sides in a dispute, but rather act as a mediator between the company and consumer to help both sides come to a resolution. Complaints the BBB tackles include misleading advertising, improper selling practices, non-delivery of goods or services, misrepresentation, unhonored guarantees or warranty, unsatisfactory service, credit/billing problems and unfulfilled contracts. They don't deal with discrimination or employment practices.

CHAPTER 6
THEATRES

Hauptmann
TimeLine Theatre

The Jeffs

Most commonly described as "Chicago's Tony's," the Joseph Jefferson Awards are named for Joseph Jefferson III, a 19th century actor best known for portraying Rip Van Winkle. Founded in 1968 at the urging of Actors' Equity Association, the first Jeff Committee was created as a way to recognize actors working in Chicago. The first awards ceremony was held in 1969, and six awards were given out to seven theatres. In 1973, the committee extended judging to non-Equity theatres by creating the Citations wing. This division continues with the Equity ceremony taking place in late fall and the non-Equity in late spring.

The Jeff Committee currently consists of up to 45 people. Some are retired theatre professionals. Some are academics. Some are simply voracious theatre-goers. In any case, these intrepid folks volunteer their time to attend a ton of theatre in the course of a year.

About six years ago, the Jeff Committee contracted an outside consultant to review the awards process and suggest improvements. One recommendation was to integrate the theatre community more fully into the award process, resulting in the creation of the Arts & Technical Team (A/T Team). Administered by the League of Chicago Theatres, the A/T Team consists of theatre professionals who attend opening night—impacting whether a show gets recommended—but have no say in the eventual voting for awards or citations.

How Can My Theatre Win A Jeff?

To be eligible, your theatre must present 18 performances over a minimum of four weeks. At least one of these performances a week must be on a Friday, Saturday or Sunday. Weekday matinees do not count towards your 18. The Jeff Committee does not judge children's theatre, performance art, opera, late nights or improvisation.

If you're non-Equity, there are a few additional criteria. You must produce within Chicago city limits (certain theatres like Circle Theatre in Forest Park were grandfathered in). You must have been in existence for at least two years and have produced at least four shows in that time span. Finally, you must continue to produce at least two shows a year to maintain your eligibility.

Equity theatres only have to exist within 30 miles of the corner of Madison and State Street and meet the performance schedule restrictions to be considered.

Assuming that you and your production are eligible, you need to register your performance with the committee before the 20th of the month that precedes the show's opening. Call them to get the proper form.

Now that you're registered, seven judges will attend opening night of your performance. Randomly selected, these judges will consist of five regular committee members and two A/T Team judges. Each Jeff judge gets a ballot and can vote for any or all of the following categories: Production, Director, Actor in a Principal Role, Actress in a Principal Role, Actor in a Supporting Role, Actress in a Supporting Role (each of the actor awards are given for both play and musical), Actor and Actress in a Revue, Cameo Performance, Ensemble, Choreography, Scenic Design, Lighting Design, Costume Design, Original Music, Musical Direction, Sound Design, New Work, Adaptation and Other (for exceptional elements that aren't covered by the existing categories—i.e. puppets, wig design, etc.). The judges call their votes in by 9 a.m. the following morning to determine whether your production will be Jeff Recommended.

The rules for determining whether a show is recommended can be best described as labyrinthine. Shows also vary by Equity or non-Equity status.

For Equity productions:

At least five judges must vote

AND

four of the judges must vote on the same category

AND

three of the judges must vote on the same second category

OR

at least five judges must vote

AND

there must be a total of 20 votes cast

OR

all seven judges must vote for the same category.

Non-Equity criteria are a little simpler to fulfill, though there are more of them:

At least five judges must vote

AND

four of the judges must vote on the same category

AND

three of the judges must vote on the same second category

OR

at least five judges vote

AND

five judges vote on the same category

AND

two judges vote on the same second category

OR

six judges vote on the same category

109

AND

at least one judge votes on a second category

OR

all seven judges vote for the same category

OR

five judges vote

AND

at least 15 total votes are cast.

Confused yet?

You're Recommended!

Congratulations! Now what? The Jeff hotline will announce your recommendation, and pretty soon the phone will start ringing. Now the show is up for viewing by the rest of the committee, and each member arrives armed with a ballot identical to that of the opening night judges. They, too, will vote, not knowing what category the opening night judges might have found exceptional.

And The Nominees Are...

At the end of the Jeff season (April 1-March 31 for non-Equity; August 1-July 31 for Equity), all the votes are tabulated. Speaking generally, the top vote-getters in each category receive nominations and go on the final ballot. While the Jeff Committee seeks to have five nominees in each category, the statistics used are more complicated. For instance, say Actor A received votes on 80 percent of the ballots cast by the Jeff judges during the run of his show, Actor B on 76 percent, Actor C on 72 percent and Actor D (the next highest vote getter) on 48 percent. In this case, even though Actor D was one of the top five vote-getters, he will not be nominated, and there will be only three nominees in this category. Similarly, suppose Designers A, B, C and D all received votes on more than 80 percent of their ballots, Designer E got 77 percent, Designer F got 75 percent and Designer G got 74 percent. In that case, Designers E, F and G are considered to be in a statistical tie, so all three would appear on the final ballot, leading to seven nominees in that category. In the end, though, you can be assured that each of the nominees received enough votes that they have a chance of winning an award or citation. It is also possible that a show might be Jeff Recommended but not receive any nominations.

You Like Me! You Really Like Me!

So, your show has survived the capricious statistics and has been nominated; how are the final recipients determined? Again, the process differs, depending on whether the production in question is Equity or non-Equity.

Equity

Each Jeff judge receives a ballot with the nominees in each category. A Jeff judge may only vote on a category if they have seen more than half of the nominees. Each judge receives as many votes as they've seen productions in the category. For instance, if Jeff judge A has seen four of the nominees for Outstanding Production, they have four votes to distribute. They could put all four towards one nominee, divide them among two or three, or even be completely equitable and give one vote to each production they saw. Each judge fills out their ballots, and the results are tabulated. The nominee with the most votes receives the Award. The only exceptions to this process occur in the New Work and Adaptation categories, which are non-competitive. Then, in a manner similar to choosing nominees, one or more productions could receive the Award.

Non-Equity

While the Equity Awards are considered competitive, the non-Equity Citations are tabbed as non-competitive. As such, there can be more than one recipient in each category. This simplifies the voting process. Each Jeff judge receives a ballot and simply checks off as many nominees in each category as he or she considers deserving. The determination of the final recipients is similar to that used to determine nominees, and one, two or even all of the ballots in a category could receive Citations.

Complaints about the Jeff Committee abound. By awarding participants in an inherently subjective art form, Jeff judges open themselves up to all sorts of criticism. However, it cannot be disputed that the process each Jeff Eligible show goes through—though Byzantine, certainly—minimize individual input, and therefore, individual biases. Certainly, deserving shows are sometimes ignored. Unworthy shows sometimes receive undeserved praise. However, Jeff Recommendations, Nominations and Awards or Citations are still sought after by theatres and theatre artists. And the Jeff Committee probably gets it right more often than they get it wrong.

The Joseph Jefferson Awards Committee
www.jeffawards.org
info@jeffawards.org

Theatres

Theatres-Equity

About Face Theatre
Heather Schmucker, Producer
1222 W. Wilson, 2nd Flr. West
Chicago, IL 60640
Phone: 773/784-8565
Fax: 773/784-8557
faceline1@aboutfacetheatre.com
www.aboutfacetheatre.com

Date of Inception: 1995

*About Face Theatre creates perform-
ances and programs that use the lens of
gender and sexual identities to examine
universal human experience. Through
commitments to artistic innovation,
community transformation, and the culti-
vation of new voices, we seek to challenge the intellects, imaginations, self-
perceptions and moral expectations of
audiences and our artists within and
beyond the lesbian, gay, bisexual, and
transgender communities.*

Actors Workshop Theatre
Michael Colucci, Artistic Director
1044 W. Bryn Mawr
Chicago, IL 60660
Phone: 312/622-1136
Fax: 847/982-1214
colucci@actorsworkshop.org
actorsworkshop.org

Date of Inception: 1994

*The Actors Workshop Theatre mission is
to produce the entire body of work of
one playwright over a theatre season or
several seasons.*

American Players Theatre
Brenda DeVita, Associate Artistic
  Director
PO Box 819
Spring Green, WI 53588
Phone: 608/588-7401
Fax: 608/588-7085
apm@americanplayers.org
www.playinthewoods.org

*American Players Theatre is a profes-
sional, equity, classical theatre located in
Spring Green, Wisconsin, 40 miles west
of Madison. The 1150 comfortably cush-
ioned theatre seats sit in a natural
amphitheater on 110 acres of woods and
meadow.*

American Theater Company
Attn: Casting
1909 W. Byron
Chicago, IL 60613
Phone: 773/929-5009
Fax: 773/929-5171
dkiely@atcweb.org
www.atcweb.org

Date of Inception: 1985

*American Theater Company is an
ensemble of artists committed to
producing new and classic American
stories that asks the question: "What
does it mean to be an American?" We
provide a truly intimate home for the
community to gather and share meaningful stories and provide a nurturing
environment for artists to take risks and
create essential work.*

Apollo Theater
Rob Kolson, Managing Director
2540 N. Lincoln
Chicago, IL 60614
Phone: 773/935-9336
Fax: 773/935-6214
info@apollochicago.com
www.apollochicago.com

Apple Tree Theatre
Barbara Harris, Casting
595 Elm Pl., Ste. 210
Highland Park, IL 60035
Phone: 847/432-8223
Fax: 847/432-5214
lbaber@appletreetheatre.com
www.appletreetheatre.com

Artistic Home
Kathy Scambiatterra, Artistic Director
1420 W. Irving Park
Chicago, IL 60613
Phone: 773/404-1100
Fax: 708/387-7286
Theartistichome@aol.com

*We are a collective of actors dedicated
to creating theatre and film. We redress
the classics and explore new works. We
give artists a home where they can
shape, develop and strengthen their
artistic voice.*

Aspect Theatre Company

Todd Hissong, Executive Director
c/o 2320 W. Sunnyside, Ste. 2E
Chicago, IL 60625
Phone: 773/784-9934
Fax: 773/784-9934
aspecttheatre@aol.com/tmhissong@aol.
com

Date of Inception: 2001

Aspect performs staged readings under the Equity Showcase Code, identifying a theme for each season and exploring diverse "aspects" of that subject. Our company prides itself on providing a respectful, joyful environment where seasoned professionals come together to work on material they might not otherwise have a chance to, and presenting these works to the community for free.

Black Ensemble Theater

4520 N. Beacon
Chicago, IL 60640
Phone: 773/769-4451
Fax: 773/769-4533
blackensemble@aol.com
www.blackensembletheater.org

Date of Inception: 1976

The Black Ensemble Theater is committed to producing entertaining, educational and enlightening African American theatre of excellence that reaches interracial audiences. We believe that theatre should serve as a cultural bridge, bringing people of all cultures together to understand, accept and celebrate the uniqueness of the human spirit.

Boxer Rebellion Ensemble

Michael S. Pieper, Artistic Director
1257 W. Loyola
Chicago, IL 60626
Phone: 773-465-7325
bspieper@aol.com
www.boxerrebellion.org

An adventurous and ambitious ensemble that produces social, thought-provoking, emotional work challenging its audiences and artists.

Broadway In Chicago

22 W. Monroe, Ste. 700
Chicago, IL 60603
Phone: 312/751-5513
www.broadwayinchicago.com

Buffalo Theatre Ensemble

Connie Canaday Howard, Artistic
Director
Fawell and Park Blvds.
Glen Ellyn, IL 60137
Phone: 630/942-3008
Fax: 630/790-9806
canaday@cdnet.cod.edu
www.cod.edu/ArtsCntr

BTE is rooted in the idea that an acting ensemble and company who have a history of working together and have developed a sense of trust and community can create better art.

Chicago Dramatists

Russ Tutterow, Artistic Director
1105 W. Chicago
Chicago, IL 60622
Phone: 312/633-0630
Fax: 312/633-0610
NewPlays@ChicagoDramatists.org
www.ChicagoDramatists.org

Date of Inception: 1979

Chicago Dramatists is a professional theatre dedicated to the nuturing of playwrights and the development and production of new plays. It offers a variety of developmental programs year-round, which include staged readings, private readings, workshops, full productions, classes, private dramaturgy, and two playwright membership programs.

Chicago Jewish Theatre at Red Hen Productions

Elayne LeTraunik, Artistic Director
5123 N. Clark
Chicago, IL 60640
Phone: 773/728-0599
Fax: 773/728-0589
chgojewishtheatr@aol.com
www.chicagojewishtheatre.com

Date of Inception: 1997

Chicago Jewish Theatre will Illuminate and celebrate the past, present, and future of the Jewish experience in America and the world.

Theatres

Chicago Shakespeare Theater
Bob Mason, Casting Director
800 E. Grand
Chicago, IL 60611
Phone: 312/595-5656
Fax: 312/595-5607
www.chicagoshakes.com

Date of Inception: 1986

The mission of Chicago Shakespeare Theater is to present the works of William Shakespeare as well as other great performances to audiences from all walks of life and from around the world.

Chicago Theatre Company
Douglas Alan-Mann, Artistic Director
500 E. 67th
Chicago, IL 60637
Phone: 773/493-0901
Fax: 773/493-0360
www.chicagotheatrecompany.com

Date of Inception: 1984

At CTC local African American artists can hone and develop their skills. We also pride ourselves on presenting universal African-American themes.

Congo Square Theatre Company
Derrick Sanders, Artistic Director
1501 W. Randolph
Chicago, IL 60607
Phone: 312/492-9359
Fax: 312/492-9360
dsanders@congosquaretheatre.org
www.congosquaretheatre.org

Date of Inception: 1999

Congo Square Theatre is an African-American acting ensemble that performs theatre from the African Diaspora.

Court Theatre
Cree Rankin, Casting Director
5535 S. Ellis
Chicago, IL 60637
Phone: 773/702-7005
info@courttheatre.org
www.courttheatre.org

Court Theatre is Chicago's premier interpreter of classic texts and redefining what it means to be 'classic.'

Drury Lane Theatre Oakbrook
Dian Van Lente, Managing Director
100 Drury Lane
Oakbrook Terrace, IL 60181
Phone: 630/530-0111
Fax: 630/530-0436
www.drurylaneoakbrook.com

5 productions per season- 4 musicals, 1 play. We use local actors and musicians.

Drury Lane Theatre Evergreen Park
Marc Robin, Director
2500 W. 95th
Evergreen Park, IL 60805
Phone: 708/422-0404
Fax: 708/422-8127
producer80@aol.com
www.drurylane.com

We are known as the theatre "Where the Stars Come Out!!!"

Equity Library Theatre Chicago
Lucinda Underwood, Producing Director
843 W. Belle Plaine, Ste. 1N
Chicago, IL 60613
Phone: 773/975-0950
eltchicago@ameritech.net

We are a showcase organization operating under special agreement with Actors' Equity Association.

European Repertory Co.
Laura Scott Wade, Casting Director
1839 W. Thomas
Chicago, IL 60622
Phone: 773/972-1678
dg930@hotmail.com

Date of Inception: 1992

ERC is commited to raising the profile of Chicago as an international theatre city through cross cultural exchange and by bringing provocative, timely, and rarely produced works of contemporary social significiance to the Chicago stage.

Famous Door Theatre Company
Hanna Dworkin, Casting Director
P.O. Box 57029
Chicago, IL 60657
Phone: 773/404-8283
Fax: 773/404-8292
info@famousdoortheatre.org
famousdoortheatre.org

Date of Inception: 1987

Famous Door is a Chicago-based ensemble of theatre artists working together to develop and produce innovative, evocative, and accessible theatre with and for the people of Chicago. We also seek to break down barriers—both real and perceived—that keep members of our community from participating in the live theatre experience.

First Folio Shakespeare Festival
Alison C. Vesely, Artistic Director
1717 W. 31st St.
Oak Brook, IL 60523
Phone: 630/986-8067
Fax: 630/455-0071
firstfolio@firstfolio.org
www.firstfolio.org

Outdoor Shakespeare on the grounds of a beautiful estate.

Goodman Theatre
Tara Lonzo, Casting Director
170 N. Dearborn
Chicago, IL 60601
Phone: 312/443-3811
Fax: 312/443-3821
staff@goodman-theatre.org
www.goodman-theatre.org

Goodman stands to be Chicago's oldest and largest non-profit theatre.

Illinois Shakespeare Festival
Cal Maclean
Campus Box 5700
Normal, IL 61790-5700
Phone: 309/438-8783
Fax: 309/438-5806
shake@ilstu.edu
www.thefestival.org

Date of Inception: 1978

The Illinois Shakespeare Festival is dedicated to producing William Shakespeare and works that relate to his productions.

Illinois Theatre Center
Etel Billig, Artistic Director
P.O. Box 397
Park Forest, IL 60466
Phone: 708/481-3510
Fax: 708/481-3693
ilthctr@bigplanet.com
www.ilthctr.org

We are the only Professional Non-Profit Equity Theatre in the south suburbs of Chicago.

Lookingglass Theatre
David Barari, Artistic/Production Assistant
821 N. Michigan
Chicago, IL 60611
Phone: 773/477-9257
Fax: 773/477-6932
contact@lookingglasstheatre.org
www.lookingglasstheatre.org

Date of Inception: 1988

Founded in 1988 by eight Northwestern students, Lookingglass Theatre Company has emerged as a dynamic and powerful

theatrical force in Chicago with a rapidly growing national reputation. At the core of the company is a multi-disciplined ensemble dedicated to the development of highly visual, physical, innovative works and experimentation for the American stage.

Madison Repertory Theatre
Anne-Marie Cammarato, Associate
  Artistic Director
211 State St., Ste. 201
Madison, WI 53703
Phone: 608/256-0029
Fax: 608/256-7433
postmaster@madisonrep.org
www.madisonrep.org

Date of Inception: 1969

Madison Repetory Theatre entertains, educates and engages diverse audiences with plays produced in an intimate setting, emphasizing newly commissioned works and re-imagined old ones, while creating a theatrical home where emerging and leading artists of the day can flourish.

Marriott Theatre in Lincolnshire
Rick Boynton, Artistic Director
10 Marriott Dr.
Lincolnshire, IL 60069
Phone: 847/634-0204
Fax: 847/634-7358
producer@marriotttheatre.com
www.marriotttheatre.com

Date of Inception: 1975

In addition to the presentation of classic American musical theatre, the Marrriott Theatre is a driving force in the development of original and re-thought musicals.

Marriott Theatre in Lincolnshire
Andy Hite
10 Marriott Dr.
Lincolnshire, IL 60069
Phone: 847/634-0204
Fax: 847/634-7358
www.MarriottTheatre.com

Theatres

Metropolis Performing Arts Centre
Corey Harrison, Production Manager
111 W. Campbell
Arlington Heights, IL 60005
Phone: 847/577-5982
Fax: 847/577-5992
info@metropolisarts.com
metropolisarts.com

Metropolis is dedicated to presenting a broad range of high-quality artistic productions in an exceptional yet intimate venue, and making a vital contribution to the quality of life in Arlington Heights and Chicago's Northwest suburbs.

Milwaukee Shakespeare Company
Robert Quinlan, Associate Artistic Director
UWM 2400 E. Kenwood Blvd.
Milwaukee, WI 53211
Phone: 414/298-9930
Fax: 414/298-9961
milwshakespeare@aol.com
www.milwaukeeshakespeare.com

We are Milwaukee's only theatre devoted to the works of William Shakespeare offering a three production season.

Moving Dock Theatre Company
Dawn Arnold, Artistic Director
2970 N. Sheridan, Ste. 1021
Chicago, IL 60657
Phone: 773/327-1572
Dawndock@aol.com

The Moving Dock Theatre Company is dedicated to exploring the actor's creative process; discovering that theatre that is created out of the expressive, imaginative actor. Our work is ensemble based, involving movement, and oriented in the acting technique of Michael Chekhov. To develop our approach, The Moving Dock offers workshops in the Chekhov technique.

Naked Eye Theatre Company
Mikhael Garver, Casting Director
1454 W. Hollywood, Ste. 3
Chicago, IL 60660
Phone: 312/409-9800
www.nakedeyetheatre.org

Naked Eye develops approximately 5-10 new scripts per year and produces 1-2 of them, in addition to one other.

Next Theatre Company
Jason Loewith, Artistic Director
927 Noyes St.
Evanston, IL 60201
Phone: 847/475-6763
Fax: 847/475-6767
nexttheatre@aol.com
www.nexttheatre.org

The Next Theatre is devoted to socially provocative, artistically challenging work.

Noble Fool Theater
Casting Department
16 W. Randolph
Chicago, IL 60601
Phone: 312/658-0094
Fax: 312/658-0274
info@noblefool.com
www.noblefool.com

Date of Inception: 1994

The Noble Fool Theater is dedicated to elevating the art of comedy in all its forms, through performance, promotion and education. The Noble Fool creates and develops ensemble driven shows, drawing from improvisation and music, and fosters an active relationship between performers and audience.

Northlight Theatre
Reetu Gowdar, Assistant to Artistic Director
9501 Skokie Blvd.
Skokie, IL 60077
Phone: 847/679-9501
Fax: 847/679-1879
rgowdar@northlight.org
www.northlight.org

Northlight Theatre is a nationally respected not-for-profit theatre company with a reputation for ambitious program-ming, quality productions, and a commit-ment to community service.

Oak Park Festival Theatre
Roxanne Fay, Producing Artistic Director
P.O. Box 4114
Oak Park, IL 60303
Phone: 708/660-0636
Fax: 708/660-0126
roxannefay@sbcglobal.net
www.oakparkfestival.com

Illinois' oldest outdoor professional theatre.

Organic Theater Company
Ina Marlowe, Producing Artistic Director
PO Box 578189
Chicago, IL 60657
Phone: 773/561-7708
Fax: 773/561-7754
organic@theatrechicago.com
www.organictheater.com

Organic Theater Company produces lasting new work and neglected classics that highlight Chicago artists.

Peninsula Players Theatre
Greg Vinkler, Artistic Director
W. 4351 Peninsula Players Rd.
Fish Creek, WI 54212
Phone: 920/868-3287
Fax: 920/868-2295
tickets@peninsulaplayers.com
peninsulaplayers.com

Date of Inception: 1935

Peninsula Players Theatre is committed to preserving America's oldest professional resident summer theatre in its unique setting along the cedar lined shores of Green Bay. The theatre's mission is to support the company; to preserve the theatre in a garden's natural beauty; and to provide artists the freedom, tools, and facilities they require to uplift and entertain our audiences.

Phoenix Theatre
Bryan Fonsesca, Artistic Director
749 N. Park Ave.
Indianapolis, IN 46202
Phone: 317/635-2381
Fax: 317/635-0010
info@phoenixtheatre.org
phoenixtheatre.com

Date of Inception: 1983

The Phoenix is proud of its unique position in the Indiana Theatre Community. We are the area's only professional company that dedicates its entire programming to contemporary, issue oriented theatre. Through the years, we have remained true to our mission—to produce plays that challenge and catalyze discussion, as well as entertain.

Piven Theatre Workshop
Jennifer Sultz, Production Manager
927 Noyes St.
Evanston, IL 60201
Phone: 847/866-8049
Fax: 847/866-6614
PivenTW@aol.com
www.piventheatreworkshop.com

Date of Inception: 1972

Piven Theatre Workshop is celebrating its 30th year as a theatre and nationally acclaimed actor training center, specializing in improvisation traingin and the story theatre form.

Red Orchid Theatre, A
Guy Van Swearingen, Artistic Director
1531 N. Wells
Chicago, IL 60610-7752
Phone: 312/943-8722
Fax: 312/943-9185
guy@a-red-orchid.com
www.a-red-orchid.com

Date of Inception: 1992

Remy Bumppo Theatre Co.
James Bohnen
3717 N. Ravenswood, Ste. 245
Chicago, IL 60613
Phone: 773/244-8119
Fax: 773/296-9243
info@remybumpo.org

Date of Inception: 1996

The Remy Bumppo Theatre Company was founded in 1996 with the mission of presenting new works written by the world's finest playwrights that demonstrate the intricate and transcendent power of language while utilizing the talents of Chicago's vast pool of veteran actors and designers. Remy Bumpo Theatre Company produces high quality, literary plays with top flight casts in an intimate setting.

Theatres

117

Rivendell Theatre Ensemble
Tara Mallen
1711 W. Belle Plaine, Ste. 3B
Chicago, IL 60613
Phone: 773/472-1169
rivtheatre@aol.com
www.rivendelltheatre.net

Our mission is to create an intimate theatre experience, which explores new voices and reflects on personal human journeys in an engaging salon environment while pursuing the talents of women theatre artists.

Roadworks
Geoffrey Curley, Artistic Director
1239 N. Ashland
Chicago, IL 60622
Phone: 773/862-7623
Fax: 773/862-7624
roadworks@ameritech.net
www.roadworks.org

Date of Inception: 1992

Roadworks has established itself as a springboard for young, emerging theatre artists as they progress to the national forefront, and has built a reputation as THE outlet for gripping plays by emerging and daring playwrights.

Running With Scissors
Attn: Casting
PO Box 408438
Chicago, IL 60640
Phone: 773/913-6471
info@rwscissors.org
www.rwscissors.org

We seek to create theatre that is inventive, timely and provocative; that speaks to the social, political, and cultural landscape of our times.

Seanachai Theatre Company
Michael Grant
2206 N. Tripp
Chicago, IL 60639
Phone: 773/878-3727
info@seanachai.org
www.seanachai.org

The mission of Seanachai Theatre Company is to return theatre to the origin of the traditional Irish Seanachai (storyteller) by creating compelling productions and programs that focus the energy of the artists towards the common goal of exceptional story

Second City
Beth Kligerman, Associate Producer
1616 N. Wells
Chicago, IL 60614
Phone: 312/664-4032
Fax: 312/664-9837
www.secondcity.com

Date of Inception: 1959

At the heart of The Second City lies improvisation. It is the root from which the talent is trained, the shows created, and the business conducted. The theatre believes that the audience is as smart as you let them be, that the actors need to work to the top of their intelligence and that the value of laughter becomes more vital with each passing year.

Second City E.T.C.
Beth Kligerman, Sr. Associate Producer
1608 N. Wells
Chicago, IL 60614
Phone: 312/664-4032
Fax: 312/664-9837
bkligerman@secondcity.com
www.secondcity.com

Date of Inception: 1982

The Second City E.T.C. is the second stage of the nation's foremost improvisation-based comedy theatre.

Shakespeare Project of Chicago
Jeff Christian, Artistic Director
2529 W. Carmen
Chicago, IL 60625
Phone: 773/334-8771
Fax: 773/334-8771
theshakespeareproject@att.net
shakespeareprojectchicago.org

We present timeless, text-driven theatrical readings of plays with Equity actors—free to the people of Chicago.

Shattered Globe Theatre
Linda Reiter, Artistic Director
P.O Box 3540
Chicago, IL 60690
Phone: 312/223-1168
Fax: 312/223-1169
bpudil@nl.edu
www.shatteredglobe.org

Date of Inception: 1989

Ensemble based theatre that explores social and political themes dealing with the American experience.

Stage Left Theatre
Attn: Casting
3408 N. Sheffield
Chicago, IL 60657
Phone: 773/883-8830
Fax: 773/472-1336
sltchicago@aol.com
www.stagelefttheatre.com

Stage Left produces and develops plays that raise debate on political and social issues.

Steppenwolf Theatre Company
Erica Daniels, Casting Director
1650 N. Halsted
Chicago, IL 60613
Phone: 312/335-1888
Fax: 312/333-0830
theatre@steppenwolf.org
www.steppenwolf.org

Date of Inception: 1975

Committed to the principle of ensemble performance through the collaboration of a company of actors, directors and designers, Steppenwolf Theatre Company's mission is to advance the vitality and diversity of American theatre by nurturing artists, encouraging repeatable creative relationships, and contributing new works to the national canon. The company, formed in 1976 by a collective of actors, is dedicated to perpetuating an ethic of mutual respect and the development of artists through on-going group work. Steppenwolf has grown into an internationally renowned company of thirty-five artists whose talents include acting, directing, playwriting, filmmaking, and textual adaptation.

Theatre at the Center
Michael Weber, Artistic Director
907 Ridge Rd.
Munster IN 46321
Phone: 219/836-0422
Fax: 219/836-0159
MWeber935@aol.com
www.theatreatthecenter.com

Date of Inception: 1991

Chicago area theatre presenting premieres and revivals of plays and musicals.

Viaduct Theater
Attn: Casting
3111 N. Western
Chicago, IL 60618
Phone: 773/296-6024
viaduct@mindspring.com
viaducttheater.com

Victory Gardens Theater
Attn: Casting
2257 N. Lincoln Ave.
Chicago, IL 60614
Phone: 773/549-5788
Fax: 773/549-2779
vgtheater@aol.com
www.victorygardens.org

Date of Inception: 1974

Victory Gardens Theater is a Tony Award winning professional theatre whose mission is the development of new plays by primarily Chicago area writers. The theatre is committed to a diverse community of artists.

Woodstock Musical Theatre Company
121 Van Buren
PO Box 613
Woodstock, IL 60098
Phone: 815/263-7658
Fax: 847/706-2945
info@woodstocktheatre.com
www.woodstocktheatre.com

The Woodstock Musical Theatre Company, founded in 1974, is a not-for-profit corporation established to provide local talent the opportunity to offer artistic theatrical productions for the viewing pleasure of area residents and to promote community theatre.

Writers' Theatre Chicago
Shade Murray, Associate Producer
325 Tudor Court
Glencoe, IL 60022
Phone: 847/242-6008
Fax: 847/242-6011
writerstheatre@aol.com
www.writerstheatre.com

Date of Inception: 1991

The Writers' Theatre is a professional company dedicated to a theatre of language and passion where the word and the artist are our primary focus.

Theatres

Theatres-Non-Equity

15 Head- a theatre lab

Joe Stanley, Artistic Director
712 Ontario Ave.W., Ste. 201
Minneapolis, MN 55403
Phone: 612/377-1200
Fax: 612/377-1203
15head@15head.org
www.15head.org

15 Head develps and produces engaging, original, company-created works marked by excellence of craft and devotion to innovative uses of movement, language, music and design.

A Reasonable Facsimile Theatre Co.

1225 W. Belmont
Chicago, IL 60657
Phone: 773/282-9728
moonmike99@yahoo.com
www.arftco.org

Concentration on new Chicago playwrights, with a focus on scripts that will spark thought and discussion. A concentration on the actor as the focus of the production over technical values.

Alchymia Theatre

Scott Fielding, Producing Artistic
  Director
2146 W. Berteau
Chicago, IL 60618
Phone: 773/755-6843
alchymia.il@netzero.net
www.alchymia.org

Alchymia Theatre was founded in 1999 with the aim of awakening people to an experience of their highest self and of nourishing their developing human potential. We produce theatre, train actors, and conduct theatre research in accord with the philosophical and methodological principles articulated by Michael Chekhov (1891-1955) in his lifelong pursuit of an ideal theatre of the future.

Alphabet Soup Productions

Snady Bergman, Stage Manager
P.O. Box 85
Lombard, IL 60148
Phone: 630/932-1555
Fax: 630/665-8465
ABSkidshow@aol.com
absproductions.com

Date of Inception: 1987

Alphabet Soup Productions provides children's theatre with a fracture of a fairy tale twist.

American Girl Theater

Scott Davidson, Theatre Director
111 E. Chicago
Chicago, IL 60611
Phone: 312/787-3883
Fax: 312/640-0461
scott.davidson@pleasantco.com
www.americangirl.com/

Date of Inception: 1986

American Girls Theatre Co. is an entertainment site for girls and their families with an one-hour live musical telling the stories from the American Girls collection.

Angels' Roost Theatre

Brandon Bruce, Artistic Director
4824 N. Damen, Ste. 202
Chicago, IL 60625
Phone: 773/784-9383
angelsroosttheatre@hotmail.com

Angels' Roost Theatre is mercilessly committed to producing theatre that transcends and challenges the standards of off-Loop theatre.

Athenaeum Theatre

2936 N. Southport
Chicago, IL 60657
Phone: 773/935-6860
Fax: 312/935-6878
www.athenaeumtheatre.com
cfoster29@surfbest.net

Attic Playhouse

410 Sheridan Rd. (performing address)
Highwood, IL 60040
Phone: 847/433-2660
atticplay@aol.com
atticplayhouse.com

Awaken! Performances

2448 W. Catalpa
Chicago, IL 60625
Phone: 773 275 2036
Fax: 773 275 4095
bspangled@aol.com

Babes With Blades
Dawn "Sam" Alden, Founder
5920 N. Paulina, Ste. 1W
Chicago, IL 60660
Phone: 773/275-0440
babeswithblades@juno.com
www.babeswithblades.org

An all-female stage combat troupe dedicated to raising the profile and increasing the opportunities for women fighters.

BackStage Theatre Company
Attn: Casting
P.O. Box 118142
Chicago, IL 60611
Phone: 312/683-5347
www.backstagetheatrecompany.org

We present new and classic plays in environmental settings.

Bailiwick Repertory Arts Center
Bo List, Associate Artistic Director
1229 W. Belmont
Chicago, IL 60657
Phone: 773/883-1090
Fax: 773/883-2017
Bailiwickr@aol.com
www.bailiwick.org

Since 1982, Bailiwick has been a daring leader of Chicago's off-Loop theatre movement, with shows that embrace the wide diversity of our community.

Theatres

Barrel of Monkeys
2936 N. Southport, Ste. 210
Chicago, IL 60657
Phone: 773/296-0218
hkays@barrelofmonkeys.org
www.barrelofmonkeys.org

Barrel of Monkeys is an ensemble of actor-educators who run creative writing workshops and perform in-school performances of children authored stories; Barrel of Monkeys also engages the broader community through public performances of their work.

Beverly Theatre Guild
9936 S. Harnew Rd. East
Oak Lawn, IL 60453
Phone: 312/409-2705
Fax: 630/435-5496
btg@urbancom.net
www.beverlytheatreguild.org

Blindfaith Theatre
Nick Minas, Artistic Director
840 W. Belle Plaine, Ste. 3W
Chicago, IL 60613
Phone: 773/250-7133
blindfaiththeatre@blindfaiththeatre.org
www.blindfaiththeatre.org

Date of Inception: 1999

Blindfaith Theatre offers an explosive, creative forum in which emerging artists can hone their craft. Performing in intimate theatre spaces throughout Chicago, Blindfaith strives to produce reexaminations of classics, bold interpretations of modern plays, and explorations of new plays whose themes and issues are of immediate concern. Blindfaith creates literate, visceral, affecting theatre that is experienced, not simply observed.

Breadline Theatre Group
Heather Carpenter, PR/Marketing
  Director
1800-04 W. Berenice
Chicago, IL 60613
Phone: 773/327-6096
breadline@breadline.org
www.breadline.org

Date of Inception: 1993

BTG produces world premieres that present social and political ideas in a vibrant theatrical style.

See our ad on page 121

Broutil and Frothingham Productions
Brian Posen, Artistic Director
1415 W. Lill
Chicago, IL 60614
Phone: 773/868-0226
Fax: 773/327-5039
BandFproductions@aol.com
BroutilandFrothingham.com

Date of Inception: 1997

B and F is a non-Equity theatre company dedicated to producing a high level of quality theatre to honor and celebrate the excellent non-union talent in Chicago. We are dedicated to an environment where actors act, directors direct and stage managers stage manage, so that actors are not soliciting money and directors are not putting up posters.

Camenae Ensemble Theatre Company
Bernadine Ann Tippit, Artistic Director
PO Box A3877
Chicago, IL 60690
Phone: 773/856-5318
camenae@comcast.net
www.camenaetheatre.org

Cantilever Network, Inc.
Priscilla Paris-Austin, Artistic Director
Hamilton Park, 513 W. 72nd St.
Chicago, IL 60621
Phone: 773/239-2495
cantilever@wideopenwest.com
www.iyanola.com/cantilever

The basic philosophy of Cantilever is to help build self-esteem, spark creativity, instill a sense of societal responsibility and foster an appreciation for the arts.

CenterLight Theatre for the Deaf
Attn: Auditions
614 Anthony Trail
Northbrook, IL 60062
Phone: 847/559-0110
Fax: 847/559-8199
icoda@aol.com
www.icodaarts.org

The only theatre in the Midwest dedicated entirley to promoting the talents of deaf, hard of hearing and hearing artists who work together to create a unique theatre experience for all audiences.

C'est La Vie Drama

Brian LaDuca, Artistic Director
4331 N. Kenmore
Chicago, IL 60613
Phone: 773/415-2538
fester1226@hotmail.com
www.cestlaviedrama.com

Date of Inception: 2001

C'est La Vie Drama Group combines what happens when MTV meets the live stage.

Chase Park Theatre

Karen Fort
4701 N. Ashland
Chicago, IL 60640
Phone: 312/742-4701
Fax: 312/742-4123
karenfort@earthlink.net
www.chicagoparkdistrict.com

Date of Inception: 1978

A community theatre for the theatre community. Two large-cast classic or master works per year. A proven launching ground for veteran actors and designers new to town or seeking a showcase for lead roles. Also casts talented beginners who exhibit commitment.

Chemically Imbalanced Comedy

Angela Farruggia, Executive Producer
Cornservatory, 4210 N. Lincoln
Chicago, IL 60618
Phone: 773/865-7731
cicomedy@hotmail.com
www.cicomedy.com

Chemically Imbalanced Comedy show-cases the best and brightest comedy from all around the city.

Chicago Actors Studio Theatre

Raymond Vanagus, Managing Director
1567 N. Milwaukee
Chicago, IL 60622
Phone: 773/735-6400
Fax: 773/767-4151
chiactorstudio@aol.com
actors-studio.net

To focus on the needs of the communtiy and student, we serve without regard for financial profit. A complete open door policy.

Chicago Kids Company

3812 W. Montrose
Chicago, IL 60618
Phone: 773/539-0455
Fax: 773/539-0452
CKCPaige@aol.com

Chicspeare Production Company

Casting,
1915 W. Summerdale
Chicago, IL 60640
Phone: 773/769-2056
Fax: 773/769-0313
chicspeare@earthlink.net
www.chicspeare.org

Chicspeare Production Company makes Shakespeare's works accessible to Chicago-area residents through touring performances and educational programs; our name reflects our commitment to both the city and the playwright.

Childrens' Theatre Fantasy Orchard

Dana Low, Artistic Director
PO Box 25084
Chicago, IL 60625
Phone: 773/539-4200
Fax: 773/539-4211
kidtheatre.com

Date of Inception: 1990

The Children's Theatre performs folk and faerie tales from around the world that reflect the cultural and ethnic diversity found in the Chicago public school children.

Chopin Theatre

1543 W. Division
Chicago, IL 60622
Phone: 773/278-1500
www.chopintheatre.com

Circle Theatre

7300 W. Madison
Forest Park, IL 60130
Phone: 708/771-0700
Fax: 708/771-1826
info@circle-theatre.org
www.circle-theatre.org

Circle Theatre is an artist-based company whose mission is to produce exciting and innovative theatre accessible to our widely diversified city and suburban audience.

Theatres

City Lit Theatre Company
Page Hearn
1020 W. Bryn Mawr
Chicago, IL 60660-4627
Phone: 773/293-3682
Fax: 773/293-3684
metapage@aol.com
www.citylit.org

Date of Inception: 1979

City Lit produces a mainstage season of 3-4 plays consisting of adaptations, classics, and new works.

ComedySportz
Tim Chidester, Artistic Director
2851 N. Halsted
Chicago, IL 60657
Phone: 773/549-8080
Fax: 773/549-8142
mattcsz@mcleodusa.net
www.comedysportzchicago.com

The ComedySportz Theatre focuses primarily on the performance of the show ComedySportz at its own theatre and touring that show abroad.

Corn Productions
Jango Van Bebo, Casting Director
Cornservatory
4210 N. Lincoln
Chicago, IL 60618
Phone: 773/868-0243
Fax: 773/868-0243
Cornproductions.aol.com
Cornservatory.org

Date of Inception: 1992

This diverse company produces bawdy comedies, raucous satire, and tongue in cheek dance parodies as well as a kid's program and dramas. Corn mounts only original works, mostly written by company members, and is always looking for theatre professionals dedicated to all aspects of the art to join their company.

Courtesy Reach Around Productions
Attn: Jeff Stebor
1402 N. Ashland
Chicago, IL 60622
Phone: 773/252-0593
crapproductions@yahoo.com

Grass Roots Political Theater

Cupid Players
Brian Posen, Artistic Director
1415 W. Lill
Chicago, IL 60614
Phone: 773/665-8899
www.cupidplayers.com
www.cupidplayers.com

We are the only group that performs musical sketch comedy where all the scenes move to song.

D.R.A.M.M.A. (The Mt. Prospect Theatre Scociety)
Janice Stone, President
420 W. Dempster
Mt. Prospect, IL 60056
Phone: 847/640-1000

D.R.A.M.M.A.'s (Dramatic Repertory for Modern Meaningful Actors) goal is to produce shows that have wide appeal.

Darknight Theatrical Productions
James Bagnall, Artistic Director
1536 Highridge Pkwy.
Westchester, IL 60154
Phone: 708/492-0273
thedarknight60@comcast.net

We are a company driven to produce the highest quality plays that touch on the universal thematic intent that lies beneath the surface; we drive this vision with the promise that we will compromise nothing for the sake of the quality of the show.

Defiant Theatre
Lisa Rothschiller, Artistic Director
3540 N. Southport, Ste. 162
Chicago, IL 60657
Phone: 312/409-0585
defianttheatre@defianttheatre.org
www.defianttheatre.org

Date of Inception: 1993

Defiant Theatre defies fear. Defiant Theatre strives to subvert the social, moral, and aesthectic expectations of mainstream artistic expression. We dare to impassion our audiences and ourselves by using any means necessary, limited only by our boundless imagination.

See our ad on page 124

DePaul University's Merle Reskin Theatre
60 E. Balbo
Chicago, IL 60605
Phone: 773/325-7938
Fax: 773/325-7938
Lgoetsch@depaul.edu
http://theatreschool.depaul.edu

One of the top-rated theatre schools in the country, with very well noted and well respected alumni including John C. Reilly, Gillian Anderson, and many of the best in the artistic field today.

Dominican University Center Stage
Laura K. Wolf, Associate Director
7900 W. Division
River Forest, IL 60305
Phone: 708/524-6516
Fax: 708/524-6517
Lwolf@email.dom.edu
www.dom.edu

Dominican University's nationally acclaimed center stage program offers an abundance of rich and varied fine performing arts opportunities including a professional series, mainstage series and a second stage series.

Dream Theatre Company
Rebecca Lincoln,
735 W. Belmont, Ste. 1F
Chicago, IL 60657
Phone: 773/865-4486
hlsamj@aol.com
www.dreamtheatrecompany.com

From its inspired beginnings at the Moscow Art Theatre in 1998, Dream Theatre has been removing the safety net of the "fourth wall" and reinventing the relationships between audience, actor and the dream world—the world of the play.

Eclipse Theatre Company
Attn: Casting
2000 W. Fulton
Chicago, IL 60612
Phone: 312/409-1687
eclipsetheatre@hotmail.com
www.eclipsetheatre.com

Date of Inception: 1992

Eclipse Theatre Company is the Midwest's only theatre to produce the works of one playwright in one single season. Featured playwrights included Jean Cocteau, Tennessee Williams, Lillian Hellman, Romulus Linney, John Guare, Neil Simon.

Theatres

125

Emerald City Theatre Co.

Heather McGinley, Production Manager
2936 N. Southport
Chicago, IL 60657
Phone: 773/529-2690
Fax: 773/529-2693
oz@emeraldcitytheatre.com
www.emeraldcitytheatre.com

Date of Inception: 1996

Emerald City is a not-for-profit children's theatre dedicated to the entertainment of families, offering magic "so close you can touch it!"

eta Creative Arts Foundation

Runako Jahi, Artistic Director
7558 S. South Chicago
Chicago, IL 60619
Phone: 773/752-3955
Fax: 773/752-8727
email@etacreativearts.org
www.etacreativearts.org

We are an African-American, culturally specific organization dedicated to "telling our own stories in the first voice."

Excalibur Shakespeare Company of Chicago

Mr. Robinson, Artistic Director/Producer
4200 W. Wilcox , 2nd Flr.
Chicago, IL 60624
Phone: 773/533-0285
sirricharddrury@yahoo.com

A 17-year-old, multiracial, non-union, professional chamber theatre dedicated to high-quality interpretations of classical and contemporary plays as well as literary adaptations for new audiences.

Experimental Theatre Chicago

Jaclyn Biskup, Artistic Director
1050 N. Honore, Ste. 1R
Chicago, IL 60622
Phone: 312/388-7660
etchicago@hotmail.com
experimentaltheatrechicago.org

We are a progressive theatre company seeking to move past the tradition of American realism.

www.factorytheater.com

PRODUCING ORIGINAL WORK SINCE 1992!

Coming November 2003 to Stage Left:

HERE COMES A REGULAR by Nick Digilio & Mike Vieau

Coming March 2004 to the Viaduct:

FACTORY CHAMPIONSHIP WRESTLING: THE PAY-PER-VIEW

by Scott OKen, Nick Digilio & Ernest Deak

Factory Theater 2936 N. Southport Chicago, IL 60657 (312) 409-3247

Factory Theater
Noah Simon, Artistic Director
2936 N. Southport
Chicago, IL 60657
Phone: 312/409-3247
noahsimon@hotmail.com
www.factorytheater.com

Date of Inception: 1992

Factory Theater produces all original material written by members of our ensemble.

See our ad on page 126

Foreground Theatre Company
Allen Jeffrey Rein, Artistic Director
P.O. Box 543369
Chicago, IL 60654
Phone: 773/604-1605
foregroundtheatre@yahoo.com
www.foreground.org

Date of Inception: 2000

Foreground's mission is to create bold, insightful, process-driven theatre; to develop an atmosphere in which artists can improve their craft; and to produce lesser known work of prominent playwrights and new work by promising playwrights.

The Free Associates
2936 N. Southport, Ste. 210
Chicago, IL 60657
Phone: 773/296-0541
Fax: 773/296-0968
freeassociates@aol.com
www.thefreeassociates.com

FreeStreet
1419 W. Blackhawk
Chicago, IL 60622
Phone: 773/722-7248
Fax: 773/772-7248
gogogo@hotmail.com
freestreet.org

Free Street opens the potential of youth and teens through theatre and writing to be creative, active participants in their own destiny.

FuzzyCo
Phone: 773/960-7855
Fax: Call for details
shaun@fuzzyco.com
www.fuzzyco.com

Cutting edge of live performance and movies

Galileo Players, Inc.
1850 N. Clark
Chicago, IL 60614
Phone: 312/944-1986
ronofeld@yahoo.com
www.galileoplayers.com

The Galileo Players develop and present original works of satirical sketch comedy that focuses on scientific and philosophical concepts.

GayCo Productions
Andrew Eninger
1450 W. Winona
Chicago, IL 60640
Phone: 773/531-5086
Fax: 773/528-0042
eningera@suba.com
www.gayco.com

Date of Inception: 1996

GayCo productions specializes in Gay and Lesbian-themed sketch comedy that begins with Gay as the given, not the punchline.

Gift Theatre Company
Michael Patrick Thornton, Co-Artistic
   Director
P.O. Box 411553
Chicago, IL 60641-1553
Phone: 312/458-9721
info@thegifttheatre.org
www.thegifttheatre.org

The Gift Theatre Company is dedicated to telling stories on stage with honesty and simplicity.

Greasy Joan and Company
Alison Dornheggen, Producer
P.O. Box 13077
Chicago, IL 60613
Phone: 773/761-8284
info@greasyjoan.org
www.greasyjoan.org

We produce classic work as well as plays that are innovative in language or style.

Griffin Theatre Company
Jon Berry, Associate Artistic Director
5404 N. Clark
Chicago, IL 60640
Phone: 773/769-2228
Fax: 773/769-2228
www.griffintheatre.com

We produce highly original new work, adaptations and classic plays that appeal to both young and old audiences, and we have a national touring company.

Theatres

HealthWorks Theatre
3171 N. Halsted
Chicago, IL 60657
Phone: 773/929-4260
Fax: 773/404-6815
hwt96@aol.com
www.healthworkstheatre.com

Hell In A Handbag Productions
Steve Hickson, Managing Director
1517 W. Rosemont , Ste. 3E
Chicago, IL 60660-1322
Phone: 312/409-4357
shickson@hotmail.com
www.handbagproductions.org

Date of Inception: 2002

Hell In A Handbag specializes in presenting live theatrical works through the prism of popular culture; productions that have popular appeal, reach across a broad spectrum of the general public and are FUN!

hic theatre company
hic theatre co., casting
1065 W. Glenlake, Ste. 1
Chicago, IL 60660
Phone: 773/561-3766
hictheatreco@hotmail.com

We produce only new work with an emphasis on one-act plays and off/late night runs.

Hi-Volt Theatre Company
Harry Bauer, Artistic Director
1844 W. Belle Plaine, Ste. 2
Chicago, IL 60613
Phone: 773/755-6959
hivolttheatre@yahoo.com
www.hivolt.org

Hi-Volt craves imagination, vitality and honesty in its productions by uncovering new ideas and putting fresh spins on old ones.

HomeGrown Theatre Company
Kipp Moorman, Managing Director
2617 W. Lawrence
Chicago, IL 60625
Phone: 773/728-6762
Fax: 773/728-6652
homegrownproductions@mac.com
www.homegrowntheatre.org

Date of Inception: 1999

HomeGrown Theatre is dedicated to providing enlightening quality entertainment through multi-media that voices different aspects of life.

The House Theatre
4344 N. Bell
Chicago, IL 60618
Phone: 773/583-5657
info@thehousetheatre.com
www.thehousetheatre.com

Date of Inception: 2001

It is the mission of The House to explore theatrical styles that recognize the presence, intelligence, and most importantly the imagination of the audience.

Hyper World Theatre Co.
4655 N. Campbell
Chicago, IL 60625
Phone: 773/784-8100
hyperworldtheatre@hotmail.com
www.hyperworldtheatre.com

As long as we have your attention, we try to make it something worth hearing.

The Hypocrites
Sean Graney, Artistic Director
P.O. Box 578542
Chicago, IL 60657-8542
Phone: 312/409-5578
info@the-hypocrites.com
www.the-hypocrites.com

Date of Inception: 1997

Noted as one of Chicago's most "inventive theatre companies" by the Chicago Sun-Times, The Hypocrites have produced everything from Ionesco, Buchner and Beckett to Chekhov, Stoppard and Mamet. In 2003, the company received six Joseph Jefferson Citations for their production of Sophie Treadwell's Machinal. In 2004 they will serve as the resident company at Gallery 37's Storefront Theatre.

ImprovOlympic
3541 N. Clark
Chicago, IL 60657
Phone: 773/880-0199
Fax: 773/880-9979
improvolymp@ameritech.net
www.improvolympic.com

Date of Inception: 1981

To further the art of long-form improvisation through education and entertainment and provide the artist with a place to create.

Infamous Commonwealth Theatre
Genevieve Hurst, Artistic Director
1604 W. Cullom, Ste. 3WC
Chicago, IL 60613
Phone: 312/458-9780
infamous_commonwealth_theatre@yaho
o.com
www.infamouscommonwealth.org

*Infamous Commonwealth selects one
topic each year and, from that, we create
a diverse season that looks at the chosen
topic from variant perspectives. This
season's topic is distorted perspectives.*

Irreverence Dance & Theatre
Amy Russell, Managing Director
5812 N. Magnolia
Chicago, IL 60660
Phone: 773/230-2168
irreverencedance@yahoo.com
www.irreverencedance.com

*Irreverence Dance + Theatre specializes
in original multi-discipline
(theatre/dance/vocal) works and serves as
a training ground for up and coming
dancers, actors, and directors.*

The Journeymen Theatre Company
Attn: Casting
3915 N. Janssen
Chicago, IL 60613
Phone: 773/857-5395
Fax: 773/529-5781
thejourneymen@aol.com
www.TheJourneymen.org

Katharsis Theatre Co.
Kyle Hillman, Artistic Director
6166 N. Sheridan, Ste. 20B
Chicago, IL 60660
Phone: 773/203-0879
katharsis@4thwall.com
www.katharsistheatre.com

Date of Inception: 2001

*Katharsis Theatre Co. is a non-profit
organization dedicated to providing
educational productions for the public
concentrating on the purification or
purgation of the emotions (especially pity
and fear) primarily through art.*

Keyhole Theatre Company
Frank Merle, Artistic Director
1536 W. North, 2nd Flr.
Chicago, IL 60622
Phone: 773/805-5055
frankmerle@juno.com
www.keyholeplayers.homestead.com

*Keyhole Theatre Company features
emerging artists in reenvisioned classics
of the highest quality.*

Lifeline Theatre
Dorothy Milne, Artistic Director
6912 N. Glenwood
Chicago, IL 60626
Phone: 773/262-3790
Fax: 773/761-4582
Dorothy@lifelinetheatre.com
www.lifelinetheatre.com

Date of Inception: 1983

*Lifeline Theatre and its artistic ensemble
of writers, directors, designers and
performers collaboratively develop
literary adaptations and original theatre.
Lifeline's innovative artistic and educational programs for adults, children and
families bring engaging and reflective
stories to life.*

Lincoln Square Theater of Chicago
Jerry Miller, Director
4754 N. Leavitt
Chicago, IL 60625
Phone: 773/275-9735
Fax: 773/784-8595
gaev5@aol.com
www.lincolnsquaretheaterofchicago.com

*Our goals are to raise consciousness
on contemporary social and religious
issues, support and encourage artists,
do outreach to the community, and
offer affordable/quality theatre to the
community.*

Theatres

Live Bait Theater
Attn: Casting
3914 N. Clark
Chicago, IL 60613
Phone: 773/871-1212
Fax: 773/871-3191
staff@livebaittheatre.org
www.livebaittheater.org

Date of Inception: 1987

Live Bait Theatre was founded in 1987 to produce new work by emerging Chicago playwrights and solo artists. Whether on our main stage or in our outreach programs, our primary goal is to encourage our resident artists and members of our community to create work that is personal, distinctive, and innovative.

L'Opera Piccola
Sasha B, Brauer
5239 N. Lacrosse
Chicago, IL 60630
Phone: 312/560-1072
Fax: 847/823-3165
sasha@loperapiccola.org
www.loperapiccola.org

Date of Inception: 1996

We strive to keep classical opera accessible to all people. Ticket prices remain at $10 so all can enjoy our diverse cast of 116 and orchestra of 43. We also hchildren's performances through our "Operatunity" program that has been featured on WGN.

The Mammals
3729 N. Ravenswood, Ste. 138
Chicago, IL 60640
Phone: 773/293-0431
bobfisher@themammals.org
www.themammals.org

Horror, Science Fiction, Phantasmagoria, New Works and Adaptation/New Investigations of Classics

Mary-Arrchie Theatre Co.
Richard Cotovsky, Artistic Director
731 W. Sheridan.
Chicago, IL 60613
Phone: 773/871-0442
Fax: 773/871-1439
coyotesky_2000@yahoo.com

Moving Dock Theatre Company
Dawn Arnold, Artistic Director
410 S. Michigan, Ste. 720
Chicago, IL 60657
Phone: 312/427-5490
Fax: 312/427-5492
contact@movingdock.org
www.movingdock.org

The Moving Dock Theatre Company explores the art of the theatre through a dedication to and practice of the actor's imaginative creative process.

Mystery Shop
Mary Heitert, Aritistic Director
551 Sundance Ct.
Carol Stream, IL 60188
Phone: 630/690-1105
Fax: 630/690-7928
TMS@themysteryshop.com
www.themysteryshop.com

Date of Inception: 1988

Mystery Shop is a traveling theatre company specializing in adult and children's partcipatory mysteries and programs. We are committed to providing quality entertainment to an active and involved audience. We stimulate the mind as well as the funnybone.

The Neo-Futurists
5153 N. Ashland
Chicago, IL 60640
Phone: 773/878-4557
Fax: 773/878-4514
info@neofuturists.org
www.neofuturist.org

The Neo-Futurists are an ensemble of artists who write, direct, and perform their own work dedicated to social, political, and personal enlightenment in the form of audience-interactive, non-illusory, conceptual theatre.

New Leaf Theatre
2045 N. Lincoln Park West
Chicago, IL 60614
Phone: 773/463-2575
Fax: 773/463-2575
newleaftheatre@hotmail.com
www.newleaftheatre.org

New Leaf Thetre is committed to immersing the audience and players in the passion and intimacy of live performance and storytelling through the exploration of new and lesser-produced works.

New Millennium Theatre Company
Chad Wise, Artistic Director
4744 N. Malden, Ste. 3
Chicago, IL 60640
Phone: 773/989-4515
Fax: 773/878-1143
info@nmtchicago.org
www.nmtchicago.org

Doing shows that we would want to see, NMTC makes theatre fun and relevant to today's complex audiences, especially those that don't regularly see theatre, by producing pop-culture-heavy shows involving familiar properties and characters.

North Shore Theater of Wilmette
Wilmette Park District
3000 Glenview Rd.
Wilmette, IL 60091
Phone: 847/256-9694
Bbierie@wilpark.org
Date of Inception: 1950

We pride ourselves on continuing to be the oldest continuing community theatre on the city's North Shore.

Odyssey Express Touring Co.
4515 N. Malden, Ste. 2C
Chicago, IL 60640
Phone: 773/784-5090
odyssey_express@yahoo.com
www.geocities.com/odyssey_express

Odyssey Express intends to mix the traditions of good storytelling, puppetry, history and education—all within a theatrical and thematic context in order to provide a quatlity theatre experience.

Open Door Repertory Company
Mary Pat Sieck, Artistic Director
P. O. Box 3547
Chicago, IL 60303 3547
Phone: 708/383-0566

We are a theatre of the community. We do work that reflects the diversity of our community; we provide opportunities for people in the communitiy to be a part of theatre and we build community within the company of Open Door.

Open Eye Productions
Sara Sevigny, Artistic Director
6214 N. Bell, Ste. 2N
Chicago, IL 60659
Phone: 773/856-5790
Fax: 773/381-8045
oep@openeyeproductions.org
www.openeyeproductions.org

Open Eye recognizes that not only are we all flawed, but that who we are is a result of how we react to our own flaws and those of others; by presenting theatrical works with strong, flawed characters, we explore how people are defined by their flaws.

Pegasus Players
Alex Levy, Associate Artistic Director
1145 W. Wilson
Chicago, IL 60640
Phone: 773/878-9761
Fax: 773/271-8057
pegasusp@megsinet.net
www.pegasusplayers.org
Date of Inception: 1978

Mostly new works and plays focusing on socially relevant works.

Performing Arts Chicago
410 S. Michigan, Ste. 911
Chicago, IL 60605
Phone: 312/663-1628
Fax: 312/663-1043
mail@pachicago.org
www.pachicago.org

PAC is an international, national, and local presenter of innovative performing arts.

Phoenix Theatre
Bryan Fonseca, Producing Director
749 N. Park Ave.
Indianapolis, IN 46202
Phone: 317/635-2381
Fax: 317/635-0100
info@phoenixtheatre.org
www.phoenixtheatre.org

We are the only professional company in the Indianapolis area that dedicates its entire programming to contemporary, issue-oriented theatre.

Theatres

Plasticene

2122 N. Winchester
Chicago, IL 60614
Phone: 312/409-0400
info@plasticene.com
www.plasticene.com

Date of Inception: 1995

Plasticene is an ensemble-based, experimental physical theatre company dedicated to the creation of original, artist-based theatre and training actors and others through the physical theatre process.

Playground Theater

Megan Pedersen, Production Manager
3341 N. Lincoln
Chicago, IL 60657
Phone: 773/871-3793
Fax: 773/913-6121
webmaster@the-playground.com
www.the-playground.com

We are the nation's only not-for-profit co-op theatre dedicated to improvisational comedy.

Porchlight Music Theatre Chicago

Walter Stearns, Artistic Director
2936 N. Southport
Chicago, IL 60657
Phone: 773/325-9884
porchlighttheatre@yahoo.com
www.Porchlighttheatre.com

Date of Inception: 1994

Porchlight produces intimate and inventive music theatre performance.

Profiles Theatre

Darrell W. Cox, Associate Artistic
  Director
4147 N. Broadway
Chicago, IL 60613
Phone: 773/549-1815
ProfilesCo@aol.com
www.Profilestheatre.org

Date of Inception: 1988

Profiles Theatre brings new works to Chicago that, Illuminate the determination and resiliency of the human spirit.

Prop Thtr

Jonathan Lavan, Executive Director
2621 N. Washtenaw
Chicago, IL 60647
Phone: 773/486-PROP
Fax: 773/486-7767
sviger@earthlink.net
www.propthtr.org

Date of Inception: 1981

Prop is solely dedicated to new plays and the yet to be discovered playwright. Prop has been creating groundbreaking cutting edge theatre with pennies for nearly a quarter of a century.

Pyewacket

Kate Harris, Artistic Director
2322 W. Wilson
Chicago, IL 60625
Phone: 773/275-2201
timothea45@hotmail.com

Date of Inception: 1997

Pyewacket was founded five years ago to recognize the very important need to connect audiences to plays that brought mature themes to life. Pyewacket continues in this vien by producing fully staged quality performances of "middle-tales" at venues across the city of Chicago.

Raven Theatre

Michael Menendian, Artistic Director
6157 N. Clark
Chicago, IL 60660
Phone: 773/338-2177
Fax: 773/508-9794
raventc1@aol.com
raventheatre.com

Raven Theatre focuses on American Theatre.

Redmoon Theater

Kristin Randall Burrello, Production
  Manager
1438 W. Kinzie
Chicago, IL 60622
Phone: 312/850-4430
Fax: 312/850-4430
info@redmoon.org
www.redmoon.org

Date of Inception: 1989

Redmoon creates theatrical spectacles that transform streets, stages and architectural landmarks into places of public celebration, utilizing an original theatrical language capable of speaking across cultural, ethnic and generational boundries.

Reverie Theatre Company

Chris Pomeroy, Artistic Director
P.O. Box 408740
Chicago, IL 60640
Phone: 312/409-6501
info@reverietheatre.com
reverietheatre.com

Reverie focuses on theatre that deals with the complexities, absurdities, and utter perplexities of love.

REVOLUTION Theatre Company

John Thurner, Artistic Director
P.O. Box 3896
Chicago, IL 60654
Phone: 312/494-2675
Fax: 312/670-0812
revolutiontheatrecompany@yahoo.com
www.revolutiontheatre.org

We produce theatre that is thought provoking and deviates from the status quo or any type of fad.

Rogue Theater Company

Nathan White, Artistic Director
840 Michigan, Ste. 14
Evanston, IL 60202
Phone: 773/450-0591
roguetheater@hotmail.com
www.roguetheater.com

We produce gender-balanced plays about rogues, rebels, misfits, and outcasts, and give away tickets to every show.

Saint Sebastian Players

1641 W. Diversey
Chicago, IL 60614
Phone: 773/404-7922
stsebplyrs@aol.com
members.aol.com/stsebplyrs

The Saint Sebastian Players produces a variety of events (including our original, yearly Monologue Matchup competition) and three mainstage productions each year for 22 seasons.

Sangfroid

Laura Millett, Artistic Director
1518 W. Schriever, Ste.1
Chicago, IL 60626
Phone: 773/973-1678
larlarland@hotmail.com

Date of Inception: 2001

Scrap Mettle SOUL

B. Micheletti, Managing Director
4600 N. Magnolia, Ste. C
Chicago, IL 60640
Phone: 773/275-3999
Fax: 773/561-3852
scrapmettle@core.com
www.scrapmettlesoul.org

Date of Inception: 1996

Scrap Mettle Soul is a community performance ensemble of all generations, integrating professionals and novices while doing plays based on true stories.

Searchlight Theatre Company

c/o Michael Garcia, Artistic Director
Phone: 773/347-1339
searchlighttheatreco@hotmail.com

Using non-traditional casting, we focus on returning older and forgotten plays to the spotlight of our current theatre.

Sense of Urgency

Edwin A. Wilson, Artistic Director
905 S. Grove, 1st floor
Oak Park, IL 60304
Phone: 708/386-6669
keitel@megsinet.net
www.senseofurgency.org

Date of Inception: 1995

Sense of Urgency is an ensemble-driven theatre. Our purpose is to unite the audience and the artist in an enriching, entertaining, communal experience by producing innovative, thought provoking theatre. Our company offers outreach programs and workshops. Our passion is to add our unique voice to the tradition of excellence, which is the trademark of Chicago Theatre.

Serendipity Theatre Company

Matt Miller, Artistic Director
1658 N. Milwaukee, Ste. 242
Chicago, IL 60647
Phone: 773/988-8480
contact@serendipitytheatre.com
www.serendipitytheatre.com

Date of Inception: 1999

Serendipity Theatre Company creates exhilarating new work for today's audiences.

Theatres

Shakespeare, Inc.
Bobby Zaman, Artistic Director
4750 N. Clarendon, Ste. 905
Chicago, IL 60640
Phone: 773/944-5247
shakespeareinc@yahoo.com
www.shakespeareinc.org

We specialize in Shakespeare's works and classic theatre only, and also do works inspired by classic texts.

Shining Through Productions
7016 N. Glenwood
Chicago, IL 60626
Phone: 773/743-3591
Muttsinc@aol.com

We the spiritual and emotional elements together that touch and change our lives.

The Side Project
Adam Webster, Artistic Director
1520 W. Jarvis
Chicago, IL 60626
Phone: 773/973-2150
Fax: 312/335-4277
adam@thesideproject.net
www.thesideproject.net

The Side Project specializes in new works that portray the human condition at the peak of adversity and examine the individual and its relation to society, striving for the betterment of both through the portrayal of life's extremes.

Signal Ensemble Theatre
Ronan Marra, Artistic Director
3023 N. Clark, Box199
Chicago, IL 60657
Phone: 773/347-1350
ronan@signalensembletheatre.com
www.signalensembletheatre.com

By focusing on a diverse slate of plays, we strive to produce clear and concise stagings of great stories.

Silk Road Theatre Project
Jamil Khoury, Artistic Director
6 E. Monroe, Ste. 801
Chicago, IL 60603
Phone: 312/236-6881
Fax: 312/357-0025
info@srtp.org
www.srtp.org

Dedicated to works by and about peoples of Asian, Middle Eastern and Mediterranean backgrounds.

Simple Theater
Laura Forbes, Artistic Director
4303 N. Winchester, Ste. 3D
Chicago, IL 60613
Phone: 773/832-0651
Fax: 773/832-0651
leadergreen@yahoo.com

The Simple Theater presents theatre as a community event—theatre is an opportunity to meet, relate and grow through the communion of people sharing a completely unique moment.

Single File Solo Festival
Attn: Submissions
1533 N. Wells, Ste. 1C
Chicago, IL 60610
Phone: 312-388-1805
info@singlefilechicago.com
www.singlefilechicago.com

Annual theatre festival features solo performances (everything from stand-up to performance art) with artists from around the world.

Smoke and Mirror Productions
Nick Jones, Artistic Director
6226 N. Clark, Ste. 3G
Chicago, IL 60660
Phone: 773/388-9590
www.smokeandmirror.org

We mutually share with our audience the experience of joy and sorrow, of mystery and fascination, of living and dying in an exhilirating visceral atmosphere.

Speaking Ring Theatre Company
Jennifer Leavitt, Artistic Director
3176 N. Broadway, Box 81
Chicago, IL 60657
Phone: 312/458-9374
info@speakingringtheatre.org
www.speakingringtheatre.org

We create a strong ensemble by using different techniques to bring out each individual's creative strengths and to blend them in order to best serve the play.

Stage Center Theatre
Rodney Higginbotham, Director
5500 N. St. Louis
Chicago, IL 60625
Phone: 773/442-5950
Fax: 773/442-5960
r-higginbotham1@neiu.edu
www.neiu.edu/~stagectr

Stage Center Theater is dedicated to teaching their liberal arts theatre program that operates a semi-professional summer theatre venue.

Stage Two Theatre Company
Wendy Kaplan, Managing Director
Estonian Lane
Lincolnshire, IL 60048
Phone: 847/432-7469
Fax: 847/982-0219
stagetwotheatre@cs.com
www.stagetwotheatre.com

We bring exceptional producions of rarely-done plays to the northern suburbs of Chicago.

Steep Theatre Company
Attn: Casting
3902 N. Sheridan
Chicago, IL 60613
Phone:
steeptheatre@hotmail.com

We bring out the everyday truth in the stories we tell through ensemble work.

Stir-Friday Night!
Jennifer Liu, Casting
P.O. Box 268560
Chicago, IL 60626
Phone: 773/973-4533
Fax: 773/761-8121
stirfridaynight@hotmail.com
www.stirfridaynight.org

A non-profit theatre organization, Stir-Friday Night! is the Midwest's premier Asian-American sketch comedy/improv troupe performing all original material.

Stockyards Theatre Project
Katie Carey Govier, Artistic Director
1300 W. Hood, Ste. 1
Chicago, IL 60660
Phone: 773/575-5942
Fax: 435/604-7736
stockyardstheatre@lycos.com
www.angelfire.com/il2/stockyards

Stockyards Theatre Project, is devoted to "improving women's lives via the theatre and performance art." A nationally recognized woman-centered theatre organization, Stockyards serves as a collaborative, ongoing theatre project whose mission is to help support and promote women as theatre and performance artists, to explore gender roles and gender issues in the theatre arts, and to explore both traditional and experimental theatre and performance art.

Strawdog Theatre Company
Jennifer Avery, Michael Dailey, co-
  Artistic Directors
3829 N. Broadway
Chicago, IL 60625
Phone: 773/528-9889
Fax: 773/528-7238
info@strawdog.org
www.StrawDog.org

Strawdog Theatre Co. is an ensemble of artists dedicated to producing provocative, inspiring theatre in an intimate setting.

Striding Lion InterArts Workshop
Annie Arnoult Beserra, Artistic Director
c/o the Vittum Theatre
1012 North Noble
Chicago, IL 60640
Phone: 773/561-0494
aberg@stridinglion.org
www.stridinglion.org

Striding Lion is a not-for-profit organization dedicated to cultivating a collaborative community through interdisciplinary arts programming. We are committed to the empowerment of the independent artist, to the enrichment and entertainment of diverse audiences, and to the evolution and advancement of American artistic expression.

Theatres

135

Studio Z
Jason A. Vales, Production Director
c/o Breadline Lab Space
1801 W. Byron
Chicago, IL 60613
Phone: 312/543-7920
info@studioz.org
www.studioz.org

Chicago's only arts organization dedicated to combining live theatre and digital multimedia.

T.U.T.A.
Zeljko Djukic, Artistic Director
3638 N. Pine Grove, Ste. 1
Chicago, IL 66714
Phone: 773/296-4887
Fax: 847/983-0529
info@tutato.com
www.tutato.com

Presenting atypical scripts, reenvigorating the theatre going experience.

TEATRO LUNA: Chicago's All-Latina Theater
Tanya Saracho
556 W. 18th
Chicago, IL 60616
Phone: 312/829-7552
teatroluna@aol.com
www.teatroluna.org

Teatro Luna is dedicated to producing original work by Latina artists.

Tellin' Tales Theatre
Tekki Lomnicki, Artistic Director
360 E. Randolph, Ste. 1006
Chicago, IL 60126
Phone: 312/540-1330
Fax: 312/540-1330
TekkiL@aol.com
Tellintales.org

Tellin' Tales Theatre's mission is to build community through the art of storytelling. Our company gathers the stories of groups or individuals-including adults and children with disabilities and creates

theatrically innovative performances using mentoring and collaboration. Tellin' Tales is dedicated to providing a venue for bringing together diverse people. Our aim is to help our audiences and our performers recognize their commonalties and build a sense of community where none existed before.

Terrapin Theatre
Jimmy Freund, Managing Director
444 N. Wabash, Ste. 410
Chicago, IL 60611
Phone: 312/464-1345
terrapintheatre@hotmail.com
www.terrapintheatre.org

Terrapin Theatre is dedicated to culti-vating new works for an audience seeking a fresh theatrical experience, rich in language and blistering with intellingence.

Theater Hikes
Nick Minas, Assistant Artistic Director
1344 E. Bailey Rd.
Naperville, IL 60565
Phone: 773/293-1358
FrankTFarrell@ameritech.net
www.theatrehikes.org

Date of Inception: 2002

Theatre Hikes performs outdoor theatre, taking an audience to different locations for each scene of a play.

Theatre Building Chicago
John Sparks, Artistic Director
1225 W. Belmont
Chicago, IL 60657
Phone: 773/929-7367
Fax: 773/327-1404
BoxOffice@TheatreBuildingChicago.org
www.TheatreBuildingChicago.org

The company maintains a steady commit-ment to the performing arts community in Chicago and strives to promote, develop and strengthen both emerging and estab-lished artists and organizations by:

• *Providing subsidized space, equipment and support for performing groups*

• *Developing and producing new musicals*

• *Providing opportunities for artists, administrators and performing groups.*

See our ad on page 136

Theatre of Western Springs
Headshots are not taken.
4584 Hampton
Western Springs, IL 60558
Phone: 708/246-4043
Fax: 708/246-4015
ad@theatrewesternsprings.com
www.TheatreWesternSprings.com

Date of Inception: 1929

Theatre of Western Springs is a commu-nity based theatre with great resouces, great facilities, and a talented ensemble.

Theo Ubique Theatre Company
Fred Anzevino, Artistic Director
1434 W. Jarvis, Ste. 2H
Chicago, IL 60626
Phone: 773/370-0235
blochbe@yahoo.com

Date of Inception: 1996

Theo Ubique Theatre, a Greek/Latin hybrid meaning "God is present every-where," reflects our belief that the self-sustaining creative force that animates all life is ever available to all of us: It is only our fears, doubts and insecurities that alienate us from its mysterious and bene-ficial power.

TimeLine Theatre Company
P.J. Powers, Artistic Director
615 W. Wellington
Chicago, IL 60657
Phone: 773/281-8463
Fax: 773/281-1134
info@TimeLineTheatre.com
www.TimeLineTheatre.com

TimeLine produces provocative theatre that illuminates the impact and resonance of history in society.

Tinfish Productions
Dejan Avramovich, Artistic Director
4247 N. Lincoln
Chicago, IL 60618
Phone: 773/549-1888
Fax: 773/549-1888
Tinfish@Tinfish.org
www.Tinfish.org

Date of Inception: 1994

To produce works by or about great European literary figures.

Theatres

Tireswing Theatre
Andrew Lines, Co-Artistic Director
850 W. Jackson, Ste. 310
Chicago, IL 60607
Phone: 312/961-5827
Fax: 312/228-4908
arl@tireswingtheatre.org
www.tireswingtheatre.org

*Tireswing is a versatile theatre group
dedicated to family oriented productions
through the use of the world's rich litera-
ture.*

Tommy Gun's Garage
Sandy Mangen, President/Gen. Mgr.
1239 S. State
Chicago, IL 60605
Phone: 312/461-0102
Fax: 312/461-9553
sandygun@earthlink.net
tommygunsgarage.com

Date of Inception: 1988

*Tommy Gun's offers a 1920's
musical/comedy revue in a "speak easy"
setting featuring gangsters, flappers, and
lots of audience participation.*

Tony 'n' Tina's Wedding
Chris Johnson, Production Manager
230 W. North
Chicago, IL 60610
Phone: 312/664-6969
Fax: 312/664-9610
www.tonyntina.com

TownSquare Players Inc.
121 Van Buren St.
Woodstock, IL 60098
Phone: 815/338-1937
Fax: 815/338-0248
LouCzarny@tspinc.org
www.tspinc.org

*Consistently highest quality community
theatre in area. Two productions at
Woodstock Opera House; one at Raue
Center for the Arts in Crystal Lake.*

Trap Door Productions
1655 W. Cortland
Chicago, IL 60622
Phone: 773/384-0494
Trapdoor@xnet.com
www.trapdoortheatre.com

Date of Inception: 1990

*Trap Door stages contemporary and
rarified works by foreign playwrights that
have hardly, if ever, been produced in the
U.S.*

TriArts, Inc.
Brian Loevner, Executive Director
5315 N. Clark, Ste. 142
Chicago, IL 60640
Phone: 773/866-8082 ext. 2
Fax: 928/395-9506
info@triarts.org
www.triarts.org

*TriArts is an ensemble based on the unifi-
cation of design, creative and technical
elements of production.*

Tripaway Theatre
Karin Shook, Aritistic Director
2714 W. Leland, Garden
Chicago, IL 60625
Phone: 773/878-7785
karin@tripaway.org
www.tripaway.org

*Tripaway Theatre uses modern theatre
tactics in order to awaken, entertain, and
inspire audiences.*

Uffda Productions
1247 W. Granville, Ste. 3E
Chicago, IL 60660
Phone: 773/856-5399
Uffda_productions@hotmail.com

*Uffda is dedicated to exploring diverse
interests through collaborations and
storytelling.*

University of Wisconsin - Parkside Theatre
Dean Yohnk, Development Director
900 Wood Rd.
Kenosha, WI 53141
Phone: 262/595-2352
Fax: 262/595-2271
yohnk@uwp.edu
www.uwp.edu/academic/theatre.arts

Our extensive undergraduate professional theatre training program maintains extensive ties with the professional theatre communities in Chicago and Milwaukee as we prepare our students for meaningful careers in the theatre.

Village Players Theatre
1006 W. Madison
Oak Park, IL 60302
Phone: 708/524-1892
www.village-players.org

Visions and Voices Theatre Co.
Brian A. Hill, Artistic Director
2007 W. Argyle, Ste. 3
Chicago, IL 60625
Phone: 773/271-9309
Fax: 773/271-6967
visionsandvoices@msn.com
www.visionsandvoices.org

Creating a balance between art and the business of art.

Vitalist Theatre
Elizabeth Carlin-Metz, Artistic Director
695 N. Broad St.
Galesburg, IL 61401
Phone: 309/343-6746
emetz@knox.edu

Visceral ensemble acting of physical theatre in the European tradition with American guts.

Vittum Theatre
1012 N. Noble St.
Chicago, IL 60622
Phone: 773/278-7471 ext. 172
Fax: 773/278-2621
info@vittumtheater.org
www.vittumtheater.org

The Vittum Theater is commited to presenting Chicago's students, educators and families with the opportunity to engage in an affordable, educational experience that is rooted in the art of performance.

VORTEX
Gary Charles Metz, Artistic Director
920 Barnsdale Rd.
LaGrange Park, IL 60526
Phone: 708/354-4580
vortexlgp@hotmail.com
www.vortexlgp.com

Vortex is a theatre that believes in chances; taking them, and giving them.

Walkabout Theater Company
Kristan Schmidt, Artistic Director
3241 N. Ravenswood
Chicago, IL 60657
Phone: 773/248-9278
Fax: 773/248-9284
kristan@walkabouttheater.org
www.walkabouttheater.com

We create all our own work, usually multi-disciplinary in nature.

White Horse Theatre Company
Jeremy Morton, Artistic Director
2089 W. Wabansia, Ste. 206
Chicago, IL 60647
Phone: 773/252-0164
admin@whitehorsetheatre.com
www.whitehorsetheatre.com

White Horse Theatre Company is dedicated to the celebration of musical theatre. In particular, WHTC seeks to revive the art of musical theatre by producing and bringing attention to the many under-appreciated, yet important musicals of our time. In addition, we serve as a forum for up and coming musical writers and composers to share and workshop their work. By sharing these stories told through music, we hope to contribute to the revitalization of this powerful artform.

Will Act for Food
Corri Feuerstein, Artistic Director
1061 W. Hollywood, Ste. 1-B
Chicago, IL 60660
Phone: 773/506-4559
corri@willactforfood.org
www.willactforfood.org

Will Act For Food supports those starving in our community—both physically and artistically—by producing thought-provoking works while collecting food for local shelters.

Theatres

139

Wing and Groove Theatre Company
Attn: Casting
1737 West Le Moyne, Garden Apt.
Chicago, IL 60622
Phone: 773/782-9476
info@wingandgroove.com
www.wingandgroove.com

The mission of Wing and Groove is:

- *To cultivate and develop an ensemble of resident theatre artists who share the values of community, accessibility, and quality in shaping all artistic programming.*

- *To present provocative plays by visionary playwrights with innovative direction and the highest possible standards of production.*

- *To engage in an agenda that furthers the art of the theatre by developing new plays and providing opportunities for emerging artists.*

- *To actively participate in the improvement of the community.*

- *To provide its staff and artists with the best working conditions possible.*

WNEP Theater Foundation
Jen Ellison, Artistic Director
3210 N. Halsted, Ste. 3
Chicago, IL 60657
Phone: 773/755-1693
hall@wneptheater.org
www.wneptheater.org

Date of Inception: 1993

WNEP Theater generates original work casting a critical eye on American values, culture, and perspectives by presenting the grotesque as beautiful, the mundane as unexpected, and asking its audience to change its role from spectator to participant.

Woodstock Opera House
Lou Czarny, Producer
121 Van Buren St.
Woodstock, IL 60098
Phone: 815/338-1937
Fax: 815/338-0248
LouCzarny@tspinc.org
www.tspinc.org

To continue being the oldest active community theatre group in McHenry County.

www.performink.com

pidollars
Performink's Online Currency

Audition notices updated twice weekly.

Photo: Margaret Lakin

CHAPTER 7

RUNNING A SMALL THEATRE COMPANY

Machinal
The Hypocrites

The Business of the Art

From Board Development to Tax Audits—Organizations Designed to Help Non-Profits

By J.L. Myers

Arts and Business Council of Chicago

Get the "know-how" for running your theatre as an effective business with the aid of the Arts and Business Council of Chicago (A&BC). Connecting business-savvy volunteers with small and medium-sized not-for-profit art groups is A&BC's mission. The council looks to cultivate communities through financially healthy art establishments, sponsoring a number of services that help theatres manage their businesses sensibly.

The council's nuclear program, Business Volunteers for the Arts (BVA), assembles "project teams" (generally two or three volunteers) prepared to identify and meet your operational challenges. Defining a new business model, executing a marketing plan or simply getting help with unruly financial systems are just a few of the services which a growing theatre might be able to hammer out with the aid of professional consultants. A small fee ($60-$100) is required, based on operational expenditures.

Need an energetic, business-oriented board member? The council's OnBOARD program trains business professionals for work as board members in the not-for-profit art world. Recruits get an overview of the arts scene in Chicago, then learn the intricacies and responsibilities of governing in the specialized art industry. After training, OnBOARD graduates are placed with an appropriate organization as "apprentice" board members for two or three months, after which you decide if your apprentice should come aboard. A small fee ($100-$150) is required, based on operational expenditures. Applications are due in February.

A&BC also hosts a number of luncheons, conferences and workshops to build not-for-profit business knowledge. Each month, the council runs a workshop focused on a particular business function like e-marketing, grant writing, branding or outreach strategies. They also maintain a resource library for answering your business and marketing questions.

The Arts Marketing Center, a former extension of A&BC dedicated to addressing marketing concerns, morphed into the National Arts Marketing Program, headed up by the organization's New York offices. Marketing resources through the program are available online at http://artsmarketing.org. For more information about A&BC of Chicago, see http://www.artsbiz-chicago.org.

CPA's for Public Interest

Did somebody call an accountant? CPA's for the Public Interest (CPAsPI) links nonprofits with volunteers who specialize in financial, tax, technical and accounting services. The group's Accounting Consultation Program and Board Service Outreach Program anchor its support services, but CPAsPI also hosts workshops and publishes a variety of works stuffed with financial and accounting tips.

Maritza Martinez, the group's manager of community service programs and volunteers, said many nonprofits contact the organization expecting a "do-it-all" accounting service. But the thrust of the group's services is to help nonprofits understand the financial, tax and accounting world. "[CPAsPI] is there to help guide nonprofits so that they can understand their accounting responsibilities," she said. For qualifying nonprofits (with annual revenues between $10,000 and $350,000), CPAsPI will help locate a volunteer accountant to assist with the installation of an accounting system.

Alongside the accounting consultation, CPAsPI also promotes openings on nonprofit boards with the Board Service Outreach Program. CPAsPI is "not match-making," Martinez said, but rather providing general referrals through its Web site.

The group also hosts occasional workshops designed for nonprofit management; the most recent dissected the audit process. Free publications include "The Audit Process" and "Tax and Reporting Guide for Illinois Not-for-Profit Charitable Organizations," both packed with important accounting tips for nonprofits. For more information, see http://www.cpaspi.org/cpaspi/index.htm.

Donors Forum of Chicago

The Donors Forum of Chicago, a grant-making and philanthropy advocacy group, offers what many theatres need most—funding information. The group is an association of hundreds of Chicago-area funding institutions and nonprofit organizations which hosts more than 100 networking and educational events each year.

As an organization connected to The Foundation Center in New York, the nation's leading philanthropy authority, the Donors Forum serves as a clearinghouse for information on foundation giving. The group's library is open to the public and houses more than 2500 volumes concerned with fundraising and not-for-profit management in the Chicago area. To ease library access in the suburbs, the Chicago-based library planted Philanthropy Centers in Glen Ellyn, Schaumburg and Chicago Heights. Stop in and start researching!

The group also offers the Grantseekers Toolbox online, a collection of tips and instructions for grant writing. Another online tool, called the Illinois Funding Source database, allows grant seekers to search through Illinois' philanthropists with targeted ease. There is a charge for an online subscription, but the service is free at the Donors Forum Library.

As part of the Donors Forum's educational outreach, it hosts a grantwriting workshop each year. The workshop walks participants through the steps of writing grants, focusing the proposal and its contents on an appropriate grant-making foundation. For more information, see http://www.donorsforum.org.

Running a Small Theatre Company

Illinois Arts Alliance/Foundation

The Illinois Arts Alliance (IAA) and the Illinois Arts Alliance/Foundation (IAA/F) are two separate organizations functioning together to promote statewide multidisciplinary arts progress. The alliance focuses on advocacy issues, maintaining a constant legislative force that guides pro-art political action, while the foundation focuses on education, research and outreach for the arts community as a whole. "We speak to the larger arts picture," said Lisa May Simpson, IAA/F's membership and development director. As part of that outreach effort, the foundation maintains the Local Arts Network, in conjunction with the Illinois Arts Council. The network serves local art groups with technical assistance and operates a peer-sharing program. By training leaders in the arts to act as consultants for their peers, the foundation seeks to foster an interconnected and thriving art scene.

The organization also sponsors a variety of workshops and conferences, including its biennial One State Together in the Arts conference. Presentations at the 2003 conference focused on best practices in fundraising, planning and marketing. But the real benefit for theatre management is to learn what leaders in different arts disciplines are doing, Simpson said. "There's this chance to break out of your normal circles that is enormously helpful."

The foundation's efforts to educate the arts community should not go unnoticed. With research into the economic impact of the arts in Illinois, the group has garnered more political clout. Another foundation study, "Arts Leadership for the 21st Century," dives into the complicated issues surrounding the new guard of arts stewards. For more information, visit http://www.artsalliance.org.

Lawyers for the Creative Arts

Lawyers for the Creative Arts (LCA) is Chicago's only pro bono legal service provider specifically geared towards arts and entertainment. "There is no one who does what we do," said executive director Bill Rattner.

In more than 30 years of service, the LCA has served tens of thousands of artists and their organizations. It connects artists and arts organizations with over 200 volunteer attorneys and law firms to meet virtually any legal concern. Get help navigating the legal quagmires surrounding issues like small business setup, copyrighting and licensing.

Arts mediation is another critical service provided by LCA. Solve disputes with other artists or arts organizations quickly, privately, economically and out-of-court with the LCA's help.

LCA also hosts regular seminars and presentations on legal issues affecting the arts community. Recent seminars focused on setup for nonprofits and obtaining tax exemptions, while another presentation explored copyright issues.

Moving into the world of financial consultation, the LCA recently assembled a list of volunteer accountants, bookkeepers and other financial specialists. Rattner said the new program will mirror the organization's legal services.

Stay abreast of upcoming seminars and workshops by signing up for the LCA's revamped newsletter. For more information, see http://law-arts.org.

League of Chicago Theatres

The League of Chicago Theatres promotes local theatre through collective advertising and marketing campaigns, and by spearheading advocacy efforts to keep Chicago theatre-friendly. "We like to see ourselves as the launch pad for giving assistance to the community as needed," said Bill Pacholski, manager for the League's member services group.

One of the League's most popular services is its Hot Tix discount ticket sales program. League members get help filling their seats with distribution of half-price, day-of-performance tickets to seven locations throughout the city and all Tower Records outlets.

Other advertising and marketing boosts: Get your theatre listed in the "Chicago Theatre Guide," reaping the benefits of its 60,000 bimonthly circulation. "Chicago Plays," another League publication, reaches 180,000 readers each month. Members can also buy discounted radio and television advertising time from the League, which buys in bulk. "It's generally about 40 percent off," Pacholski said.

Even non-members reap the benefits of some League activities. The organization runs a variety of promotion campaigns for the Chicago theatre scene, including television public service announcements and its Street to Seats campaign. For more information, see http://www.chicagoplays.com.

Nonprofit Financial Center

Part bank, part school and part service center, the Nonprofit Financial Center (NFC) helps nonprofit organizations with lending and financing, while also providing a plethora of seminars, workshops, publications and consulting services aimed at improving nonprofit management. If your theatre is hit by cash flow problems, check with NFC promptly.

Lending to nonprofits can be risky because often their collateral cannot be liened, zapping traditional credit routes. But nonprofits need credit too. What do you do if your grant is waylaid and you can't pay your staff? Anne Willmore, NFC's senior outreach associate, said the organization started out lending to nonprofits stuck in similar predicaments. "A lot of times, groups are just waiting for the check from the state," she said. "But they've got to keep going."

NFC offers three types of loans to nonprofits: short term emergency loans, collateral-based longer term loans (no longer than one year), and a special loan for technology and office equipment purchases. Check into using your promised grant or contract as collateral.

Soon after starting, NFC realized nonprofits need more than just lending help, Willmore said. Among the many training and consulting services offered by NFC, a three-day bootcamp for nonprofit financial and managerial officers is exceedingly popular. Willmore said it's a chance for officers to learn the best practices and new techniques for operating their nonprofit enterprise.

NFC also released a new, second edition of its nonprofit bible, "Do It Right the First Time: Starting a Nonprofit Organization in Illinois." Approaching nonprofit startups from an Illinois-centric perspective, the book helps newcomers get it right from the word "go."

Running a Small Theatre Company

Theatre Communications Group

The Theatre Communications Group (TCG), publisher of "American Theatre Magazine," offers dozens of services aimed at increasing "organizational efficiency" to theatre groups of all sizes. Did we mention they also grant money? In 2002-03, TCG gave $4.4 million to theatres and individual artists through its artistic programs awards.

TCG administers seven artistic programs for theatres, including actor and playwright residency programs and a mentoring program for theatre professionals. One such program, called the New Generations Program, is "designed to cultivate future leaders" by granting $65,000 to awarded theatres for employing a protégé during a two-year stint, said Joan Channick, TCG's deputy director. The program helps emerging theatre leaders "cover some of the financial barriers" associated with entry into the theatre industry while learning through close ties with a theatre's mentors, she said. The New Artistic Leader Institute is another program specifically tailored for new theatre administrators. "It's a kind of bootcamp offered every other year," Channick said. "It's designed to help people who are a first-time artistic director...or prospective artistic directors." Channick said participants learn the ropes of managing in a creative position.

TCG hosts other professional development events, too. Twice a year, the group teleconferences with members, administering five-hour-long discussions to explore marketing, development and other management issues.

TCG also conducts extensive research on the American theatre scene. Through a series of fiscal surveys, the organization produces its popular "Theatre Facts" each year, loaded with information about the market's vital signs. Other publications utilizing TCG research include the "TCG Bulletin" and letters from the group's executive director, Ben Cameron. Both feature analysis of the trends shaping the field. "Centerpiece" is also published, featuring coverage of the issues affecting theatre management most directly. For more information, see http://www.tcg.org.

Helpful Organizations

The Actor's Fund
203 N. Wabash, Ste. 2104
Chicago, IL 60601
Phone: 312/372-0989
Fax: 312/372-0272

Arts and Business Council of Chicago
70 E. Lake, Ste. 500
Chicago, IL 60601
Phone: 312/372-1876
Fax: 312/372-1102
www.artsbiz-chicago.org

Association of Consultants to Nonprofits
P.O. Box 2449
Chicago, IL 60690-2449
Phone: 312/580-1875
www.ACNconsult.org

Center for Communication Resources
1419 W. Blackhawk
Chicago, IL 60622
Phone: 773/862-6868
Fax: 773/862-0707
www.bham.net/soe/ccr

Chicago Department of Cultural Affairs
Phone: 312/742-1175
www.ci.chi.il.us/CulturalAffairs

Community Media Workshop at
Columbia College
600 S. Michigan
Chicago, IL 60605
Phone: 312/344-6400
Fax: 312/344-6404
www.newstips.org

CPA's for Public Interest
222 S. Riverside Plaza, 16th Flr.
Chicago, IL 60606
Phone: 312/993-0393
Fax: 312/993-9432
www.cpaspi.org

Cultural Facilities Fund
78 E. Washington, Ste. 250
Chicago, IL 60602
Phone: 312/372-1710
Fax: 312/372-1765

Department of Revenue
Phone: 312/747-3823
www.ci.chi.il.us/Revenue

Donors Forum of Chicago
208 S. LaSalle, Ste. 735
Chicago, IL 60604
Phone: 312/578-0175
Fax: 312/578-0158
Info@donorsforum.org
www.donorsforum.org

Executive Service Corps of Chicago
25 E. Washington, Ste. 1500
Chicago, IL 60602
Phone: 312/580-1840
Fax: 312/580-0042
www.esc-chicago.org

Illinois Alliance for Arts Education
200 N. Michigan, Ste. 404
Chicago, IL 60601
Phone: 312/750-0589
Fax: 312/750-9113
www.artsmart.org

Illinois Arts Alliance
200 N. Michigan, Ste. 404
Chicago, IL 60601
Phone: 312/855-3105
Fax: 312/855-1565
www.artsalliance.org

Illinois Arts Council
100 W. Randolph, Ste. 10-500
Chicago, IL 60601
Phone: 312/814-6750
Fax: 312/814-1471
www.state.il.us/agency/iac

League of Chicago Theatres
228 S. Wabash, Ste. 300
Chicago, IL 60604
Phone: 312/554-9800
Fax: 312/922-7202
www.chicagoplays.com

National Dinner Theatre Association
P.O. Box 726
Marshall, MI 49068
Phone: 616/781-7859
Fax: 616/781-4880
www.ndta.com

Nonprofit Financial Center
29 E. Madison, Ste. 1700
Chicago, IL 60602
Phone: 312/606-8250
Fax: 312/606-0241
www.nonprofitfinancial.org

The Saints (Volunteers
for the Performing Arts)
Athenaeum Theatre
2936 N. Southport, Rm. 203
Chicago, IL 60657
Phone: 773/529-5510
Fax: 312/372-0272
www.saintschicago.org
info@saintschicago.org

Season of Concern
203 N. Wabash, Ste. 2104
Chicago, IL 60601
Phone: 312/332-0518
Fax: 773/529-5512
www.seasonofconcern.org

Society of Stage Directors
and Choreographers
(SSDC)
1501 Broadway, Ste. 1701
New York, NY 10036
Phone: 212/302-6195
Fax: 212/391-1070

Women's Theatre Alliance
P.O. Box 64446
Chicago, IL 60664-0446
Phone: 312/408-9910
www.wtachicago.org

Running a Small Theatre Company

147

A 12-Step Program to Organize Your Business

By Greg Mermel, CPA

Almost all nonprofit theatre companies start small, typically founded by a small group of people with something in common. Maybe they all went to school together or are obsessed with Shakespeare, Brecht or new works. Maybe they suffered together under the same clueless director. Or, perhaps, they were all frustrated by not being cast elsewhere.

Whatever the bond, they talked. And talked. And then started a company. A nonprofit corporation was created. Internal Revenue Service (IRS) recognition of exempt status was obtained. Families and friends were turned into contributors, and savings from day jobs were thrown into the financial pot. From the chaos emerged a show. And lo, it was good. (At least in this example it was good, or the narrative would end here.) Then came another show and a third. Before the founders realized it, the company had a style and a reputation, something to build on.

By the time a company is three or four years old, however, changes typically start to happen. The founders may discover that they do not know each other as well as they thought. Some move on after disagreements over artistic affairs, or the end of a love affair or being cast in bigger or better paying parts elsewhere. Those remaining may feel betrayed or relieved, proud of their erstwhile colleagues' success or envious of it, despairing or energized by the changes—often all at the same time. The company may still have lofty goals and ambitions, but not have the money or knowledge to achieve them. It is like being a teenager again, without the acne.

And, as those four high school years can set patterns that last a lifetime, what happens during these few years will shape much of the future of the theatre company. Here are some events that will almost certainly happen during these awkward years:

1. Someone is put in charge. Most small theatres start with collective policy-making and management tasks being parceled out among the group, whether by accident ("Hey, kids! Let's put on a show!") or design ("We're a manifesto-issuing Marxist/feminist/vegetarian cooperative"). Group management does not work, at least not for long. Too much time gets spent avoiding hurt feelings and reaching consensus, and not enough time gets spent on art.

You will also find that you need people with non-artistic skills. If a gifted director proves to be a good administrator, or a talented playwright is a capable grant-writer, you got lucky. And even if so, those may not be the best uses of their limited time. If you bring in extra people for these important functions, they need the authority to act without hindrance from the original crew. Otherwise, you will waste their time and your money.

2. You need to have actual employees, or you might need Equity actors. (Remember those founders who have been working elsewhere? Guess what? They joined the union.) Along with that comes payroll taxes and deadlines for filings and payment. In addition to the federal and state income taxes and Social Security tax withheld from employees' paychecks, the employer has to pay an equal amount of Social Security tax along with unemployment taxes. There are both state and federal unemployment taxes, but nonprofit organizations are exempt from the federal tax.

3. You discover some financial chaos and realize that nobody quite knows how the money has been spent, or if any has been misspent. Bring in competent help to fix this, pronto. You must have good financial records to be able to plan and to raise money.

4. Nonprofit organizations whose annual gross receipts are normally under $25,000 do not have to file annual federal tax returns; over that amount, you must file a form 990 each year. If your financial records are in chaos, you may not realize that you have hit this mark.

Also, forms 990 are public records. You are required to have a copy available for inspection at all times, and the curious can obtain copies from the IRS.

5. If you have not done so already, this would also be an excellent time to register the theatre with the Charitable Trusts division of the Illinois Attorney General's office and start filing the annual reports that you should have been filing since the day your company was formed.

6. During your fifth year of operation, you will receive a confusing notice from the IRS talking about private foundation status and including references to many obscure parts of the Internal Revenue Code. Do not panic: You did nothing wrong. The IRS classifies non-profit organizations operating under Section 501(c)(3) of the Code as either private foundations or public charities. Private foundations are those organizations largely or entirely funded by the contributions of a few individuals, like the Bill & Melinda Gates Foundation, while public charities are (surprise!) supported by the public. Your theatre company is not a private foundation, and you do not want it to be. Different, complex and unpleasant tax rules apply to private foundations.

If you were prompt in applying for IRS recognition of exempt status, your company did not have enough operating history at the time to prove it was publicly supported. The IRS would have issued an advance ruling, based on your projected financial information, saying that they will assume for five years that you are not a private foundation. This notice asks for actual information so that they can issue a definitive ruling. Routine stuff.

7. You have to extend fundraising beyond family and friends. Even if they can afford bigger contributions, they get tired of giving and giving, and they start dropping hints about your giving up acting and going to law school so you can earn a decent living like your brother. There is an important lesson to be remembered here for later fundraising, which is donor fatigue. The most prosperous people and deep-pocketed foundations will not support the same organizations forever. For some, like Chicago Community Trust, it is a matter of policy. Others simply find their interest shifting to other companies or causes.

Running a Small Theatre Company

149

This means, unfortunately, that donor development is a never-ending task.

8. These new prospective donors will want to see something you do not yet have: financial statements. Do them. Properly, a full set of financial statements for a nonprofit organization includes four statements: (a) a balance sheet showing the company's assets, liabilities, and various classes of net assets, (b) a statement of activity showing the various types of revenue and support, and categories of expenses, (c) a statement of changes in net assets which might be combined with the statement of activity in a simple organization, and (d) a statement of cash flows, showing the sources and uses of cash. To be in conformity with generally accepted accounting principles, all of these statements would need to have certain explanatory notes and follow a semi-standard format. If your budget is still under $100,000, you may be able to get by with a simplified set. Eventually, though, you will need the involvement of an independent Certified Public Accountant (CPA) to help you comply with the accounting principles, and to provide either a review or audit.

9. Payroll taxes and 990s involve deadlines—serious ones. This is not stuff to fool around with. Engage a CPA to do the 990s, to file extensions if necessary, and to make sure they are filed when due. Use a reputable payroll processing service (not a paymaster) to pay the employees, and let them transfer the payroll taxes and file the returns electronically.

For organizations of this size, the penalty for not filing a 990 on time is $20 per day, to a maximum of $10,000 for each tax year. The IRS will waive the penalty once with almost any kind of excuse if you convince them it won't happen again. They dislike recidivists, and the second or third time, you'd better meet the narrow technical definition of reasonable cause. I know of one nonprofit organization that has been paying penalties at $500 per month for three years, with several more to go.

The consequences of not paying the payroll taxes are even worse. The IRS can permanently close recalcitrant, delinquent businesses, and has done so with at least one well-established Chicago theatre. They also can effectively impose personal liability on anyone with signature authority on the company's bank account or who had the authority to see that the taxes were paid and did not, which means your officers and board and key employees.

10. Your board expands beyond the insiders. As you start getting significant money from people who are not family and friends, these new donors will, literally, want a seat at the table. Give it to them. If they have money, so do their friends. The more your donors identify with—even bond with—the company, the more they are willing to get contributions from people they know.

11. You want to start keeping serious records. A database of who gave how much, when, names and addresses, etc., will be of immeasurable value—not just for going back to those donors, but for being able to demonstrate to grantors that, yes, you do have a broad base of support.

12. Turn those boxes of old stuff into a proper archive. If the company really grows and prospers, those old production photos, programs, press releases, design sketches and reviews will be important.

Finding and
Maintaining Space

By Kevin Heckman

Chicago has its share of theatre companies and then some, but while most outsiders think of Steppenwolf and the Goodman when they think of theatre—and even Chicagoans don't necessarily get past Victory Gardens and Court—the vast bulk of Chicago's theatres are itinerant. From space to space they roam, producing a show here or a show there. Many theatres with permanent homes supplement their income by renting their space out to those itinerant companies. Both sides of the renting coin have their own troubles and concerns.

Renting? In the current political climate, you'd best be sure the theatre from which you're renting has their Public Place of Amusement (PPA) license. This permits the venue to host entertainment events, and without it the space can be shut down without notice. You can actually find out whether a given theatre has its PPA by going to www.cityofchicago.org/Revenue/License/License.html and clicking on Business License Holders Search. Of course, you needn't only trust the city's Web site. This should be the first question for the company from whom you're considering renting.

Aside from the legality of the space, be sure you understand what you else get. Technical supplies? Box office support? Signage? How might you be limited? Will they permit changes in the seating arrangement? Altering the light plot? Food? Smoke? Are there any additional charges, aside from the (usually weekly) cost of renting? Above all else, get a written agreement and read it carefully.

As a renter, of course, everything becomes more complicated. Dealing with the city alone, particularly if your space has just opened, can be a major undertaking. Your number one resource will be your alderman. (S)he has the clout to make your life easier and, most likely, the interest in seeing your business succeed.

The trick to renting is balancing the needs of your theatre with the needs of the renter. The more you put down on paper, either in a contract or in a handbook for the space, the less likely the chance of a misunderstanding. Of course, many renters won't read everything you give them, but if there's advance notice of shutdown and start-up procedures, required cleaning or maintenance, and charges for failing to do any of these things, your relationship will be that much clearer.

For both sorts of theatres, brand recognition is a crucial aspect of a rental relationship. A rentee wants patrons to follow the company, not the space. A renter doesn't want its patrons to confuse its work with that of guest artists in the theatre. As a rentee, how will your show be presented? Is it part of the guest theatre's season? Do they advertise you to their patrons? As a renter, do you limit the use of your name and/or logo in the rentee's advertising?

Obviously, successful rental relationships take place everyday and form the bedrock of Chicago theatre. The key to that success lies in taking care of your company and your show. A little caution will go a long way to ensuring that your theatre can have the best opportunity to succeed.

Running a Small Theatre Company

Rehearsal Space Rental

Alphabet Soup Productions
P.O. Box 85
Lombard, IL 60148
Phone: 630/932-1555
Fax: 630/665-8465
ABSkidshow@aol.com
absproductions.com

American Theater Company
1909 W. Byron
Chicago, IL 60613
Phone: 773/929-5009
Fax: 773/929-5171
dkiely@atcweb.org
www.atcweb.org

Artistic Home Acting Ensemble, The
1420 W. Irving Park
Chicago, IL 60613
Phone: 773/404-1100
Fax: 708/387-7286
Theartistichome@aol.com

BackStage Theatre Company
P.O. Box 118142
Chicago, IL 60611
Phone: 312/683-5347
www.backstagetheatrecompany.org

Bailiwick Repertory Arts Center
1229 W. Belmont
Chicago, IL 60657
Phone: 773/883-1090
Fax: 773/883-2017
Bailiwickr@aol.com
www.bailiwick.org

Breadline Theatre Group
1802 W. Berenice
Chicago, IL 60613
Phone: 773/327-6096
breadline@breadline.org
www.breadline.org

C'est La Vie Drama
4331 N. Kenmore
Chicago, IL 60613
Phone: 773/415-2538
fester1226@hotmail.com
www.cestlaviedrama.com

Chicago Actors Studio Theatre
1567 N. Milwaukee
Chicago, IL 60622
Phone: 773/735-6400
Fax: 773/767-4151
chiactorstudio@aol.com
actors-studio.net

Chicago Dramatists
1105 W. Chicago
Chicago, IL 60622
Phone: 312/633-0630
Fax: 312/633-0610
NewPlays@ChicagoDramatists.org
www.ChicagoDramatists.org

ComedySportz
2851 N. Halsted
Chicago, IL 60657
Phone: 773/549-8080
Fax: 773/549-8142
mattcsz@mcleodusa.net
www.comedysportzchicago.com

Corn Productions
Cornservatory
4210 N. Lincoln
Chicago, IL 60618
Phone: 773/868-0243
Fax: 773/868-0243
Cornproductions.aol.com
Cornservatory.org

Court Theatre
5535 S. Ellis
Chicago, IL 60637
Phone: 773/702-7005
info@courtheatre.org
www.courtheatre.org

Defiant Theatre
3540 N. Southport, Ste. 162
Chicago, IL 60657
Phone: 312/409-0585
defianttheatre@defianttheatre.org
www.defianttheatre.org

Eclipse Theatre Company
2000 W. Fulton
Chicago, IL 60612
Phone: 312/409-1687
eclipsetheatre@hotmail.com
www.eclipsetheatre.com

European Repertory Co.
1839 W. Thomas St
Chicago, IL 60622
Phone: 773/972-1678
dg930@hotmail.com

GayCo Productions
1450 W. Winona
Chicago, IL 60640
Phone: 773/531-5086
Fax: 773/528-0042
eningera@suba.com
www.gayco.com

Griffin Theatre Company
5404 N. Clark
Chicago, IL 60640
Phone: 773/769-2228
Fax: 773/769-2228
www.griffintheatre.com

HomeGrown Theatre Company
2617 W. Lawrence
Chicago, IL 60625
Phone: 773/728-6762
Fax: 773/728-6652
homegrownproductions@mac.com
www.homegrowntheatre.org

House Theatre
4344 N. Bell
Chicago, IL 60618
Phone: 773/583-5657
info@thehousetheatre.com
www.thehousetheatre.com

ImprovOlympic
3541 N. Clark
Chicago, IL 60657
Phone: 773/880-0199
Fax: 773/880-9979
improvolymp@ameritech.net
www.improvolympic.com

Journeymen Theatre Company, The
3915 N. Janssen
Chicago, IL 60613
Phone: 773/857-5395
Fax: 773/529-5781
thejourneymen@aol.com
www.TheJourneymen.org

Lifeline Theatre
6912 N. Glenwood
Chicago, IL 60626
Phone: 773/262-3790
Fax: 773/761-4582
Dorothy@lifelinetheatre.com
www.lifelinetheatre.com

Live Bait Theater
3914 N. Clark
Chicago, IL 60613
Phone: 773/871-1212
Fax: 773/871-3191
staff@livebaittheatre.org
www.livebaittheater.org

Lookingglass Theatre
821 N. Michigan
Chicago, IL 60611
Phone: 773/477-9257
Fax: 773/477-6932
contact@lookingglasstheatre.org
www.lookingglasstheatre.org

L'Opera Piccola
5239 N. Lacrosse
Chicago, IL 60630
Phone: 312/560-1072
Fax: 847/823-3165
sasha@loperapiccola.org
www.loperapiccola.org

Mammals, The
3729 N. Ravenswood, Ste. 138
Chicago, IL 60640
Phone: 773/293-0431
bobfisher@themammals.org
www.themammals.org

Neo-Futurists, The
5153 N. Ashland
Chicago, IL 60640
Phone: 773/878-4557
Fax: 773/878-4514
info@neofuturists.org
www.neofuturist.org

Piven Theatre Workshop
927 Noyes
Evanston, IL 60201
Phone: 847/866-8049
Fax: 847/866-6614
PivenTW@aol.com
www.piventheatreworkshop.com

Playground Theater, The
3341 N. Lincoln
Chicago, IL 60657
Phone: 773/871-3793
Fax: 773/913-6121
webmaster@the-playground.com
www.the-playground.com

Profiles Theatre
4147 N. Broadway
Chicago, IL 60613
Phone: 773/549-1815
ProfilesCo@aol.com
www.Profilestheatre.org

Redmoon Theater
1438 W. Kinzie
Chicago, IL 60622
Phone: 312/850-4430
Fax: 312/850-4430
info@redmoon.org
www.redmoon.org

Remy Bumppo Theatre Co.
3717 N. Ravenswood, Ste. 245
Chicago, IL 60613
Phone: 773/244-8119
Fax: 773/296-9243
info@remybumppo.org

Running a Small Theatre Company

Roadworks
1239 N. Ashland
Chicago, IL 60622
Phone: 773/862-7623
Fax: 773/862-7624
roadworks@ameritech.net
www.roadworks.org

Sangfroid
1518 W. Schriever, Ste. 1
Chicago, IL 60626
Phone: 773/973-1678
larlarland@hotmail.com

Second City
1616 N. Wells
Chicago, IL 60614
Phone: 312/664-4032
Fax: 312/664-9837
www.secondcity.com

Second City E.T.C.
1608 N. Wells
Chicago, IL 60614
Phone: 312/664-4032
Fax: 312/664-9837
bkligerman@secondcity.com
www.Secondcity.com

Shattered Globe Theatre
P.O Box 3540
Chicago, IL 60690
Phone: 312/223-1168
Fax: 312/223-1169
bpudil@nl.edu
www.shatteredglobe.org

Stage Left Theatre
3408 N. Sheffield
Chicago, IL 60657
Phone: 773/883-8830
Fax: 773/472-1336
sltchicago@aol.com
www.stagelefttheatre.com

Steep Theatre Company
3902 N. Sheridan
Chicago, IL 60613
steeptheatre@hotmail.com

Strawdog Theatre Company
3829 N. Broadway
Chicago, IL 60625
Phone: 773/528-9889
Fax: 773/528-7238
info@strawdog.org
www.strawdog.org

Studio Z
c/o Breadline Lab Space
1801 W Byron
Chicago, IL 60613
Phone: 312/543-7920
info@studioz.org
www.studioz.org

TEATRO LUNA
556 W. 18th
Chicago, IL 60616
Phone: 312/829-7552
teatroluna@aol.com
www.teatroluna.org

Theatre Building Chicago
1225 W. Belmont
Chicago, IL 60657
Phone: 773/929-7367
Fax: 773/327-1404
BoxOffice@TheatreBuildingChicago.org
www.TheatreBuildingChicago.org

Theatre of Western Springs
4584 Hampton
Western Springs, IL 60558
Phone: 708/246-4043
Fax: 708/246-4015
ad@theatrewesternsprings.com
www.TheatreWesternSprings.com

Theo Ubique Theatre Company
1434 W. Jarvis, Ste. 2H
Chicago, IL 60626
Phone: 773/370-0235
blochbe@yahoo.com

Tinfish Productions
4247 N. Lincoln
Chicago, IL 60618
Phone: 773/549-1888
Fax: 773/549-1888
Tinfish@Tinfish.org
www.Tinfish.org

Trap Door Productions
1655 W. Cortland
Chicago, IL 60622
Phone: 773/384-0494
Trapdoor@xnet.com
www.trapdoortheatre.com

University of Wisconsin - Parkside Theatre
900 Wood Rd.
Kenosha WI 53141
Phone: 262/595-2352
Fax: 262/595-2271
yohnk@uwp.edu
www.uwp.edu/academic/theatre.arts

Viaduct Theater
3111 N. Western
Chicago, IL 60618
Phone: 773/296-6024
viaduct@mindspring.com
viaducttheater.com

Victory Gardens Theater
2257 N. Lincoln
Chicago, IL 60614
Phone: 773/549-5788
Fax: 773/549-2779
vgtheater@aol.com
www.victorygardens.org

Vittum Theatre
1012 N. Noble
Chicago, IL 60622
Phone: 773/278-7471 ext. 172
Fax: 773/278-2621
info@vittumtheater.org
www.vittumtheater.org

WNEP Theater Foundation
3210-3209 N. Halsted
Chicago, IL 60657
Phone: 773/755-1693
hall@wneptheater.org
www.wneptheater.org

Production Space Rental

Alphabet Soup Productions
P.O. Box 85
Lombard, IL 60148
Phone: 630/932-1555
Fax: 630/665-8465
ABSkidshow@aol.com
absproductions.com

American Theater Company
1909 W. Byron
Chicago, IL 60613
Phone: 773/929-5009
Fax: 773/929-5171
dkiely@atcweb.org
www.atcweb.org

Athenaeum Theatre
2936 N. Southport
Chicago, IL 60657
Phone: 773/935-6860
Fax: 312/935-6878
www.athenaeumtheatre.com
cfoster29@surfbest.net

Bailiwick Repertory Arts Center
1229 W. Belmont
Chicago, IL 60657
Phone: 773/883-1090
Fax: 773/883-2017
Bailiwickr@aol.com
www.bailiwick.org

Breadline Theatre Group
1802 W. Berenice
Chicago, IL 60613
Phone: 773/327-6096
breadline@breadline.org
www.breadline.org

Broadway In Chicago
22 W. Monroe, Ste. 700
Chicago, IL 60603
Phone: 312/751-5513
www.broadwayinchicago.com

Chicago Actors Studio Theatre
1567 N. Milwaukee
Chicago, IL 60622
Phone: 773/735-6400
Fax: 773/767-4151
chiactorstudio@aol.com
actors-studio.net

Chicago Dramatists
1105 W. Chicago
Chicago, IL 60622
Phone: 312/633-0630
Fax: 312/633-0610
NewPlays@ChicagoDramatists.org
www.ChicagoDramatists.org

Chopin Theatre
1543 W. Division
Chicago, IL 60622
Phone: 773/278-1500
www.chopintheatre.com

ComedySportz
2851 N. Halsted
Chicago, IL 60657
Phone: 773/549-8080
Fax: 773/549-8142
mattcsz@mcleodusa.net
www.comedysportzchicago.com

Corn Productions
Cornservatory
4210 N. Lincoln
Chicago, IL 60618
Phone: 773/868-0243
Fax: 773/868-0243
Cornproductions.aol.com
Cornservatory.org

Court Theatre
5535 S. Ellis
Chicago, IL 60637
Phone: 773/702-7005
info@courtheatre.org
www.courttheatre.org

Dominican University Center Stage
7900 W. Division
River Forest, IL 60305
Phone: 708/524-6516
Fax: 708/524-6517
Lwolf@email.dom.edu
www.dom.edu

European Repertory Co.
1839 W. Thomas
Chicago, IL 60622
Phone: 773/972-1678
dg930@hotmail.com

Griffin Theatre Company
5404 N. Clark
Chicago, IL 60640
Phone: 773/769-2228
Fax: 773/769-2228
www.griffintheatre.com

HomeGrown Theatre Company
2617 W. Lawrence
Chicago, IL 60625
Phone: 773/728-6762
Fax: 773/728-6652
homegrownproductions@mac.com
www.homegrowntheatre.org

The House Theatre
4344 N. Bell
Chicago, IL 60618
Phone: 773/583-5657
info@thehousetheatre.com
www.thehousetheatre.com

ImprovOlympic
3541 N. Clark
Chicago, IL 60657
Phone: 773/880-0199
Fax: 773/880-9979
improvolymp@ameritech.net
www.improvolympic.com

Journeymen Theatre Company, The
3915 N. Janssen
Chicago, IL 60613
Phone: 773/857-5395
Fax: 773/529-5781
thejourneymen@aol.com
www.TheJourneymen.org

Live Bait Theater
3914 N. Clark
Chicago, IL 60613
Phone: 773/871-1212
Fax: 773/871-3191
staff@livebaittheatre.org
www.livebaittheater.org

Lookingglass Theatre
821 N. Michigan
Chicago, IL 60611
Phone: 773/477-9257
Fax: 773/477-6932
contact@lookingglasstheatre.org
www.lookingglasstheatre.org

The Neo-Futurists
5153 N. Ashland
Chicago, IL 60640
Phone: 773/878-4557
Fax: 773/878-4514
info@neofuturists.org
www.neofuturist.org

Noble Fool Theater
16 W. Randolph
Chicago, IL 60601
Phone: 312/658-0094
Fax: 312/658-0274
info@noblefool.com
www.noblefool.com

Phoenix Theatre
749 N. Park Ave.
Indianapolis IN 46202
Phone: 317/635-2381
Fax: 317/635-0100
info@phoenixtheatre.org
www.phoenixtheatre.org

Playground Theater
3341 N. Lincoln Ave.
Chicago, IL 60657
Phone: 773/871-3793
Fax: 773/913-6121
webmaster@the-playground.com
www.the-playground.com

Profiles Theatre
4147 N. Broadway
Chicago, IL 60613
Phone: 773/549-1815
ProfilesCo@aol.com
www.Profilestheatre.org

Sangfroid
1518 W. Schriever, Ste. 1
Chicago, IL 60626
Phone: 773/973-1678
larlarland@hotmail.com

Shattered Globe Theatre
P.O Box 3540
Chicago, IL 60690
Phone: 312/223-1168
Fax: 312/223-1169
bpudil@nl.edu
www.shatteredglobe.org

Running a Small Theatre Company

157

the side project
1520 W. Jarvis
Chicago, IL 60626
Phone: 773/973-2150
Fax: 312/335-4277
adam@thesideproject.net
www.thesideproject.net

Stage Left Theatre
3408 N. Sheffield
Chicago, IL 60657
Phone: 773/883-8830
Fax: 773/472-1336
sltchicago@aol.com
www.stagelefttheatre.com

Steep Theatre Company
3902 N. Sheridan
Chicago, IL 60613
steeptheatre@hotmail.com

Strawdog Theatre Company
3829 N. Broadway
Chicago, IL 60625
Phone: 773/528-9889
Fax: 773/528-7238
info@strawdog.org
www.StrawDog.org

Studio Z
c/o Breadline Lab Space
1801 W. Byron
Chicago, IL 60613
Phone: 312/543-7920
info@studioz.org
www.studioz.org

TEATRO LUNA:
556 W. 18th
Chicago, IL 60616
Phone: 312/829-7552
teatroluna@aol.com
www.teatroluna.org

Theatre of Western Springs
4584 Hampton
Western Springs, IL 60558
Phone: 708/246-4043
Fax: 708/246-4015
ad@theatrewesternsprings.com
www.theatrewesternsprings.com

Theo Ubique Theatre Company
1434 W. Jarvis, Ste. 2H
Chicago, IL 60626
Phone: 773/370-0235
blochbe@yahoo.com

TimeLine Theatre Company
615 W. Wellington
Chicago, IL 60657
Phone: 773/281-8463
Fax: 773/281-1134
info@TimeLineTheatre.com
www.TimeLineTheatre.com

Tinfish Productions
4247 N. Lincoln
Chicago, IL 60618
Phone: 773/549-1888
Fax: 773/549-1888
Tinfish@Tinfish.org
www.Tinfish.org

Trap Door Productions
1655 W. Cortland
Chicago, IL 60622
Phone: 773/384-0494
Trapdoor@xnet.com
www.trapdoortheatre.com

**University of Wisconsin-
Parkside Theatre**
900 Wood Rd.
Kenosha WI 53141
Phone: 262/595-2352
Fax: 262/595-2271
yohnk@uwp.edu
www.uwp.edu/academic/theatre.arts

Viaduct Theater
3111 N. Western
Chicago, IL 60618
Phone: 773/296-6024
viaduct@mindspring.com
viaducttheater.com

Victory Gardens Theater
2257 N. Lincoln
Chicago, IL 60614
Phone: 773/549-5788
Fax: 773/549-2779
vgtheater@aol.com
www.victorygardens.org

Vittum Theatre
1012 N. Noble
Chicago, IL 60622
Phone: 773/278-7471x172
Fax: 773/278-2621
info@vittumtheater.org
www.vittumtheater.org

WNEP Theater Foundation
3209 N. Halsted
Chicago, IL 60657
Phone: 773/755-1693
hall@wneptheater.org
www.wneptheater.org

Audience Development

By Christina Biggs

The question of the new millennium for performing arts organizations is how to fill all the empty seats created by a post-9/11 economy. And the answer appears to be a surprising mix of traditional Marketing 101, combined with new technologies and just a bit of creativity.

"The key to audience development is research, research, research. It is the building block of all marketing efforts," says Tres MacDonald, assistant director of programs for the Arts & Business Council of Chicago. "Without research and an understanding of who your audience is and how they behave, an organization is not able to make 'smart' decisions on how to buy media or develop communications for a specific target audience."

Such marketing research generally falls into two categories: primary and secondary. Primary can subsequently be broken down into qualitative (focus groups, in-depth interviews, observational research) and quantitative (surveys by fax, phone, or exit; tracking studies; database mailing).

The sources of secondary research are nearly endless. Some of the more useful include census data (www.census.gov), local library reference desks, the Metropolitan Chicago Information Center (www.mcic.org) and Lexis Nexis (lexis-nexis.com), as well as syndicated data such as Arbitron (www.arbitron.com), SPSS (www.spss.com), American Demographics Magazine or PR Week. Before consulting organizations such as the Arts Marketing Center of Chicago (www.artsbiz-chicago.org/AMC/amchome.htm) or the Arts Marketing Program (www.artsmarketing.org.)—who can offer help in utilizing your research—it is helpful to browse some of these sites and become acquainted with their content and its limits.

For a marketing plan to prove effective, the strategy needs to address basic behaviors in the particular audience group you define. "One thing people always forget is that different groups act differently. Older patrons are more likely to use subscriptions and younger audiences, such as Gen X and Gen Y, have different purchasing habits," says MacDonald. To help identify both the product you are attempting to sell and the specifics that best appeal to your audiences, check out Brand Channel (www.brandchannel.com) and the trending experts at www.faithpopcorn.com.

Free resources from the Arts & Business Council of Chicago include a collection of texts on audience development with titles like E-loyalty, Email Marketing and Permission Marketing. They also offer the Business Volunteers for the Arts program, which recruits, develops and pairs experienced business professionals with appropriate projects. "At Arts & Business Council, we are able to assist organizations with the help of professional consultants," says Macdonald. The volunteers work as pro bono consultants for small to mid-sized arts organizations in areas such as strategic marketing and financial planning. Contact Ebony Vincent at 312/372-1876 ext 229 or evincent@artsbiz-chicago.org for more information.

A&BC also holds monthly workshops for between $35-$50 that are specifically designed to address a range of marketing issues identified by the Chicago arts community. The topics include Market Research and How to Use It, Branding Your Organization and E-Marketing. Call 312/372-1876 ext 229 for more information on this program.

If you do not already belong, you might consider joining the League of Chicago Theatres (www.chicagoplays.com), who provide audience development services for members only. These services include their monthly program book, Chicagoplays; the bi-monthly Chicago Theatre Guide listings; Hot Tix, which sells more than 75,000 half-price day-of or week-of show tickets annually; Play Money gift certificates; and Theatre Fever, a day of free workshops, demonstrations, and other hands-on events to encourage patrons to visit Chicago area theatres. "The League's new strategic plan has given us a sharper focus on audience development and marketing, and we're using every tool in the drawer, from our slick new TV PSAs starring George Wendt and Meshach Taylor and our expanded website to Chicagoplays, the magazine that now serves as the theatre program for more than 50 companies," says Marj Halperin, president and CEO of the League.

The League upped its visibility post-9/11 with the launch of their Streets to Seats program and additional placement of news and feature stories as well as print ads. USA Today called it "the most visible campaign outside New York encouraging theatre attendance after September 11."

Individual theatres also reacted. "Location can be a challenge. And, frankly, it's because of 9/11," says Northlight marketing director Kathy Van Zwoll. "People are choosing to stay closer to home, in the neighborhood." Northlight has spent the past five years marketing to attract hip, city consumers to its Skokie-based theatre. Post-9/11, however, Van Zwoll has also begun teaming up with community partners to bring in their closest potential patrons. One of her newest techniques is placing ads and vouchers in the brown bag promotional stuffers distributed at Old Orchard Shopping Center events across the street from the theatre.

Places like Theatre Building Chicago, who have also seen a hit in their subscription sales since 9/11, are now using their location (on Belmont in Lakeview) to help develop a new local brand. "The audience that currently comes to TBC are the 'true believers,'" says executive director Joan Mazzonelli. "Now we're trying to drive deeper. Attract folks in the neighborhood. Make it a local theatre."

TBC has converted their lobby to a jazzed-up cabaret space and added varied programming, such as a morning matinees series for seniors and an ongoing late night show. "The whole point of the late night cabaret is buzz. This is the hot new place to be—Theatre Building Chicago. It's casual, cheap, and has a local movie feel. But it's live," adds Mazzonelli.

E-marketing has also changed the way theatres sell their shows. It outdoes traditional mail in speed, affordability and effectiveness. The most important tool in an effective email campaign, however, is the use of permission-based marketing. "We're very careful who we send the e-newsletter to," says Goodman marketing director Patricia Nicholson. "I understand. I probably hate spam more than junk mail and telemarketing combined."

E-newsletters allow organizations to do one amazing thing that snail mail never could: look at box office sales the day before a show and offer last-minute, selective savings to only those that are not selling well. "We rigged the computer to bang out a long list to tell us who phoned in or used the Web site or online ticketing services, and found out that we've been getting about a 1 percent return from our e-newsletter," says Nicholson. While that might seem like a miniscule number, 1 percent from something that costs virtually nothing to create and distribute, and adds revenue to production dollars already spent, in reality is quite powerful.

If you are unsure of how to best implement an e-marketing campaign, there are organizations that provide assistance. Arts Eventures (www.artseventures.com) offers e-solutions for and from "people passionate about the arts." They provide services like strategic email marketing, website design and development, strategic consulting and list development services. Also check out their three-volume online Arts Marketing Guidebook, with sections on advice, methods and tales from the field. Target X (www.targetx.com) is another authority in email marketing. They provide a user-friendly, web-based application called eXpress that allows their customers to target and personalize newsletters, track the results and measure the effectiveness.

Chicago-favorite Stagechannel.com, which continues to grow in popularity since its inception last year, is a listings Web site that features minute-long video previews of theatre performances. All productions listed on www.stagechannel.com can also include links to an online ticketing service, the "tell a friend" feature, special online discounts and a complete statistic tracking system that allows organizations to separate hits from different marketing initiatives (postcard mailings, e-newsletters, posters, print ads). "We believe it is essential to create a new 'visual vocabulary' for performing arts marketing, and to provide theatrical coverage on the viewer's schedule," says Marty Higginbotham of the Stage Channel. "Our goal is to continue to develop products and services whose prices can be scaled according to the size of the venue or that can even be subsidized through revenue streams outside of the venues themselves." Call 877/893-8494 for more information.

Running a Small Theatre Company

Press Play: A Guide to PR

By Jill Evans

To properly publicize your production, it is best to retain a public relations firm with a proven track record of generating media placements for similar theatrical events.

These professionals possess the expertise and relationships needed to draw the theatre press' attention to your production. If your budget will not allow for you to hire public relations professionals, you can undertake the following steps to garner publicity for your show.

I. The Press Release

A press release is sometimes your first and most important tool for introducing you, your company or your production to the media. It is also your first chance to get the media excited about your event. It is crucial that the release is accurate, factual and as detailed as possible, but should generally not exceed two pages.

A good format to follow for a press release is below:

FOR IMMEDIATE RELEASE
Date of Release

Contact: Your Name
Your Company
Your phone number
Your email address

THE HEADLINE SHOULD STATE THE MOST IMPORTANT FACTS ABOUT YOUR PRODUCTION

Include the location and the date(s) in the subhead, as well as any special feature that was not highlighted in the headline.

The opening paragraph of a press release should include the title, a brief one-sentence description of the project, any well-known names involved in the production, and date, time and location. The description in this paragraph and the well-known names are going to be what intrigues the reporter to read the rest of the release.

The second paragraph should again include the title of the play, as well as a more in-depth description. This description may go into the third paragraph. Be sure to be as concise as possible, offering as much information as you can about the production without editorializing. Stick to the facts and allow the journalist to form opinions about your show. These paragraphs, as with the entire release, should be well written with correct grammar, accuracy and factual information. A reporter will be very suspicious or dismissive if they come to realize the release has any inaccuracy.

Don't forget that the descriptive paragraphs are what make the reporter excited about your play. These paragraphs can also provide a starting ground for creating story angles. There are many different sections to a newspaper where your play might fit in to a story. Keep potential story angles in mind when thinking about who will receive your release.

Brief biographies of those involved in the production should be mentioned toward the end of your release. All actors involved in the production should be mentioned by name and character. Include in the bios any career highlights or awards the cast or creative team may have received. If notable, mention other companies or productions they might be involved with, especially if that company has a good reputation in Chicago. Don't forget to include the director's name and brief bio and any company information you would like to mention.

The final paragraph of the press release should restate the vital facts. Name of production, the company and producer of the production, and dates, times, location, ticket price and box office number should be included. If there is a Web site to purchase tickets or receive more information, include that here as well.

II. Media Database

Knowing the media is key to the success of your campaign. Reading the newspapers daily and researching the types of articles written by reporters covering the arts beat is the first and best place to begin. Your press release should go to the major arts critics, editors, photo editors, feature reporters, calendar listing editors and freelancers. It sounds like a big list, but every writer has different areas of accountability, and you never know who is going to be interested in your play. Calendar listing editors alone will ensure your placement in the listings for theatre events. You can receive editor contact information in the paper, usually located on the inside cover of the section you are pitching.

Don't forget about the smaller neighborhood and targeted publications when distributing your release. These publications are usually very supportive of arts events and are a great way to obtain local coverage. Pick up papers wherever you see them and read through the publication to determine if the paper covers events similar to yours. If so, look for the box of editorial information and include that publication on your mailing list. Always send your information to the editor if you are unsure who should receive your release. Once you begin pitch calls, you can have a conversation with the editor about who else might be interested in receiving the release in the future.

Once you have mailed your press release and begin follow-up calls, you will soon see how quickly your database grows. One talk with an editor could lead you to a features reporter, which could lead you to a freelancer. Take good notes about the reporters you talk to and be sure to get their full names, phone number, email, address and preferred method of communication. It is also helpful to inquire about the publication's deadlines. Add this information to your database.

III. The Pitch

Once the press release is sealed, stamped and delivered, it is time to begin the pitch calls. If you don't have the phone numbers of the people you are pitching, dial the general number of the publication and ask for the editor by name. When you get the reporter on the phone, remember to clearly state who you are and why you are calling. Let the reporter know why your play is special. Add

Running a Small Theatre Company

163

any of the highlighted information in the press release. Be enthusiastic, but understand that the reporter might be on deadline and may have to call you back. Be knowledgeable about what the reporter covers.

Know your play and the cast. A million possible angles can be found in the play alone, not to mention the cast. If the play has an issue that is topical, trendy, controversial, etc., you potentially have a feature story on your hands! The media might not see this angle just from reading your press release (and you can't be sure they all read your press release!), so it is important you stress your pitch. The cast can also be where a feature story is found. A good idea is to pass out PR questionnaires to all of the cast and production team. General questions can be asked in the questionnaire—for example, hometown, local address, ethnicity, past plays, companies, awards, movie/commercial history, etc. There are numerous niche publications that will feature a member of your team in their publication if it is of interest and relates to their audience.

IV. Photographs

A strong, professionally shot photograph is a very important part of a successful campaign. Publications love to run a striking image. It is sometimes hard to fit a photo shoot into your production budget, but know that if you have a strong image, it will get printed, along with your show information. If you have it in your budget, it is smart to send images out with your press releases. One image per editor will do, if you are worried about quantity. Since email has become an increasingly popular and reliable way to communicate, you can save money by distributing digital images. Nearly all publications have a way to receive images by email. This will again require a call to the editor to inquire about proper email addresses to send images. Some publications are very specific about where to send images, due to inbox overload.

There are many photographers in the city to fit every budget, so don't forget how important it is to have photographs shot for your production.

V. The PR Timeline

Develop a timeline to follow that begins at least three months prior to the opening of your play.

Three months out: Press releases go out to monthly publications.
Photo shoot takes place.

Ten weeks out: Follow up calls to monthly publications. Be sure they are at least including your play in the calendar listings. Ask if they would like a photo, and what their deadline is to receive it (usually about 6 weeks before going to press).

Begin to identify your target media for the weekly and daily media.

Six weeks out: Press releases and images go out to all weekly and daily print media and all arts-related Web sites, radio and television stations.

Create your hit list for the pitch calls. Begin with the publications in which you most want to be included.

Five weeks out: Pitch calls begin to all daily and weekly media. If you do not get a reporter on the phone, leave a brief message explaining the reason for your call and where you can be reached.

Four weeks out: Continue pitching. Some reporters won't return your call, so it is important to follow up on your messages but avoid being too pushy.

Distribute a professional-looking opening night invitation to reviewers.

Three weeks out: By this time, you should have a good idea of who is interested in covering your play. Keeping good contact with these reporters is essential to locking in your story. Make sure they have everything they need, help set up interviews, provide additional information, etc. Their deadline will be coming up, so make sure you know when it is and what they'll need.

Two weeks out: Interviews will be happening, and the reporters will probably need additional photos mailed or original photos re-mailed. Begin contacting the media for reviews. Don't forget the Internet media, as they now play an important role in reviewing as well.

One week out: Prepare for opening night. Blow up any advance stories you may have to decorate your lobby, and prepare press kits.

VI. Press Kits

Your press kit should be offered to members of the media who attend your performance. You should hand the press kit to the reporter with his or her ticket to the play. A press kit should include:

- Press Release
- Company Bio
- Cast Bio
- Program
- Photographs
- Any past media highlights you wish to include or company history information.

Running a Small Theatre Company

PR Firms

Carol Fox & Associates
1412 W. Belmont
Chicago, IL 60657
Phone: 773/327-3830
Fax: 773/327-3834

GSA Advertising
211 E. Ontario, Ste. 1750
Chicago, IL 60611
Phone: 312/664-1999
Fax: 312/664-9017

Jay Kelly- off Loop PR
2254 W. Grand
Chicago, IL 60612
Phone: 312/633-1992
Fax: 312/633-1994
offloop@earthlink.net

K.D.—P.R.
2732 N. Clark
Chicago, IL 60614
Phone: 773/248-7680
Fax: 773/883-1323

Margie Korshak, Inc.
875 N. Michigan, Ste. 2750
Chicago, IL 60611
Phone: 312/751-2121
Fax: 312/751-1422

PitBull PR
3210 N. Halsted, Ste. 3
Chicago, IL 60657
Phone: 773/879-4610
hall@wneptheater.org

PitBull PR offers the small theater owner: press releases and follow-up, graphic design for posters, postcards and ads, web design and web banners, flexible pricing.
See our ad on page 63.

Beth Silverman
1 E. Superior, Ste. 104
Chicago, IL 60611
Phone: 312/932-9950
Fax: 312/932-9951

Andra Velis Simon
Phone: 773/278-3243

Tree Falls Productions
Karin McKie
Phone: 773/276-3434
kmckie@msn.com

Running a Small Theatre Company

CHAPTER 8
LIVING

The Seagull
Redmoon Theatre

Health Insurance—
Don't Live Without It

By Christina Biggs

Artists know all too well about the healthcare crisis in America. More than 30 percent of them are underinsured or living without coverage altogether. For many, the search for suitable, affordable insurance is hopeless and overwhelming. But there is a dedicated group of administrators, advocates and physicians in Chicago who are working hard to help artists make well-informed decisions about their well-being.

The best place to begin a search for healthcare information is on the Web at the **Artists' Health Insurance Resource Center** (AHIRC), accessible through the **Actors' Fund** site (www.actorsfund.org/ahirc). AHIRC is an online database with 12 sections and more than 60 categories of information not only about getting and keeping health insurance, but also about receiving financial assistance for medical bills, choosing a doctor or medical group, understanding benefits complaints and appeals, and advocating for change in the healthcare system.

Once there, look over the general information section to learn about consumer rights and protections in Illinois and guides to types of insurance. If you are uninsured, AHIRC managing director Jim Brown suggests determining if you are a candidate for a government program. "First, look to see if you're eligible for free or subsidized," he says. "It's the least costly and it's not just Medicaid or Medicare. Many people mistakenly think they're not eligible for that type of plan, yet they still may be."

The AHIRC site includes links to programs for low-income people (including Medicaid), seniors (including Medicare) and children, as well as eligibility calculators and worksheets, Illinois state and county health departments and other state-sponsored plans. Another general resource for these types of benefits is the **State of Illinois Department of Insurance** (www.ins.state.il.us).

If you do find, after all, that you are not eligible for a government-subsidized plan, the next best thing is a group plan. Organizations that frequently offer such plans include employers, chambers of commerce, unions and fraternal groups. "Group plans are a better option because they're less expensive and more benefit rich," says Brown.

If you are not a member of a union, you should probably not consider joining for insurance benefits alone. The cost of membership ($1,000 at Equity) will not be well spent if you are not in need of the union's other advantages. "Membership in Equity doesn't provide insurance," says Kathryn Lamkey, Actors' Equity's Central Regional Director. "It does open the opportunity to work under contract that can lead to qualification for insurance."

But if union membership is something you have been considering, union benefit packages are high quality and generally at the top of members' priority lists. "Members find access to health insurance to be of such importance that many of our contracts have health insurance rates (paid in total by the producer) that represent 60 percent of the weekly salary. We have given it such great importance that we have often sacrificed salary gains to improve the health payment—to keep as many actors qualified for the insurance, and to make that insurance coverage as comprehensive as possible," adds Lamkey.

Benefits and eligibility vary from union to union. SAG/AFTRA eligibility is based on earnings, while Equity requires their members to work a defined number of hours. For a complete list of unions, visit the AFL-CIO Web page at www.aflcio.org. AHIRC also provides a list of links to entertainment industry unions and guilds, as well as chambers of commerce brokers and other artist groups.

One such artist group listed on AHIRC is the Chicago Artists' Coalition (www.caconline.org), a non-profit service organization open to all artists. CAC provides a full spectrum of benefits, from Blue Cross and Fortis to Golden Rule, Unicare and United Health Care. Benefits vary from a traditional (choosing any doctor or hospital) to an HMO (a health maintenance organization offering preventive and wellness benefits through specific doctors and hospitals). They also offer short-term and international health plans and dental care.

The least attractive and most expensive option in health insurance is direct purchase. AHIRC provides information on the types of direct-purchase health insurance out there, insurers and managed care companies in Illinois, dental and vision providers, and health insurance agents and internet insurance brokers. But this is one area where it may be more prudent to seek professional, face-to-face advice. "Investigate who is eligible, what your rights and protections are, and insurance companies' current rates," warns Brown. "Most people believe that with direct purchase they don't have rights and protections. Know what's permitted before you buy."

One of the foremost experts on the topic in Chicago is Lenore Janecek of Lenore Janecek & Associates, Ltd. (LJA). She helped create AHIRC by obtaining an NEA grant and is the author of the book "Health Insurance: A Guide for Artists, Consultants, Entrepreneurs and Other Self-Employed." LJA provides cost-effective health care and employee benefits for both businesses and individuals. "We found that one size doesn't fit all," says Janecek. So she begins every consultation with a barrage of questions, ranging from "Do you travel for work?" to "Are you expecting full-time employment in the near future?"

"We have a myriad of products, up to 15 actually. By asking the questions, we can get that down to two or three. Then they can do the shopping here, so to say." To contact Janecek, call 312/214-3532 or e-mail her at ljanecek@aol.com.

Just because you obtain insurance, however, does not necessarily mean you are getting quality healthcare. AHIRC includes a general guide to using your health insurance effectively and navigating the health care system. There is also information on the site about donated services, community clinics and prescription drug programs.

Living

The best resource for free and sliding scale clinics in Chicagoland is the **Gilead Outreach and Referral Center** (www.gileadcenter.org), which connects uninsured and underinsured individuals and families throughout metropolitan Chicago with affordable health care benefits and the services for which they are eligible. They also tout publicly supported health insurance options, help eligible residents enroll and obtain benefits, and help residents find and receive affordable primary and preventive healthcare.

Community Health Center (CHC) is the place to get affordable health care through Gilead. Care is offered to all individuals, regardless of health insurance status, income level or residency status. They provide primary health care, pediatrics, internal medicine, obstetrics and related testing and laboratory work, and they accept private and public insurance, as well as an income-based sliding fee from persons without health insurance.

While CHCs are low-cost, they are not free in most cases. Some charge a flat amount per visit that varies depending on income, and others offer discounted rates that also vary based on income. If you do not have insurance, bring proof of income (a recent check stub or your W-2 form), proof of address (utility bill or rent receipt) and photo identification to your appointment (make sure to call ahead). There are literally dozens of CHCs in the Chicago metropolitan area. A complete list is available on Gilead's Web site, from the Illinois Primary Health Care Association at 312/692-3000 or the Gilead Outreach and Referral Center at 312/906-6024.

One other program that offers help specifically for people in the arts is the **Health in the Arts Program** (HARTS at www.uic.edu/sph/glakes/harts/). This program was founded by Dr. David Hinkamp, former chair of the Arts-Medicine Section of the American College of Occupational and Environmental Medicine, and Dr. Katherine Duvall, on faculty at UIC's School of Public Health and currently researching the health needs of artists. Their mission is to diagnose, treat and prevent arts-related disorders among people working in the arts and to address the special risks that arts workers face, from exposure to toxic materials to hazardous physical conditions and repetitive motion disorders.

Dr. Hinkamp and Dr. Duvall practice occupational medicine and, therefore, do not offer primary care. "We're donating time, so we have limits and must confine our practice to arts-related problems, not general care. We don't want to mislead people that they can come for anything," says Dr. Duvall. HARTS is located at 901 S. Wolcott, Room #E144, in Chicago. To schedule an appointment or to obtain additional information, call 312/996-7420.

The Actor's Tax: A Guide for the Perplexed

By Greg Mermel, CPA

You finished your degree and moved to the Big City to pursue your dream. On arrival, you may have even flung your hat off and started doing your version of Gene Kelly's "Gotta Dance" number—until you realized it played a lot better at the drama department's graduation party than in Chicago's Greyhound bus station. Soon, though, your enthusiasm is tempered by the discovery that there is a lot to this business of being an actor that you never learned in school.

The business of being an actor is, in fact, almost never taught by universities. Most come no closer than teaching audition technique. Some offer elective courses with titles like "Professional Survival for the Actor," but as a frequent guest lecturer in those classes, I know that most students choose not to take them. The business part is something generally learned in a haphazard manner, often from those who know little more than you do.

Some of the folk wisdom is pretty good: "Always be nice to the lobby monitors at auditions because their feedback will reach the director." Some is plausible, if slightly dubious: "Always show teeth in your headshot, or casting directors will assume you have bad teeth." And, then, there is the tax and finance folklore. Some of it is felonious, much of it merely dumb, and none of it repeated here for fear people will act upon it. Here are some tax and business points you did not learn in school:

Report All Of Your Income On Your Tax Returns

There is always the temptation to leave out the undocumented stuff, either amounts too small for the payer to need to issue a 1099 form, or those that you are assured are "under the table." Resist the temptation. Not only are you an honest person, but there are also good, practical reasons.

You want to be able to deduct the expenses you incur as an artist. To be deductible, expenses must be incurred in a present trade or business of yours; the cost of entering a new trade or business is not deductible. So when, exactly, do you become a professional actor? When you were first paid for your work is one logical marker, though not the only usable one. Reporting that one or two hundred dollars of income may justify thousands of dollars in deductions. Similarly, you may eventually have the really skimpy year, when you live on the earnings from your civilian job. It is much easier to reassure the Internal Revenue Service (IRS) that you are still in the trade or business of being an actor if the income line bears a figure other than zero.

Be especially wary of the theatre producer or restauranteur who assures you that money is being paid "under the table," and therefore need not be reported. The

Living

producer might merely be naive, but the restauranteur is almost certainly dishonest. If you're not reporting the income, it helps the payer hide his tax fraud—and if he or she gets caught, you could be criminally liable. More likely, you would be paying off back taxes and penalties for a very long time. The same applies if you get audited. They will check for unreported income, both by asking you to explain every single deposit in your bank account and by testing whether you can live where and how you do on your reported income and assets.

Know Which Expenses You Can Deduct

The basic concept is that you can deduct ordinary and necessary expenses incurred in your trade or business. But before you start interpreting those three simple words, "ordinary and necessary," remember that the IRS and the federal courts have been doing exactly that for almost 90 years. In their view (the only one that matters), an expense is "ordinary" if it is either (a) customary or usual in the taxpayer's business, or (b) an unusual expense reasonably related to the taxpayer's trade or business. A "necessary" expense is one that is appropriate and helpful in developing the taxpayer's business, or so you thought at the time. Expenses that turn out to be unwise, or even stupid, can still be deductible.

The ordinary and necessary nature of some expenses is obvious and should present no problem to the IRS: agents' commissions, headshots, PerformInk subscriptions. In other areas, though, the line between personal and business expenses can be fuzzy. Federal authorities have established many rules that either (a) try to draw a clear, if arbitrary, line or (b) require specific documentation. Clear rules include those governing home office deductions (allowed if certain requirements are met) and appearance enhancing medical procedures, such as tooth veneers or Botox® (not deducible). Business meals and entertainment expenses are among those with special documentation rules. And automobile expenses have both types of restrictions.

Make Clear Distinctions Between Your Varied Trades Or Businesses

If you are a performer with a day job, you have at least two trades or businesses, and probably no more than two. Stage actor, voice-over artist, hand model, trade show spokesperson, cabaret singer, composer, director, stage manager, set designer, dramaturg, and vocal coach are really all part of a single activity in your life, clearly differentiated from waiter or office temp or network administrator. Don't waste energy attempting to make nuanced distinctions that would tax a Talmudic scholar.

Keep Good Records

Some performers, in a burst of insecurity, believe they are the only people in the world who do not keep precise, neat, perfectly balanced records of the money they spend, and that the IRS has therefore reserved a special section of hell for them. Actually, the only person I have ever known who knew, to the penny, exactly how and where he spent every bit of money was a fellow certified public accountant. For him, it was a form of obsessive-compulsive behavior. I once saw him spend an hour laboring over his figures, trying to account for 35 cents out of a $50 check he had cashed a week earlier. This is not normal.

Focus instead on the information you need for your taxes (such as income and deductible expenses) and to manage your life (you can't budget if you don't have a fair idea of what you are spending). Within this, differentiate data from documentation. To prepare a tax return, I need to know what my client spent on each type of deductible expense he or she has; I do not need the shoebox full of small bits of paper. But if the IRS comes a-knocking, those receipts, canceled checks and credit card statements are needed to prove not only how much you spent, but where, when and why.

If you make a habit of using checks or credit cards for deductible expenses and jotting down the few out-of-pocket cash ones, you can pretty easily assemble expense data that is at least 98 percent complete, and that is close enough.

Clients sometimes present me with lists of deductible expenses in which every amount ends in "00." I know, even before asking, that they have estimated these numbers. There is nothing inherently wrong with that. There is even an old Supreme Court case that allows you to estimate, provided that you can otherwise demonstrate that you spent the money. Demonstrating that, however, may not be easy. The court's ruling is really meant to cover documentation lost in catastrophes, not laziness. I always caution these clients to be sure they have underlying documents that, when added, will come close to the estimates.

There Are Records You Must Keep

Keep your tax returns forever. Keep the documents supporting the figures in the returns for seven years from when the return was due or when you actually file it, whichever is later. For long-lived assets, figure the seven years from when you sell it or when it is fully depreciated.

Live Beneath Your Means

Not within them, beneath them. Hard as it may be when you are not making much money, keeping some around is vital for staying focused on your professional goals. Taking whatever work comes along because you are dead broke is not a way to build a career. Until the first time you do it, you cannot imagine what a luxury turning down an ill-conceived or unsuitable project can be.

Be Honest With Yourself In Financial Matters

Particularly at the fuzzy edge between personal and business expenses, consider the expenditure carefully. If you are not comfortable saying it was for business, don't deduct it. Pay attention to what you make, and to what you spend, and to what you owe in taxes. Denial is no healthier here than in any other aspect of life.

Trust Everyone, But Cut The Cards

Living

Accountants and Tax Preparers

American Express Tax and Business Services
30 S. Wacker, Ste. 2600
Chicago, IL 60606
Phone: 312/634-4318
Fax: 312/207-2954

Bob Behr
4738 N. LaPorte
Chicago, IL 60630
Phone: 773/685-7721
Fax: 773/283-9839

David P. Cudnowski, Ltd.
70 W. Madison, Ste. 5330
Chicago, IL 60602
Phone: 312/759-1040
Fax: 312/759-1042
www.lawyers.com/talentlaw

David Turrentine, E.A.
Income Tax Service
3907 N. Sacramento
Chicago, IL 60618
Phone: 773/509-1798
Fax: 773/509-1806

Gerald Bauman & Company
75 E. Wacker, Ste. 400
Chicago, IL 60601
Phone: 312/726-6868
Fax: 312/726-3683

H&R Block
179 W. Washington
Chicago, IL 60602
Phone: 312/424-0268
Fax: 312/424-0278
www.hrblock.com

H. Gregory Mermel
2835 N. Sheffield, Ste. 311
Chicago, IL 60657
Phone: 773/525-1778
Fax: 773/525-3209

Joel N. Goldblatt, Ltd.
100 N. LaSalle, Ste. 1910
Chicago, IL 60602
Phone: 312/372-9322
Fax: 312/372-2905

Katten, Muchin & Zavis
525 W. Monroe, Ste. 1600
Chicago, IL 60661
Phone: 312/902-5200
Fax: 312/902-1061

Weiner & Lahn, PC
900 Ridge Rd., Ste. F
Munster, IN 46321
Phone: 708/895-6400

Attorneys

Chicago Bar Association
Lawyer Referral
321 S. Plymouth
Chicago, IL 60604-3997
Phone: 312/554-2000
Fax: 312/554-2054
www.chicagobar.org

Chicago Volunteer Legal Services
100 N. LaSalle, Ste. 900
Chicago, IL 60602
Phone: 312/332-1624

Dale M. Golden
25 E. Washington, Ste. 1400
Chicago, IL 60602
Phone: 312/201-9730
Fax: 312/236-6686
www.dalegoldenlaw.com

David P. Cudnowski, Ltd.
70 W. Madison, Ste. 5330
Chicago, IL 60602
Phone: 312/759-1040
Fax: 312/759-1042
www.lawyers.com/talentlaw

Fred Wellisch
1021 W. Adams, Ste. 102
Chicago, IL 60607
Phone: 312/829-2300
Fax: 312/829-3729

Jay B. Ross & Associates, PC
838 W. Grand, Ste. 2W
Chicago, IL 60622-6565
Phone: 312/633-9000
Fax: 312/633-9090
www.jaybross.com

JoAnne Guillemette
311 S. Wacker, Ste. 4550
Chicago, IL 60606
Phone: 312/697-4788
Fax: 312/697-4799

Joel N. Goldblatt, Ltd.
100 N. LaSalle, Ste. 1910
Chicago, IL 60602
Phone: 312/372-9322
Fax: 312/372-2905

Katten, Muchin & Zavis
525 W. Monroe, Ste. 1600
Chicago, IL 60661
Phone: 312/902-5200
Fax: 312/902-1061

Lawyers for the Creative Arts
213 W. Institute, Ste. 401
Chicago, IL 60610
Phone: 312/944-2787
Fax: 312/944-2195
www.cityofchicago.org/culturalaffairs/Cul
turalProg

Mangum, Smietanka & Johnson, LLC
35 E. Wacker, Ste. 2130
Chicago, IL 60601
Phone: 312/368-8500

Timothy S. Kelley
55 E. Washington, Ste. 1441
Chicago, IL 60602
Phone: 312/641-3560

Robert Labate
Holland Knight, LLC
131 S. Dearborn, Ste. 3000
Chicago, IL 60603
Phone: 312/263-3600

Tom Fezzey
600 W. Roosevelt Rd., Ste. B1
Wheaton, IL 60187
Phone: 630/909-0909
Fax: 630/839-1923
www.lawyers.com/fezzey

William Borah and Associates
39 S. LaSalle, Ste. 915
Chicago, IL 60611
Phone: 708/799-0066

Insurance

Myers-Briggs and Company, Inc.
125 S. Wacker, Ste. 1800
Chicago, IL 60606
Phone: 312/263-3215
Fax: 312/263-0979
Paczolt Financial Group
913 Hillgrove
LaGrange, IL 60525
Phone: 708/579-3128
Fax: 708/579-0236
www.paczolt.com

Ronald Shapero Insurance Associates
260 E. Chestnut, Ste. 3406
Chicago, IL 60611
Phone: 312/337-7133

Movie Theatres

Davis Theatre
4614 N. Lincoln
Chicago, IL 60625
Phone: 773/784-0893

Esquire Theater
58 E. Oak
Chicago, IL 60611
Phone: 312/280-0101

Facets Multimedia
1517 W. Fullerton
Chicago, IL 60614
Phone: 773/281-9075
Fax: 773/929-5437
www.facets.org

Fine Arts Theatres
418 S. Michigan
Chicago, IL 60611
Phone: 312/939-3700

Logan Theatre
2646 N. Milwaukee
Chicago, IL 60647
Phone: 773/252-0627

Music Box
3733 N. Southport
Chicago, IL 60613
Phone: 773/871-6604
www.musicboxtheatre.com

The Vic Theatre (Brew & View)
3145 N. Sheffield
Chicago, IL 60657
Phone: 312/618-VIEW
www.victheatre.com

Three Penny Theatre
2424 N. Lincoln
Chicago, IL 60614
Phone: 773/935-5744

Village North
6746 N. Sheridan
Chicago, IL 60626
Phone: 773/764-9100
www.villagetheatres.com

Living

Village Theater
1548 N. Clark
Chicago, IL 60622
Phone: 312/642-2403

Thrift Stores

Ark Thrift Shop
1302 N. Milwaukee
Chicago, IL 60622
Phone: 773/862-5011
www.arkchicago.org

Ark Thrift Shop
3345 N. Lincoln
Chicago, IL 60657
Phone: 773/248-1117
www.arkchicago.org

Brown Elephant Resale
3651 N. Halsted
Chicago, IL 60657
Phone: 773/549-5943

Brown Elephant Resale
3939 N. Ashland
Chicago, IL 60657
Phone: 773/244-2930

Disgraceland
3338 N. Clark
Chicago, IL 60657
Phone: 773/281-5875

Kismet Vintage Clothing and Furniture
2923 N. Southport
Chicago, IL 60657
Phone: 773/528-4497

Ragstock
812 W. Belmont, 2nd Flr.
Chicago, IL 60657
Phone: 773/868-9263
Fax: 773/868-6819
www.ragstock.com

Salvation Army Thrift Store
Phone: 773/477-1771
www.salvationarmy.org

*There are more than 20 Salvation Army
stores in Chicago. Visit their Web site to
find a convenient location.*

Threads
2327 N. Milwaukee
Chicago, IL 60622
Phone: 773/276-6411

Unique Thrift Store
3000 S. Halsted
Chicago, IL 60608
Phone: 312/842-0942

White Elephant Shop
2380 N. Lincoln
Chicago, IL 60614
Phone: 773/883-6184

Acupuncture

Advance Center
55 E. Washington, Ste. 1310
Chicago, IL 60602
Phone: 312/553-2020
Fax: 312/553-5128

American Acupuncture Association
65 E. Wacker
Chicago, IL 60601
Phone: 312/853-3732

Chicago Acupuncture Clinic
3723 N. Southport
Chicago, IL 60613
Phone: 773/871-0342
Fax: 773/871-0348

East Point Associates, Ltd.
1525 E. 53rd, Ste. 705
Chicago, IL 60615
Phone: 773/955-9643
Fax: 773/955-9953

Chiropractic Chicago
407 W. North
Chicago, IL 60610
Phone: 312/255-9500

Graham Chiropractic
5344 N. Lincoln
Chicago, IL 60625
Phone: 773/769-6666
Fax: 773/334-1696

Franklin D. Ing
2451 N. Lincoln
Chicago, IL 60614
Phone: 773/525-2444
Fax: 773/525-9989

**Progressive Chiropractic
Rehabilitation & Wellness Center**
2816 N. Sheffield
Chicago, IL 60657
Phone: 773/525-WELL
Fax: 773/525-9397
www.progressivechiro.net

Seaman Chiropractic Center
4941 W. Foster
Chicago, IL 60630
Phone: 773/545-2233
Fax: 773/545-8383

Ton Shen Health, Inc.
2131 S. Archer, Ste. B&C
Chicago, IL 60616
Phone: 312/842-2775
Fax: 312/842-1553

AIDS Resources

Harambee Wellness Center
1515 E. 52nd, 2nd Flr.
Chicago, IL 60615
Phone: 773/925-6877

Horizons Anti-Violence Hotline
Phone: 773/871-2273
www.horizonsonline.org

Horizons Community Service
961 W. Montana
Chicago, IL 60614
Phone: 773/472-6469
Alt. Phone: 800/AID-AIDS
www.horizonsonline.org

Howard Brown Health Center
4025 N. Sheridan
Chicago, IL 60613
Phone: 773/388-1600
www.howardbrown.org

Test Positive Aware Network
5537 N. Broadway
Chicago, IL 60657
Phone: 773/989-9400
Fax: 773/989-9494
www.tpan.com

Chiropractors

Advance Center
55 E. Washington, Ste. 1310
Chicago, IL 60602
Phone: 312/553-2020
Fax: 312/553-5128

Belmont Health Care
2110 W. Belmont
Chicago, IL 60618
Phone: 773/404-0909

Chicago Chiropractic Center
30 S. Michigan, Ste. 400
Chicago, IL 60603
Phone: 312/726-1353
Fax: 312/726-5238

Chicago Neck and Back Institute
5700 W. Fullerton, Ste. 1
Chicago, IL 60639
Phone: 773/237-8660
Fax: 773/237-3159

Chiropractic Chicago
407 W. North
Chicago, IL 60610
Phone: 312/255-9500

Chiropractic Health Care
911 W. Belmont
Chicago, IL 60657
Phone: 773/665-4400

Chislof Chiropractic Center
7448 N. Harlem
Chicago, IL 60631
Phone: 773/763-0400

Graham Chiropractic
5344 N. Lincoln
Chicago, IL 60625
Phone: 773/769-6666
Fax: 773/334-1696

Greater Chicago Chiropractic
561 W. Diversey, Ste. 221
Chicago, IL 60614
Phone: 773/871-7766
Fax: 773/871-0781

Franklin D. Ing
2451 N. Lincoln
Chicago, IL 60614
Phone: 773/525-2444
Fax: 773/525-9989

Progressive Chiropractic Rehabilitation & Wellness Center
2816 N. Sheffield
Chicago, IL 60657
Phone: 773/525-WELL
Fax: 773/525-9397
www.progressivechiro.net

Seaman Chiropractic Center
4941 W. Foster
Chicago, IL 60630
Phone: 773/545-2233
Fax: 773/545-8383

Stiles Chiropractic Offices
48 E. Chicago
Chicago, IL 60611
Phone: 312/642-1138

Living

Counselors

A Creative Change
111 N. Wabash, Ste. 1320
Chicago, IL 60602
Phone: 312/939-9394
Fax: 312/939-9594
www.reducestress.com

Chicago Women's Health Center
3435 N. Sheffield
Chicago, IL 60657
Phone: 773/935-6126

Great Lakes Psychological Providers
111 N. Wabash, Ste. 1408
Chicago, IL 60602
Phone: 312/443-1400
Fax: 312/443-1307

Ann L. Hammon, MD
550 W. Surf, Ste. 101C
Chicago, IL 60657
Phone: 773/296-2195

Harambee Wellness Center
1515 E. 52nd, 2nd Flr.
Chicago, IL 60615
Phone: 773/925-6877

Hartgrove Hospital
520 N. Ridgeway
Chicago, IL 60624
Phone: 773/722-3113
Fax: 773/722-6361

Howard Brown Health Center
4025 N. Sheridan
Chicago, IL 60613
Phone: 773/388-1600

Institute for Psychoanalysis
122 S. Michigan, Ste. 1300
Chicago, IL 60603
Phone: 312/922-7474
Fax: 312/922-5656

Ruth Landis
5054 N. Hamlin
Chicago, IL 60625
Phone: 773/732-3183
Fax: 773/463-3683

Build inner safety so that creativity flows naturally and spontaneously while preparing the actor technically for auditions (monologues, on-camera, cold-reading) and performance experience. As a longtime acting coach and certified body-psychotherapist and hypnotherapist, we explore mind/body/emotion

awareness around performance anxiety, blocks, and creating ease with self using work rooted in Alexander, Feldenkrais, and Gestalt therapy. Ruth coaches actors, is in private practice, and has taught as Victory Gardens, Northwestern, Columbia and Roosevelt University.

Carol Moss
LCSW, Life Coach
847/251-7248
csmoss@aol.com
www.carolmoss.com

Anxiety - Overcome performance fears
Body Image - Feel at home in your body

See our ad on page 182.

Panic Anxiety Recovery Center
680 N. Lake Shore, Ste. 1325
Chicago, IL 60611
Phone: 312/642-7954
Fax: 312/642-7951

Health Clubs

Bally Total Fitness
2828 N. Clark
Chicago, IL 60657
Phone: 773/929-6900
www.ballytotalfitness.com

Chicago Fitness Center
3131 N. Lincoln
Chicago, IL 60657
Phone: 773/549-8181
Fax: 773/549-4622
www.chicagofitnesscenter.com

Crunch
2727 N. Lincoln
Chicago, IL 60614
Phone: 773/477-8400
Class hotline: 800/409-4550

Know No Limits
5121 N. Clark
Chicago, IL 60640
Phone: 773/334-4728

Lehmann Sports Club
2700 N. Lehmann
Chicago, IL 60614
Phone: 773/871-8300
Fax: 773/871-3506
www.lehmannsportsclub.com

One on One Fitness
Personal Training Service, Inc.
Phone: 312/642-4235
Fax: 312/642-7686

Webster Fitness Club
957 W. Webster
Chicago, IL 60614
Phone: 773/248-2006
Fax: 773/248-3195
www.websterfitness.com

Women's Workout World
208 S. LaSalle
Chicago, IL 60604
Phone: 312/357-0001
www.w3body.com

World Gym
909 W. Montrose
Chicago, IL 60613
Phone: 773/348-1212

New City YMCA
1515 N. Halsted
Chicago, IL 60622
Phone: 312/440-7272
www.ymca.net

*For other YMCA locations, visit their
Web site.*

Health Food Stores

Life Spring
3178 N. Clark
Chicago, IL 60657
Phone: 773/327-1023
Fax: 773/327-1030

Sherwyn's
645 W. Diversey
Chicago, IL 60614
Phone: 773/477-1934

Whole Foods Market
1000 W. North
Chicago, IL 60622
Phone: 312/587-0648
www.wholefoods.com

Whole Foods Market
3300 N. Ashland
Chicago, IL 60657
Phone: 773/244-4200
www.wholefoods.com

Living

Hypnotists

A Creative Change
111 N. Wabash, Ste. 1320
Chicago, IL 60602
Phone: 312/939-9394
Fax: 312/939-9594
www.reducestress.com

Associated Psychologists and Therapists
77 W. Washington, Ste. 1519
Chicago, IL 60602
Phone: 312/630-1001
Fax: 312/630-1342
www.psychologists.org

Gerald Greene, PhD
500 N. Michigan, Ste. 542
Chicago, IL 60611
Phone: 312/266-1456

Sun Center
1816 N. Wells, 3rd Flr.
Chicago, IL 60614
Phone: 312/280-1070
wholisticlifecenter.com

Massage

American Massage Therapy Association
Phone: 708/484-9282
Fax: 708/484-8601

A Thousand Waves
1212 W. Belmont
Chicago, IL 60657
Phone: 773/549-0700
thousandwavesspa.com

Bodyscapes, Inc.
1604 Sherman Ave., Ste. 210
Evanston, IL 60201
Phone: 847/864-6464

Chiropractic Chicago
407 W. North
Chicago, IL 60610
Phone: 312/255-9500

Chislof Chiropractic Center
7448 N. Harlem
Chicago, IL 60631
Phone: 773/763-0400

Hair Loft
14 E. Pearson
Chicago, IL 60611
Phone: 312/943-5435

Greater Chicago Chiropractic
561 W. Diversey, Ste. 221
Chicago, IL 60614
Phone: 773/871-7766
Fax: 773/871-0781

Know No Limits
5121 N. Clark
Chicago, IL 60640
Phone: 773/334-4728

Leslie Kahn
1243 N. Damen
Chicago, IL 60622
Phone: 773/276-4665

Mario Tricoci Hair Salon & Day Spa
900 N. Michigan
Chicago, IL 60611
Phone: 312/915-0960
Fax: 312/943-3138

Massage Therapy Professionals
3047 N. Lincoln, Ste. 400
Chicago, IL 60657
Phone: 773/472-9484
Fax: 773/472-8590

Progressive Chiropractic Rehabilitation & Wellness Center
2816 N. Sheffield
Chicago, IL 60657
Phone: 773/525-WELL
Fax: 773/525-9397
www.progressivechiro.net

Rodica European Skin & Body Care Center
845 N. Michigan, Ste. 944E
Chicago, IL 60611
Phone: 312/527-1459
www.facialandbodybyrodica.com

Seaman Chiropractic Center
4941 W. Foster
Chicago, IL 60630
Phone: 773/545-2233
Fax: 773/545-8383

Cindy Unger
Phone: 773/848-0705

Meditation

Peace School
3121 N. Lincoln
Chicago, IL 60657
Phone: 773/248-7959
Fax: 773/248-7963

Vajrayana Buddhist Center
1116 Lake, 3rd Flr.
Oak Park, IL 60301
Phone: 708/763-0132
www.vajrabc.org

**Zen Buddhist Temple
(Chinese Culture Academy)**
608 Dempster
Evanston, IL 60202
Phone: 847/869-0554

Naprapaths

Belmont Health Care
2110 W. Belmont
Chicago, IL 60618
Phone: 773/404-0909

Chicago National College of Naprapathy
3330 N. Milwaukee
Chicago, IL 60641
Phone: 773/282-2686
Fax: 773/282-2688
www.naprapathy.edu

Karen L. Bruneel
4770 N. Lincoln, Ste. 6
Chicago, IL 60625
Phone: 773/769-1133
Fax: 773/769-1134

Lake Shore Naprapathic Center
3166 N. Lincoln, Ste. 410
Chicago, IL 60657
Phone: 773/327-0844

Nutritionists

Advance Center
55 E. Washington, Ste. 1310
Chicago, IL 60602
Phone: 312/553-2020
Fax: 312/553-5128

Lake Shore Naprapathic Center
3166 N. Lincoln, Ste. 410
Chicago, IL 60657
Phone: 773/327-0844

Rose Quest Nutrition Center
200 N. Michigan, Ste. 404A
Chicago, IL 60602
Phone: 312/444-9234

Physicians

Harambee Wellness Center
1515 E. 52nd, 2nd Flr.
Chicago, IL 60615
Phone: 773/925-6877

Howard Brown Health Center
4025 N. Sheridan
Chicago, IL 60613
Phone: 773/388-1600

Living

Religious Groups

Chicago Genesis
Phone: 773/592-2003
www.chicagogenesis.org

Congregation Or Chadash
656 W. Barry
Chicago, IL 60657
Phone: 773/248-9456

Dignity Chicago
3023 N. Clark, Box 237
Chicago, IL 60657
Phone: 773/296-0780
www.dignitychicago.org

Grace Baptist Church
1307 W. Granville
Chicago, IL 60660
Phone: 773/262-8700

HAVURA
7316 N. Tripp
Lincolnwood, IL 60712
Phone: 847/679-8760

Holy Trinity Lutheran Church
1218 W. Addison
Chicago, IL 60613
Phone: 773/248-1233
www.holytrinitychicago.org

The Ethical Humanist Society of Greater Chicago
7574 N. Lincoln
Skokie, IL 60077
Phone: 847/677-3334
www.ethicalhuman.org

Vajrayana Buddhist Center
1116 Lake, 3rd Flr.
Oak Park, IL 60301
Phone: 708/763-0132
www.vajrabc.org

Wellington Avenue United Church of Christ
615 W. Wellington
Chicago, IL 60657
Phone: 773/935-0642
Fax: 773/935-0690

Tai Chi

Dan Guidara
3052 N. New England
Chicago, IL 60634
Phone: 773/745-6442

Michael McGinn
Phone: 847/864-8180

Tim Wang
Phone: 773/363-7607
www.Chicagohealers.com

Weight Control

A Creative Change
111 N. Wabash, Ste. 1320
Chicago, IL 60602
Phone: 312/939-9394
Fax: 312/939-9594
www.reducestress.com

Professional Weight Clinic
200 E. Ohio, Ste. 501
Chicago, IL 60611
Phone: 312/664-2255

Weight Watchers
Phone: 800/651-6000

Women's Workout World
208 S. LaSalle
Chicago, IL 60604
Phone: 312/357-0001

Yoga

Bodyscapes, Inc.
1604 Sherman, Ste. 210
Evanston, IL 60201
Phone: 847/864-6464

Peace School
3121 N. Lincoln
Chicago, IL 60657
Phone: 773/248-7959
Fax: 773/248-7963

Global Yoga and Wellness Center
1823 W. North
Chicago, IL 60622
Phone: 773/489-1510

NU Yoga Center
3047 N. Lincoln, 3rd Flr.
Chicago, IL 60657
Phone: 773/327-3650
www.yogamind.com

Sivananda Yoga Center
1246 W. Bryn Mawr
Chicago, IL 60660
Phone: 773/878-7771
www.sivananda.org/chicago

Temple of Kriya Yoga
2414 N. Kedzie
Chicago, IL 60647
Phone: 773/342-4600
Fax: 773/342-4608

Yoga Circle
401 W. Ontario, 2nd Flr.
Chicago, IL 60610
Phone: 312/915-0750
www.yogacircle.com

Dentists

Belmont Dental Care
3344 N. Lincoln
Chicago, IL 60657
Phone: 773/549-7971
Fax: 773/348-7544

Dr. Craig Millard, DDS, PC
30 N. Michigan, Ste. 920
Chicago, IL 60602
Phone: 312/726-5830
Fax: 312/726-7290

Dr. David B. Drake
739 W. Belmont
Chicago, IL 60657
Phone: 773/248-8813
Fax: 773/248-8898

Dr. Gray Vogelmann
155 N. Michigan, Ste. 325
Chicago, IL 60601
Phone: 312/819-1104

Dr. Leva Wright
333 N. Michigan, Ste. 2900
Chicago, IL 60601
Phone: 312/236-3226
Fax: 312/236-9629

Dr. Jeffrey Gaule
3120 N. Ashland
Chicago, IL 60657
Phone: 773/281-7550
Fax: 773/281-0808

Dr. Joseph S. Toups
25 E. Washington, Ste. 1325
Chicago, IL 60602
Phone: 312/263-6894

Dr. Marianne W. Schaefer
4801 W. Peterson, Ste. 502
Chicago, IL 60646
Phone: 773/777-8300
www.the-toothfairy.com

Dr. Martin Lieberman
& Dr. William T. Tetford
5419 N. Sheridan, Ste. 105
Chicago, IL 60640
Phone: 773/728-9200

Dr. Roger M. Wills
30 N. Michigan, Ste. 1414
Chicago, IL 60602
Phone: 312/332-7010
Fax: 312/332-1812

Gold Coast Dental Associates
1050 N. State, Mezzanine
Chicago, IL 60610
Phone: 312/654-0606
Fax: 312/654-1606

Lincoln Park Columbus Dental Associates
2551 N. Clark, Ste. 700
Chicago, IL 60614
Phone: 773/348-7008
Fax: 773/348-5810

Lincoln Park Cosmetic and General Dentistry
424 W. Fullerton
Chicago, IL 60614
Phone: 773/404-0101

Ravenswood Dental Group
1945 W. Wilson
Chicago, IL 60640
Phone: 773/334-3555
Fax: 773/334-5771

Salons

Alfaro Hair Design
3454 N. Southport
Chicago, IL 60657
Phone: 773/935-0202

Big Hair
2012 W. Roscoe
Chicago, IL 60618
Phone: 773/348-0440

Curl Up and Dye
2837 N. Clark
Chicago, IL 60657
Phone: 773/348-1000
Fax: 773/348-2802
www.curlupdye.com

Living

Diamond Beauty Clinic
151 N. Michigan, Ste. 1018
Chicago, IL 60601
Phone: 312/240-1042

J. Gordon Designs, Ltd.
2326 N. Clark
Chicago, IL 60614
Phone: 773/871-0770
Fax: 773/871-2514

Molina Molina
54 W. Maple
Chicago, IL 60610
Phone: 312/664-2386

Nancy Angelair Salon
1003 N. Rush
Chicago, IL 60611
Phone: 312/943-3011

Niko's Day Spa
2504 N. Clark
Chicago, IL 60657
Phone: 773/472-0883

Orbit Salon
3481 N. Clark
Chicago, IL 60657
Phone: 773/883-1166

Paul Rehder Salon
939 N. Rush
Chicago, IL 60611
Phone: 312/943-7404

Philip James
710 W. Diversey
Chicago, IL 60614
Phone: 773/248-9880

Salon Absolu
1216 W. Belmont
Chicago, IL 60657
Phone: 773/525-2396

Timothy Paul Salon
200 E. Delaware
Chicago, IL 60611
Phone: 312/944-5454
Fax: 312/944-5460

TRIO Salon, Ltd.
11 E. Walton
Chicago, IL 60611
Phone: 312/944-6999
Fax: 312/944-9572
www.triosalon.com

"Chicago models turn to TRIO...for many of the shortest, coolest looks seen on the hottest new faces in town...(TRIO) has been recognized nationally for its creative and technical works...(the) name (being) synonymous with flattering, precision cuts and picture perfect stylings." MODERN SALON

Skin Care

Hair Loft
14 E. Pearson
Chicago, IL 60611
Phone: 312/943-5435

Mario Tricoci Hair Salon & Day Spa
900 N. Michigan
Chicago, IL 60611
Phone: 312/915-0960
Fax: 312/943-3138

Rodica European Skin & Body Care Center
845 N. Michigan, Ste. 944E
Chicago, IL 60611
Phone: 312/527-1459
www.facialandbodybyrodica.com

Biographies

Christina Biggs is an Evanston-based freelance writer whose work has appeared in the Chicago Tribune, Stagebill Magazine (where she was previously an editor), the Chicago Theatre Guide and PERFORMINK, where she currently writes the "Behind the Curtain" column. Biggs has also written lyrics for two musicals produced in Chicago, *Trouble in Rummyville* (New Tuners Theatre) and *Brave New Kitchen* (New Tuners Theatre in conjunction with the Columbia College Chicago theatre department). She attended the University of California-Santa Cruz and DePaul University. Presently, Biggs is writing book and lyrics on a third musical project, *The Vineyard,* with composer Paul Libman.

Becky Brett has been writing for PERFORMINK newspaper for the past three years. She is also a freelance production and event manager, having recently associate produced the 2003 Chicago Improv Festival. Prior to assuming the utterly carefree lifestyle of a contract worker, Brett was the full-time production manager for the Chicago Humanities Festival. She also spent several years as the production coordinator for Lyric Opera of Chicago's Center for American Artists. She is active in everything from politics to guitar playing, trusting that one day it will all come together.

Jen Ellison has worked with PERFORMINK since 2001. In that time she has been the advertising manager, operations manager, and project manager for this edition of "The Book." Ellison is also the artistic director of WNEP Theatre in Lakeview.

Christine Gatto holds a BFA in acting from Northern Illinois University and an MFA in acting from Pennsylvania State University. Currently, she is the artistic director of City at Peace—Chicago, a national youth organization dedicated to teaching social action through theatre. As an actor, she has worked with many theatres in and around the city, including Stage Left, First Folio Shakespeare, Breadline Theatre, Circle Theatre, Irish Repertory, Trapdoor, SummerNITE, and the Candlelight Forum Theatre.

Jennifer Gehr has been the advertising manager for PERFORMINK since December 2002. Gehr is a member of Defiant Theatre where she served as their managing director for almost 10 years. She recently joined Open Eye Productions as their development director and has worked on and off stage with many Chicago companies including: Factory, Tri-Arts, Hi-Volt and WAFF.

Jenn Goddu is a full-time freelance journalist who primarily covers theatre and the arts. She reviews regularly for the Chicago Reader and is a frequent contributor to the CHICAGO TRIBUNE'S REDEYE, PERFORMINK, DIGITAL CITY CHICAGO and other regional publications. Her writing has also been published in AMERICAN THEATRE MAGAZINE. She is a graduate of Smith College's theatre department and has a Master's degree in Journalism. She was a fellow at the O'Neill Critics Institute in 2002.

Arlo Guthrie's design skills have been utilized (and/or exploited) by many theatre companies—including Steppenwolf, Lookingglass, The Midnight Circus, Defiant, Hi-Volt, The Hypocrites, and Factory—over the past seven years. He has also designed advertising, collateral, and online materials for the real estate, human resource, and restaurant industries. He is currently pursuing a BFA at the Illinois Institute of Art in Visual Communications. He hopes to finish arlodesign.com some time this decade.

Kevin Heckman edited the first four editions of "The Book" and has been involved in some way with every edition since. He also writes the "Review Round-Up" column for PERFORMINK. Heckman serves as the managing director at Stage Left Theatre, where he is also a member of the artistic ensemble, and is a board member of the League of Chicago Theatres. The rest of the time he works around Chicago as a director, actor, light designer and fight choreographer. Heckman graduated from Wesleyan University in Middletown, CT where he earned degrees in theatre and mathematics.

Claire Kaplan has proofread all six editions of "The Book" as well as the inaugural edition of "The Kids Book," and PERFORMINK newspaper. With her trusty red pen in hand, she is at peace knowing her college and graduate English degrees are put to good use. After finishing Second City's conservatory program, she has been improvising with groups like the Free Associates, TheatreSports and performing one-woman shows. She also has been teaching improvisation and musical theatre at the Old Town School of Folk Music for the past four years.

Carrie L. Kaufman is the publisher of PERFORMINK newspaper, PERFORMINK books and PI ONLINE. She's also won a few journalism awards for her writing.

Bob Labate is a partner at the law firm of Holland & Knight, LLC, was selected as a Leading Business Lawyer in the practice area of Media & Entertainment Law in Illinois by Chambers USA. Representations include: Chicago-based production companies for film and television; talent agreements; screenwriters, best selling authors, talent agencies and talent, in a broad spectrum of contract, financing, distribution, copyright and right of publicity issues. He is also the co-creator and moderator of an annual five-part seminar series, "The Business of Independent Film Production" sponsored by Columbia College and by the Independent Feature Project/Chicago. Labate writes the "Law & Entertainment" column for PERFORMINK newspaper.

Greg Mermel, PERFORMINK'S "Money and Taxes" columnist since 1991, is a certified public accountant whose practice includes many individuals, businesses and organizations involved in the arts. He has produced and directed theatre (with both posters and Jeff Citations on the wall of his office to prove it) and has taught in the management program of Columbia College. He has a B.A. from the University of Texas at Austin, an M.B.A. from the University of Chicago, and a Certificate from Harvard University's Institute in Arts Administration.

Mechelle Moe serves as the editor for PerformInk newspaper, "The Book" (fifth & sixth edition) and PI Online. She is also the executive director of The Hypocrites, a Chicago-based theatre company. As an actor, Moe has worked with Lifeline, Prop, The Factory, A Red Orchid, Writers' Theatre, etc. In 2003, she was awarded a Jeff Citation and After Dark for Principal Actress for her role in *Machinal,* produced by The Hypocrites.

Marty McNulty has designed and typeset all six editions of "The Book." He graduated from University of Illinois in 1994 with a degree in news-editorial journalism, and has since made a career in print graphic design. A native of the Kankakee area, he now lives in Chicago. His best claim to fame, was winning all six buckets on the Bozo show's Grand Prize Game at age 9.

John Myers studied journalism at Michigan State University, where he wrote about the local arts scene for the student newspaper. After graduating, he moved to New York and found work in media publishing. But the Midwest beckoned and he enrolled in Columbia College Chicago's graduate journalism program to boost his writing career in 2002. He has written for a variety of community newspapers, art publications and 'zines.

Rachael Patterson, director of The Audition Studio, has been teaching audition technique for film, industrials and commercials for 13 years. Formerly a partner in Brody/Patterson Casting, she cast numerous films, television pilots and commercials. Patterson trained at The American Conservatory Theatre in San Francisco. She is also a private coach, and teaches film workshops at various universities, and teaches commercial directors how to effectively work with actors.

Index

B

C

D

E

F

G

H

I

J

K

L

M

N

O

P

Q

R

S

T

U

V

W

Y

Z

Advertiser's Index

Order more copies of

The Book:
An Actor's
Guide to Chicago!

Every religion has its text, Chicago theatre has *The Book!*